T0277902

Surviving Genocide: Personal Recollections

By Donna Chmara

Foreword by historian Norman Davies
Including an interview with Nobel Laureate in
Literature Czesław Miłosz

Surviving Genocide: Personal Recollections by Donna Chmara
Cover - Polish nationality tag from the Holocaust Museum, Washington DC
This edition published in 2023

Winged Hussar is an imprint of

Winged Hussar Publishing, LLC
1525 Hulse Rd, Unit 1
Point Pleasant, NJ 08742

Copyright © Winged Hussar Publishing
ISBN 978-1-950423-80-4 Hardcover
ISBN 978-1-950423-81-1 E-Book
LCN 2022932116

Bibliographical References and Index
1. History. 2. Poland. 3. World War II
Winged Hussar Publishing, LLC All rights reserved
For more information
visit us at www.whpsupplyroom.com

Twitter: WingHusPubLLC
Facebook: Winged Hussar Publishing LLC

Dedication

I dedicate the years of research that culminated in this record of survival to my parents Helena and Michał Chmara through whose sacrifice my brothers and sisters, and I, came through the war alive.

I honor my Uncle Henry Mara and his wife Minnie Mara who opened their hearts and their home to my family of eight.

My words are my heart's embrace to all the people who lived and died during the hell on earth that was World War II.

Surviving Genocide: Personal Recollections

TABLE OF CONTENTS

Appendices

Foreword
Adversity and Triumph

By Norman Davies

The history of the Second World War is usually remembered in separate compartments. Americans remember American experiences. The British remember British experiences. Russians remember events in the Soviet Union. Jewish people remember the Holocaust. But, regrettably, not all of the wartime tragedies are remembered on an equal basis. The Polish experience in particular has often been minimized. Poland, during the War, was an Ally of the Western powers, but after the War, fell under the domination of the Soviet Union. As a result, many aspects of wartime Poland have remained little known and poorly presented.

What is more, wartime Polish history is not well suited to the simple stories that people generally prefer. It was, in fact, rather complicated. For one thing, Poland possessed a multi-ethnic society, which contained large numbers of Ukrainians, Jews, Germans, Lithuanians, and Belarussians, as well as Catholic Poles. All of them suffered appalling losses. For another, it was invaded and conquered in 1939 both by Hitler's Germany and Stalin's Soviet Union. As a result, it was subjected to a double dose of repression from the two most murderous regimes in Europe's past. Different groups were victimized in different ways and in different degrees, according to the shifting balances of the Nazi-Soviet power struggle.

More than 60 years after the end of the War, the number of survivors who can bear witness to the events of 1939-1945 is dwindling. If their memories are not recorded soon, they never will be. For this reason, Donna Chmara's collection of personal reminiscences is most moving and valuable. The testament of individuals is always more telling than faceless statistics.

The emphasis in this book is on Polish Christians. They died in huge numbers, probably losing five to six million if one takes the victims of the German and the Soviet

zones of occupation together. They were viewed with hostility both by the Nazis, who saw Catholicism as a mainstay
of Polish nationality, which they intended to crush; and by
the Soviets, who were doubly suspicious of everything Polish,
both on ideological and historical grounds. Fortunately, as
this book reveals, there were enough survivors to bear witness and tell the tale to the world. This is a story of adversity
and triumph.

Norman Davies is an English historian of Welsh descent
known for his publications on the history of Poland, the
United Kingdom and Ireland, and Europe. He is a Super-
numerary Fellow at Wolfson College at Oxford University, a
Fellow of the British Academy, Fellow of the Royal Historical
Society, and Professor Emeritus of London University. Professor Davies has written the two-volume definitive history
of Poland, *God's Playground*. His most recent works include
*Rising '44. The Battle for Warsaw; Europe East and West: A
Collection of Essays on European History;* and *Europe at War
1939-1945: No Simple Victory.*

*The author's visit with British historian Norman Davies. Wolfson College,
University of Oxford, 2000*

Introduction
Our Shared Humanity

The eyewitnesses you are about to meet demonstrate the danger of identifying solely with a group or ideology rather than with the fact of our shared humanity. They survived both Nazi and Soviet attempts to destroy the Polish nation. On November 24, 1945, *The New York Times* stated that, "German documents read at the Nuremberg war criminals' trial...revealed that Hitler had ordered his generals to kill without mercy all the men, women, and children of the Polish race or language."

British sources translate Hitler's speech to his generals in Obersalzberg, Germany on August 22, 1939, as, "I have put my death-head formations' in place with the command to relentlessly and without compassion to send into death men, women and children of Polish origin and language. Only thus we can gain the living space (lebensraum) we need." *Documents on British Foreign Policy. 1919-1939.* Eds. E. L. Woodward and Rohan Riftlep; 3rd series (London: HMSO, 1954), 7:258-260.

On September 1, 1939, Germany invaded Western Poland.

My Heart Remembers

As a child, I survived the attempted genocide of the Polish nation. As an adult, my nightmares continued to be as real as any thriller on television: It is World War II. Drenched in sweat, I run for my life from men in uniform. My husband Henry taps my arm to assure me that I am safe. Sometimes he wakes me as the hissing bomb descends, or before I plunge off a steep cliff. The relief of being in my own bed is like discovering that the firing squad had changed its mind.

During the day, I teach, run meetings, make decisions. At night, the war returns. As a child, I had crossed the Atlantic Ocean for the safety of America. As an adult, I still shiver in the bunkers of Europe while the shrill sinking bombs announce that someone among us will die.

To confront these nightmares, I began looking for daytime triggers. Turns out, they showed up when I was assertive, stood up to a bully, or saw human suffering – real or on the screen. The fear of being killed for becoming visible, for finding my own voice, lay dormant. It took two journeys – one inner, one outer – to reach freedom.

First, the inner journey. During therapy, I faced the cold and thirst when talking about the war, the dread I still felt at the wail of an ambulance. I spoke to the dead soldiers I had seen sprawled out on the bloody cobblestone next to their horses whose guts were spilling out on the street. I gave them a proper burial by bringing them into the daylight and covering them with my tears.

Then, the outer journey. I was ten weeks old when my Polish town of Naliboki in Eastern Europe disappeared. It had been home to farming families like mine for 800 years. We were exiled, reduced to poverty, and like sturdy trees, took root and blossomed in new soil. So why the nightmares? To find out, I spoke with family and friends born in Poland or what had been Poland before the war. They had been assaulted by war, yet they taught me about survival, forgiveness, and love.

You will get to know them by looking into world events of their time. As I wrap the fabric of history around each person, you will discover how the good will, or distorted egos of world leaders changed lives far from the seat of power. Not so different from the world of today.

Some people were deported to the Soviet Union, others to Germany. Some stayed home, became Soviet subjects, and survived winters in underground holes. Some risked their lives to work within the Polish Underground. Some endured medical experiments on their bodies. A different war for each, with one thing in common, they knew that ultimate defeat is bitterness of heart. They knew that reclaiming our humanity puts us back into the land of the living.

My Aunt Mania reclaimed her humanity through forgiveness. She was kidnapped at age nineteen to work in a German munitions factory. When I asked if she hated her abductors, she said, "...and forgive us our trespasses as we forgive those who trespass against us." Amazing.

Each person you will meet helped me give a proper burial to the wounds in my psyche. The nightmares no longer disturb my sleep, nor did they continue to wake my husband.

Part One: From the East: Soviet Tanks Bring Communism, 1939

Those Who Were Abducted

Chapter 1 Stefania: The Frozen Arctic of Russia
Chapter 2 Alicja: The Parched Steppe of Kazakhstan

Those Who Stayed

Chapter 3 Janusz: Not Enough Strong Backs
Chapter 4 Stanisław: Always a Sorrow
Chapter 5 Jadwiga: Between God and Party

Those Who Were Forced to Return

Chapter 6 Weronika: Beware the Enemy, Beware the Ally

Chapter 1 Stefania
The Frozen Arctic of Russia

For my family, World War II did not begin on September 1, 1939, when Germany invaded Poland from the west. It began on September 17, 1939, when the Soviet Union invaded Poland from the east. German soldiers first appeared in our town when Germany invaded its Soviet ally in 1941. Our neighbors were intent on destroying us.

My father's brother, Józef Chmara, and family were deported to Russia during the Soviet occupation before I was born. Years later, in the 1960's, while teaching in Turkey, I became curious about my relatives scattered by war around the globe. Returning home from Turkey in 1968, I arranged to meet Józef and family in Nottingham, England where they had resettled.

When I knocked on his door, Józef greeted a stranger. I called him uncle and reached out to hug him. He backed away and stood gazing at my face. Was I at the wrong place? Then seeing his brother Michał's cheekbones in me, he grinned and said, "So, you are Danusia. Come in my girl."

We crossed the threshold arm in arm. His wife Józefa, daughter Stefania, and her husband Tadek were waiting for me. Józefa said, "Come sit at our table. You must be hungry travelling so far."

They were made homeless by a war I never heard of in school. We think of World War II as guns on the ground and bombs in the air over Europe and the Pacific. But Stalin had them kidnapped into the thick forests of Russia near the Arctic Circle. Two years later, they crossed the vastness of Asia to reach Iran. Then, as my uncle joined the British army to fight Germany, his wife and daughter were evacuated to Africa. Eight years. Two continents. Ten countries. Thousands of miles.

I returned to England in 1999. Stefania's parents had passed away, but she was robust, in her 60's, with full rosy cheeks. Once, as we lingered over a cup of tea, I dared ask the painful questions. She sat demurely wearing a creamy wool sweater with a delicate string of pearls, soft brown skirt, and stylish, but sensible shoes. Hard to imagine this refined English lady had once resembled a corpse.

Poland in 1939 *(Historical Atlas of World War II)*

Henry the Maverick

I will look after all of you from afar.

My grandparents Stefan and Emilia had ten children born in Naliboki (currently in Belarus) between 1888 and 1910. Three died in infancy from whooping cough, five were exiled by war, two left by choice. After the oldest daughter Urszula married a Russian soldier and left for Russia, eight people – parents, four sons, two daughters – lived in the small wooden house with a barn, chicken coops, and a toilet in the field.

The oldest son Henryk had his own ideas that were hurtful to his family. He agonized for months until one Sunday, he gathered them in the kitchen and said, "I have decided to leave Naliboki."

"Leave Naliboki!" His father said. "Do you have a girl in one of the villages you want to marry?"

"No girl. I'm going to America."

"Where did my son get such a crazy idea? Our family has lived in Naliboki for generations. We tend their graves. Only war takes someone away from us."

"That's why I'm leaving. It's always some kind of war. Some lord over us. Kissing their soft hands. And we work from morning to night."

My grandmother Emilia stepped in, "You are the oldest. When we are gone, you will be the head of this family. Your sister Józefa is three, Maria is eight. Your brother Michał ten. They will need you."

"I'm twenty-one. I can make something of myself in America. I'll send packages of food and clothes. I will look after all of you from far away."

Henryk Chmara left the bonds of blood in 1913 to seek peace and prosperity. The immigration clerk in New York harbor heard "Henry Mara" and that became his name. At first, he did odd jobs and put aside a few dollars for his family. The delicacies he sent like coffee, sugar, and chocolate did not make up for his absence. His three brothers, Józef, Jan, and my father Michał, bonded deeply to make up for the one who had left. Like our people for centuries, the Chmara boys became farmers.

World War I erupted in Europe in 1914, a year after Uncle Henry reached the United States. When his new country of choice entered the war in 1917, the army welcomed this healthy young man with open arms. As a Polish man, he had resented being a soldier in the Russian army that had occupied his homeland, but he gladly fought on behalf of the American Expeditionary Forces in France.

Sleeping Beauty Awakens: A History Lesson

If that happened, where would I find a daddy?

As his older brother Henry became a proud American soldier, Józef was an unwilling conscript in the Soviet army. He also made a gutsy decision that shocked his parents. He abandoned the czar's army to fight for an independent coun-

Having served in the US Army, Henry Mara married Minnie Pasternak. They stand in front of the home he built. Cranbury, NJ 1950's

try of Poland. The repercussions came decades later.

While Józef Chmara was in the thick of battle during World War I, his father Stefan passed away. With the rebirth of Poland, Józef came home to be the family patriarch, and at age 24, it was time to settle down. The Chmara men were tall and handsome, and besides being farmers, they were also carpenters in demand for their skilled labor – you would say a good catch. Single girls sat up front in church to be noticed by these bachelors. But Józefa Hodyl was not one of them.

Józefa sat with her parents in pews warmed by generations of her family. People got around by horse, wagon, and foot, and she felt Józef's gaze as she walked past his house on the way to church. If he wanted her, he would have to catch her. And catch her he did. At age 26, Józef was the last of the three brothers to marry.

Sorrow touched Józef and his bride early in their marriage when their firstborn died of whooping cough. Their second daughter, Stefania, was healthy, it was a time of peace, and harvests were plentiful. When she was eight, they were leaving Naliboki, but not across an ocean like brother Henry had done before World War I. They were building a new household 18 miles north in the village of Mir, in what was Poland before the boundaries changed. By spring 1939, Józef opened the rich black soil with horse and plow while Józefa walked behind scattering seed.

In this multi-ethnic region, they agreed to share half the grain with their Belarussian neighbor for tending the land until they moved in by fall. But when Adolf Hitler and Joseph Stalin invaded Poland from two directions, the Soviet occupation of eastern Poland on September 17, 1939, emboldened the farmer. He said Józef did not deserve the land or crops because he had fought against Russia. Proud of her father's bravery, Stefania would curl up on his lap and ask him to tell another soldier story.

He would begin, "Once before you were born, I was almost killed near the Lithuanian border."

She asked, "Oh, no. If that happened, where would I find a daddy?"

He laughed and said, "Go ask your mother about those kinds of things."

Stefania was confused by the neighbor saying bad things about her father being a soldier. Was Józef a patriot or an enemy? The answer lies in Poland's disappearance, with its fertile soil, from the map of Europe for 123 years. In the late eighteenth century Poland was like a luscious pie cut three ways by its neighbors, Prussia (became Germany in 1871), Austria-Hungary, and Russia. Each consumed a large chunk across three partitions and made Poland disappear. After this feast, quality of life depended on how the pie was divided.

Prussia was a developed country. The Polish people and their land became part of a solid economy. Those absorbed by Austria-Hungary saw poverty and corruption. And my region was invaded by Russia, the harshest landlord of the neighbors that had feasted on Poland. Polish men were drafted into the czar's army, the army that had invaded their homeland and never left. This national wound had rankled with resentment for generations. Then comes a savior.

Józef the Rebel

They'll get even – sooner or later. They always do.

Before Józef became a family man with a wife and a daughter, he resented being a soldier in the Russian army of Czar Nicholas II. Going home on leave, he and a fellow conscript kept hearing about Józef Piłsudski (1867 – 1935) and his Legionnaires. Like the prince who kissed Sleeping Beauty to life, Piłsudski was the man who gave Poland the kiss of life. As he shouted independence, the festering wound of resentment in men like my uncle began to itch.

British historian Margaret MacMillan writes, "Piłsudski had spent much of his life trying to re-create a country that had disappeared at the end of the eighteenth century. Now, with the destruction of its great enemies – Austria-Hungary, Germany, and Russia – Poland's chance had come...On November 10, 1918 he arrived in the old Polish capital of Warsaw. Poland...had...no clearly defined borders, no government, no army, no bureaucracy. In the next three years Piłsudski made a country."

MacMillan continues, "Piłsudski...was born into the Russian part of Poland... His mother...taught him the history of his tragic country, from the great days of the sixteenth and seventeen centuries, when the Polish – Lithuanian commonwealth stretched from the Baltic almost to the Black Sea...and when Polish republican government, Polish learning, Polish cities were the admiration of Europe; to the partitions of the 1790's, when Poland vanished into the hands of its neighbors..."[1]

Three weeks into World War I, August 1914, Piłsudski declared that three brigades were ready to put Poland back on the map of Europe. Spurred on by such brashness, like his brother Henry in America, Józef followed his dream. He would help Piłsudski give Poland the kiss of life. Home on leave, he spit out the painful news to his parents. He said, "I buried my Russian uniform."

Stefan blurted out, "You defy the Russian army? This is rebellion. You put us in danger!"

Emelia insisted, "Where is it? Your father will dig it up. I'll clean it good. No one will know."

"I won't tell you. When the Russian soldiers come for me, you won't know anything."

His father said, "I suppose you got caught up with Piłsudski fever."

"On our way home we heard that men are swarming from all over occupied Poland to join Piłsudski."

Stefan said, "I can't blame you my boy. Do you think I like my son fighting in the Russian army to keep our people down? We lost one son to America. Now you're chasing some wild dream of Poland being reborn. Think of your mother."

Emelia knew, "You won't get away with it. They'll get even – sooner or later. They always do."

The next day, Józef and the other young man packed food and fed their horses. Józef hugged his little brothers and sisters and knelt in front of his parents. He said, "I may never see you again. I ask your blessing. When my life is in danger, I must know you have forgiven me for this."

Stefan and Emelia prayed over their kneeling son. Swinging a sack of food and warm clothes over his back, he walked out the door. With the Russian uniform buried, Józef and the other rebel pushed westward. Stopping at dusk, Józef asked a farmer if they could water the horses and sleep in his barn. Hearing their Polish with an eastern drawl, he said, "What are you lads doing so far from home?"

With a young man's fervor, Józef said, "We're joining Piłsudski. We're getting back our country."

The farmer offered, "In that case, the barn won't do. Come inside and sleep by the fire. In the morning, my wife will fix you bread and a slab of fatback to take on your journey."

Invoking the name of Piłsudski, the two patriots and their horses received food and shelter each night as they galloped across occupied Poland. Reaching the city of Kraków, they joined Piłsudski's Legionnaires. To the czar's army, Józef was an enemy. To the Polish people, Józef was a hero. Piłsudski had stirred long-suppressed national feelings as the invaders – Prussia, Austria-Hungary, and Russia – were having indigestion. Shifting allegiances and World War I ended the old order and cleared the way for the rebirth of Poland. Piłsudski's volunteers became regular army, won the 1920 Battle with Russia, and secured Poland's borders. Sleeping Beauty was awake and safe. For now.

With Poland reborn, Piłsudski rewarded his men with land in the eastern part of reborn Poland. Józef was an Osadnik, men who got land for their service, in Józef's case, the land in Mir. His wife was a warrior in her own fashion. When the Belarussian farmer kept the crops from the farm in Mir, Józefa fought back. She took the case to court and got a favorable ruling. But they never baked bread with the grain. They never slept in the home they built. They never saw their farm again.

A Personal Grudge

**We sit up to make sure they don't throw us out onto the
frozen ground with the corpses.**

According to British historian, Laurence Rees, "There
were to be four major waves of deportation from Soviet-oc-
cupied eastern Poland, each separately motivated. The first
began on the night of 10 February 1940 and targeted in particular a group of people against whom Stalin had a personal
grudge – veterans of the 1920 war between Poland and the
new Bolshevik state, known as Osadniks."[2]

The war ended in 1918, but Józef came home in 1922
after he fought to secure Poland's borders. By 1940, the three
brothers had built a house for Jan, and a two-family dwelling
across the road for Józef and Michał and their families. This
way they would always be together. Years later, when Józef
received property for his service to Poland during World War
I, they helped him cultivate the land.

Naliboki within Belarus 2023 *(Wikipedia)*

With strong backs and skilled hands, the three brothers tamed acres of wild shrub. They built barns, animal shelters, and a one-family house for Józef. But before Józef could move, everyone in the two-family house in Naliboki was awakened in the middle of the night. They heard angry pounding on Józef's side of the house, and yelling in Russian, "Open up, Józef Chmara. We know you live here."

Two men shoved the door open, pushed him at gunpoint against the wall. He remembered his mother Emelia's words spoken twenty-five years ago: "They'll get even – sooner or later. They always do." He turned pale; his hands shook. The intruders ransacked the house for weapons and money. Józefa told Stefania, "Hurry. Put on all your warm clothes. I'll grab as much bread and meat we can carry."

Józefa wrapped eight-year-old Stefania into a goose down quilt like a package to be mailed. The intruders pushed them into a horse-drawn cart, jeering they were going to a better place. As they rode, the rising sun revealed frosted windows but no chimney smoke of morning fires. Between February 1940 and June 1941, thousands of families whose men had fought for Polish independence two decades earlier were abducted in the middle of the night into the Soviet Republics. This was Stalin's personal grudge.

My family was taken to the Stołpce station, 25 miles south of Naliboki, and packed so tightly into a cattle car they slept sitting up. A hole in the floor was the toilet. A tiny stove mocked the cold. Their food was gone before the train began to roll a week later. Stefania said, "Women prayed and cried. Men asked, my God, where are they are taking us?"

On the coldest night of the year, began eight years of homeless exile, never to see Naliboki again.

During a stop, Józefa asked the engineer if she could run to get warm water from the locomotive. Yes. She stepped off the train. He whistled. The train left. Seeing her standing alone in the snow, the sentry told her, "... skip the next train for Polish deportees. Take the one for Russian soldiers. They have food. Come inside the hut. Here's an old cloth to keep you warmer. And when that train comes, avoid the officer's car. They won't let you get on."

Józefa jumped onto a car full of Russian boys. First time far from home. Just learning to shave. Mothers praying hard for them. They gave Józefa warm clothes, bread, and nine rubles in money. When officers did inspections, they hid her under a pile of coats. Stefania mused, "They were decent to mother, those Russian boys going to the front to kill and be killed."

The train stopped at a massive railroad junction. Cattle cars marked "Polish Transport" led Józefa to a soup line. She searched frantically for familiar faces, until she saw Józef and Stefania!

The next train was pushing toward Archangel, a seaport in northwest Russia near the Arctic Circle. Stefania said, "We were less crowded as people died. The cattle car doors rumble open. Guards stomp in. A shuffle of bodies. We sit up to make sure they don't throw us out onto the frozen ground with the corpses. Doors slammed shut. I was eight. I still wake up at night frozen with fear, not able to move."

A month later, horse-drawn sleds took them from the Vologda train station to designated work sites. My family was taken 200 miles with 300 families to a communal farm, *Kolkhoz #21*, near the village of Zielony Bor. They lived with a couple and their two children, six people in one room. When a new barrack was built near the lake that froze by October, they got their own room. Józefa cleared lumber in the forest. Józef's work crew put up new barracks as more prisoners arrived. Stefania went to school where children were taught the virtues of Stalin.

Oppression by Design
Dear Lord, what happened to my husband?

Józef put Stefania in line before food ran out and hurried to work. They got one liter of soup per person each day, and nine pounds of bread for the week. More work meant more soup and bread. Families scoured fields for mushrooms, berries, sorrel leaves, but single people were fenced in. With no children, they could run away. (One single man who did escape survived the blizzards and wild animals of Manchuria and the Gobi Desert. Slavomir Rawicz described his ordeal in the book *Długi Marsz – The Long Walk*. It was made into a film, "The Way Back" with Colin Farrell and Ed

Harris.)

"Medical care" meant permission to rest. One morning, Józef's kidneys were so inflamed from the cold, his feet went numb, and he could not stand up. Józefa said, "Dear Lord, what happened to my husband? Your feet are swollen like balloons. I'll run to tell the commandant, or they'll come with clubs and beat you for not going to work."

The commandant stomped in, yanked the cover, saw Józef's feet, and left. As soon as he could walk, Józef returned to the construction crew building more barracks for more prisoners. For Stefania's aunt, lack of medical care was fatal. After giving birth to twins in a bleak room with no doctor and no medical sup-

Józef Chmara, wife Józefa, and daughter Stefania before their exile. Naliboki 1940

plies, her babies were left without a mother. Her husband covered her body with branches on the frozen ground in the woods. She became food for wolves. He was left to raise four children.

An occasional summer wagon brought supplies, packages, and letters. One package had warm clothes, grain, honey, smoked bacon, and a delicate white dress. Stefania quivered, "It had a blue sash with needle and thread to sew onto the waist. I put it on and ran to show my mother working in the forest. I fell into a puddle and cried."

She continued, "Your parents sold a cow to send us 300 rubles. Our aunt had four children, a sick husband, yet they helped. So did your Uncle Jan and my mother's family. Someone out there cared about us. Those packages saved us, but I can't speak calmly about that dress even now."

Groups watched films in the main building with its one movie projector, one radio, and one telephone. The films explained to cold and hungry prisoners why they should be enthusiastic about the revolution that had exiled them from home. Stefania said, "We prayed secretly and fervently - 'Jak trwoga to do Boga' (When in fear, we want God to be near). But meeting for prayer and friendship was forbidden. They had no God. They would say we were starting a revolt. The punishment would be brutal."

Fear solidified like concrete as some prisoners began policing others. Józef showed a letter he got with criticism of Soviet crimes to a fellow prisoner, expecting sympathy. Desperate to survive, or perhaps for some bread, the man told the commandant, who was himself a victim of an earlier deportation. From the 1830's and up to Stalin's regime, thousands of Polish citizens were deported to Russia. Rather than give Józef a beating, he warned him to keep his mouth shut.

Józef knew to take his advice. The NKVD, the secret police that became the KGB, had arrested ten men for criticizing the Soviets. Children were finishing the school day when nine of them returned. The most vocal man who had cursed his oppressors was gone. Stefania said, "We were leaving school and saw nine dirty men dragging themselves along the road below the school. They were beaten so badly, my friends didn't know their own fathers."

The Hidden Icon

My children might report me for praying.

When Stefania got chicken pox, the commandant released Józefa from work to care for Stefania, enabling her to leave the compound. In springtime the winds were strong as she made her way to a nearby village. A grandmother peeked through a crack in the door. Józefa said, "My child is sick. Do you have some milk, fish, or cheese to nourish her back to health? I have warm clothes to trade."

Eastern Poland was an ethnic crossroad where people spoke, or at least understood, each other's languages. Józefa spoke Russian, but not this dialect. About to close the door, the woman said, "You must be from the Polish at the *kolkhoz* by the lake. I can't talk to you. Our government says you are our enemies. Go away."

"Are you and I different? I'm a poor woman with a sick daughter. Your family could use warm clothes. Talk of enemies is for governments. We're just people, you and I, trying to survive."

At the chance of warm clothes, the woman opened the door and told Józefa to sit by the fire. They bartered a thick warm sweater and hand-knitted wool socks for carrots from the family's cold storage hut and large slab of cheese. Satisfied with their "shopping," the grandmother offered Józefa a glass of hot tea and bread. Józefa gratefully accepted and asked, "Who lives here with you?"

The woman stiffened. She thought for a moment, then reached under the little cot where she slept near the fire. She pulled out a neatly folded pile of clothes that were her wardrobe. She unwrapped a small Byzantine icon of the Blessed Mother. She said, "I hide this from my son-in-law. He's a communist. My daughter and grandchildren belong to the party. They can't know I have this. If they find out, my children might report me for praying. I'll get some kind of punishment."

"You pray alone secretly. Let us pray together. For my sick daughter. For your family."

They sat in the little hut by the fire away from the howling wind. They prayed, they talked, and opened their hearts. The woman invited Józefa to come back. Józefa was no longer her enemy.

Józefa returned a month later. The grandmother opened the door with a nervous look of apology. She wasn't alone. There would be no tea, no prayer, no nourishing human warmth. They exchanged knowing glances. Józefa trudged through the snow to the next distant dwelling. Stefania added, "On one of her visits to the villages, mother got me shoes. One was bigger than the other. What could I do? I was growing. I wore them in that cold. I couldn't go barefoot."

The packages helped Stefania beat chicken pox, but they briefly landed Józef in jail. With money from home, he was accused of laziness and no enthusiasm for the revolution. Armed guards bullied the workers, so being lazy was impossible. Józefa stood in line with that money to buy *walonki*, warm felt boots for dry snow, and a *fufajka*, a quilted jacket that reaches the chin. Stefania would need warm clothes if they were ever to become free to leave behind enthusiasm for the revolution.

Freeze or be Eaten by Wolves

I wish I didn't see this.

After the German and Soviet invasions of Poland in 1939, Germany turned on its former ally in 1941 and invaded Soviet-controlled lands. Humiliated by Germany, Stalin was welcomed by the two Allied superpowers, United States and Britain. They wanted something he had – thousands of virile young men from the Soviet republics to be sacrificed to the ravenous maw of war.

This new allegiance thrust Poland, also an Allied member, onto the same side as Russia. And it led to Soviet control of Poland for five decades. But first, Stalin released some Polish prisoners to fight Germany. The commandant of *Kolkhoz #21* called them together in August 1941 and announced, "Our governments have negotiated your release. You must find a way to leave in groups."

Find a way? Brought in by force, they had to get themselves out. Or remain forever. Their only hope was walking 200 miles to Vologda through deep glaring snow and hungry wolf packs. Stefania said, "Those dear poor people in the villages. They said our government cares enough to get us out, but their government doesn't care about them. They were good people, but oh so poor."

While Józef Chmara joined the Second Polish Corps of the British Eighth Army, Stefania and Józefa Chmara were evacuated from Iran to Tanzania, Africa. 1942

British journalist Neal Ascherson wrote, "...the Siberian and Asian prison camps swung open, and hun-

dreds of thousands of Poles – soldiers, women, officials,
priests, even orphaned children – began to make their way
toward the centers where the new Polish army was being
gathered. Many had already died; many were not released.
But the rest set out on the journey by rail, sledge, river raft,
or on foot...the Soviet authorities gave them little assistance
or food, and thousands perished..."[3]

Polish-American historian, Marek Tuszynski, told me
one reason Stalin let them leave was to transfer the burden
of housing and feeding to his British ally. Until they reached
Iran, the hunger was deliberate. Stalin allocated food rations for an army of 40,000 ethnic Poles, knowing that Polish citizens deported to the Soviet Union included Russian,
Belarussian, Ukrainian, Jewish, and other minority groups.
Stalin refused to increase provisions for an army that grew
to 71,000 troops, and with civilians, totaled 115,000. This
meager food allocation was shared by all of them.[4]

On New Year's Day 1942, eighteen families left *Kolkhoz #21*. Józefa and Stefania left the day before while Józef
remained to help prepare supplies. Wearing her new *walonki* and *fufajka*, ten-year-old Stefania needed a head start to
walk 200 miles, but this was not like daytime visits with
the grandmothers. By late afternoon, Józefa knocked on the
door of a hut. A man opened it a crack. She said, "I'm walking with my child to the Vologda train station. Can we rest
by your fire for the night?"

He opened the door wider to see the woman. He said,
"You're from the Polish at the *kolkhoz*. I can't help you. Authorities will hear that I helped a fugitive escape. My family
will be punished."

She pleaded, "Your government is letting us leave.
We're walking to the train station. Vologda. My child is with
me. Can't walk in one day. We mean no harm. We just want
to go home."

He said, "I didn't hear about that. Helping a runaway
is big punishment," and slammed the door.

Józefa knocked on two more doors. One was slammed,
one was gently closed with regret. This was not malice. It
was paralyzing fear. She knew kindness in villages where
she had bartered clothes for food. She also knew their fears.
The sun was setting. Knowing they could freeze to death or

be eaten by wolves, Józefa tried to hide her desperation from Stefania.

Józefa tottered with relief when a man in a position of authority opened the door and let them come in. He assured his wife that Stalin had freed them. Józefa told them she was meeting up with the rest of her group the next day. The wife pointed to the fire and left. She came back with hot tea for Józefa, warm milk for Stefania, some bread, and a blanket. Before saying good night, she added a log to the fire and said its best they won't be alone tomorrow. The wolves tend to stay away from a large group.

At daybreak, Józefa studied the faces of the Russian couple. They would be in her prayers forever.

Stepping into the winter harshness, they met up with Józef and the other 17 families. Pulling supply sleds, their feet pounded for days through blinding snow toward the Vologda train station. At dusk, men set up shelters, lit fires, and took turns standing watch for wolves. Women rationed supper and huddled with their children through the black night punctuated by a piercing serenade of wolves.

At the train station, a clerk took two weeks to gather transit documents and stamp them with red ink until they seemed to bleed. Like penguins shielding their young, parents put children between them and slept crouched against a building with no place to wash. During the day, they rationed food, bought juice in a canteen, and boiled snow to drink. She said, "Corpses lay around the station. Died of hunger and cold waiting for their train. We were looking gray like them. I wish I didn't see this."

The Sands of Persia

We ate every day for the first time in three years.

In January 1942, the group of 18 families boarded a train of cattle cars, slept on wooden boards, huddled near a tiny stove, and pretended no one was squatting over the hole in the floor. The Polish army, including female units, formed in two places – southern Russia and the Soviet Republic of Uzbekistan. They went southwest across Russia and Kazakhstan to reach Uzbekistan.

When they stumbled from the cattle car in March, the Polish army took my family to a flimsy cabin on an Uzbek donkey farm with two other families, as more refugees were on the way. Their only food for two weeks were wild leaves they gathered in the fields and cooked. As they lay in a stupor, life fading from them, some saw a ghost, or was it a man? The soldier *was* flesh and blood. The army was ready to lead them out of Asia to join the British in Iran. They must hurry.

Józef said, "We're barely alive. Some of us don't have the strength to walk."

The soldier said that the commander of Polish armed forces, Gen. Władysław Sikorski, had chosen Gen. Władysław Anders to lead them out of Uzbekistan. It's urgent to leave quickly. Stalin could shut the borders any time. Stefania said, "The soldier pulled out a package of rice. Oh, my God! Our first solid food in weeks! We shared it with the other two families. In the morning, we left for the army. The Uzbek farmer didn't like it, but the soldier had borrowed a wagon to carry out the weak ones."

Sikorski was right. The door slammed shut in 1943. Stalin acted indignant over accusations that 22,000 Polish military had been murdered in the Katyń forest region of Russia. He blamed the murders on Germany and broke off diplomatic relations with the Polish government-in-exile in

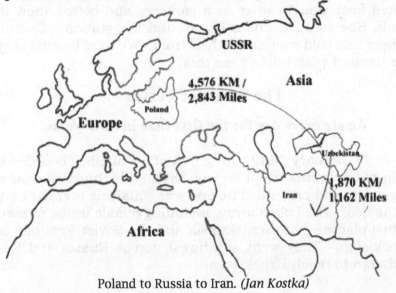

Poland to Russia to Iran. *(Jan Kostka)*

London. In 2010, the Russian government admitted that Stalin had ordered these murders – too late for thousands who were stranded in the Soviet republics forever.

The exiles left Uzbekistan in a convoy of trucks across the desert of Turkmenistan. At Krasnovodsk (now called Türkmenbaşy) on the Caspian Sea, an old Russian ship took them south to Iran. Stefania said, "In Iran, the British gave us tents and clean clothes. We ate every day for the first time in three years – bread for breakfast, rice and lamb for dinner. They lit a pile of our rags. I asked father why he was so fascinated by the fire."

He said, "Hear that popping sound from the fire? That's the lice that lived on us."

She added, "We got to Iran in April 1942. Soon the British hired local drivers to take us to a larger camp near the city of Tehran. Some trucks slid off on those treacherous mountainous roads. The truck in front of us went over the edge. The local driver was drunk. The people were killed."

In the larger camp, children got paper and pencil, sat on rocks, and school was in session. Friendships grew. Priests who had eluded concentration camps said Mass outdoors. But caught between Soviet and German forces, this hint of normal life was short lived. Polish historian Tadeusz Piotrowski explains that they left Iran because of the hostility of the Soviet army occupying northern Iran and the threat of the German armies which had already reached the Caucasus.

The Sun of Africa

When this is over, I want you to be the same man you are today.

Józef had been a Russian conscript, a volunteer in Piłsudski's Legions, and a soldier in the Polish army before returning in 1922 to Naliboki and marrying Józefa. While in Iran during the fall of 1942, my 46-year-old uncle again put on a uniform as a member of the Polish Second Corps of the British Eighth Army. As his dependents, his wife and daughter were among the Polish citizens scattered around the globe for their safety to places like Palestine and Lebanon, as Piotrowski describes below.

"Some exiles also found asylum in India...In mid-1944,
East Africa hosted over 13,000 Polish citizens in the British colonies of Uganda, Kenya, and Tanganyika. South
Africa, North Rhodesia, and South Rhodesia also became
the home of Poles. ...Polish schools, churches, hospitals,
civic centers, and manufacturing and service coopera-
tives were founded and Polish culture prospered. African
radio stations ran programs in the Polish language and
there was even a Polish press. In South Africa alone there
were 18 Polish schools with about 1,800 students in at-
tendance...A large Polish settlement was also founded in
Mexico."[5]

As his family was evacuated for safety, Józef squeezed
his little Stefania and, seemingly sure of surviving the next
battle, he said, "When I see you again, I'll have more soldier
stories to tell you."

He took his wife in his arms and said, "If we live, we'll
find a quiet place to be together in peace."

Józefa said, "Don't be too brave. When this is over, I
want you to be the same man you are today."

The trucks carrying women and children maneuvered
precarious mountain passes to reach southern Iran. They
then boarded an English ship. Some disembarked in India,
others continued south. She said, "Soviet authorities hated
teachers as leeches on society for doing mental, not physical work. They grabbed them in huge numbers. Right away,
these teachers set up school on the ship."

Hope turned to dread as they learned that a silent
enemy was waiting for them. They had entered waters full of
mines. Teachers tried to keep the children busy with lessons
all day. For a month, the ship crawled along the Arabian
Sea, then twisted vigilantly through the Indian Ocean. Each
rationed meal could be their last. Reaching land at Dar es
Salaam in what is now Tanzania felt like reaching heaven.
But they were still nomads.

These hardy souls joined a camp with 800 other wom-
en and children. Having seen too much, Stefania was savvy
beyond her tender years. She told her mother, "I can't stay
here. I hear there's a larger camp. They have schools, grade

Iran to Tanzania. *(Wikipedia)*

school and high school.

Józefa said, "You're only 12. How can I let you out of my sight? It's dangerous out there."

Stefania said, "I might still be alive when the war ends. What will I do without any education?

Józefa said, "Where is your father? Somewhere with the British. I'll be here. You'll be gone. Aren't families meant to be together?

Stefania answered, "If we live, we will be together again. But if I don't go to school, I will be the person Stalin and Hitler want me to be. I will only be fit for low menial labor."

Her words convinced Józefa to let her angel fly away. Not yet a teenager, Stefania was on her own with 5,000 refugees from the four major deportations into the Soviet Union. She said, "They grabbed us in February 1940, others in April 1940, June and July 1940, and July 1941. We were all in that camp, Polish Christians, Polish Jews, Ukrainians. We had two churches and a synagogue."

As schools were set up in smaller camps, mother and child reunited and Stefania continued her education. She said, "Mother's legs were swollen from working in the Russian cold. Now, with three growing seasons a year, she grew vegetables and peanuts for the camp kitchen. She knitted wool socks and wore them to sweat the cold out of her. Her legs healed in Africa."

Together Again

Your father is here. He sees you. He's coming toward you. Run. Run. Run to him.

Józefa grew vegetables in Africa and kept writing the Red Cross about her husband's whereabouts. The Polish Second Corps was marching with the British through the Middle East and Egypt toward the bloody Battle of Monte Cassino in Italy. It was best Józefa did not know this.

I asked Stefania if, at age 46, her father was expected to fight. She said, "The older men were essential. My father was setting up outdoor bathing facilities for the men during their long marches. Cold water and soap. Soldiers need cooks, medical care, shelter. At Monte Cassino in spring 1944, father's job was dangerous. He distributed ammunition on the front."

She added, "No one could remove the Germans deep in the mountains, not the English, nor Canadians, nor Americans. It was the Polish army that took Monte Cassino and raised the Polish flag. This opened the road to Rome, letting the Allies reach Europe, and turned the tide of the war."

British author Matthew Parker captures the moment, "Section Leader Czech played the Kraków Hejnał, a medieval Polish military signal, on the bugle. Section Leader Choma recalled the moment: "There was a lump in my throat as, through the echo of the cannon's roar, the notes of the Hejnał rang out from the abbey...These soldiers, hardened by numerous battles, only too well acquainted with the shocking wastefulness of death on the slopes of Monte Cassino, cried like children, as, after years of wandering, they heard not from the radio, but from the previously invincible German fortress, the voice of Poland, the melody of the Hejnał.... The Battle of Monte Cassino was at an end."[6]

Józef had survived his final battle, had worn his last military uniform. As the war ended, the British were building resettlement camps for thousands of military dependents who still had a husband, father, or brother to embrace. As part of the British military, Józef waited three years in England to be reunited with his wife and daughter.

Stefania and Józefa left Africa from Mombasa, Kenya with 2,000 British soldiers and 300 military dependents. The ship Scythia plowed through staggering distances: down the Indian Ocean, around Africa, and up the Atlantic. But no water mines. She said, "We were treated well. They organized dances and invited our grown-up girls. A month later, two orchestras, English and Scotch, greeted the victorious army. With great ceremony, we were served tea with milk, English of the first order."

She added, "There were friendships and maybe some marriages. Those handsome British boys and pretty Polish girls on a ship for a month together."

Exile from Naliboki on February 10, 1940, ended for Józefa and Stefania in Liverpool, England on July 1, 1948. They were given a room and a date to be reunited. Stefania said, "Father was northwest of Liverpool near the town of Blackshaw Moor. I was so excited I couldn't sleep the night before. When he came to our resettlement camp, mother saw him first. She said, 'Your father is here! He sees you. He's coming toward you. Run. Run. Run to him.'"

Six years without them, Józef Chmara, the unbroken soldier, began to shake and sob as he enveloped his wife and daughter. Stefania said, "He looked much older, but oh so happy!"

They lived in one room in Józef's resettlement camp. At age 17, Stefania operated a sewing machine in a clothing factory. Józef worked in a lime processing plant. She said, "We got the worst jobs. But when I learned English, I did quality control for a drug company."

Stefania was almost a woman when she met Tadek Kuryło. His abduction was different from hers, but they were both used for someone else's gain. Captured near the Polish city of Kraków, Tadek was given to a wealthy Austrian landowner as a reward for the man's services in Hitler's elite killing squad. The SS man became even wealthier by the forced labor of four Polish and three Ukrainian prisoners who built houses and barns on his extensive properties.

Tadek and Stefania found love and security, but when he offered to start their new lives as husband and wife, she hesitated. She said, "I can't leave my parents. They lost everything, the farm in Mir. In Africa, we didn't know if father was alive. We need to always be together."

Tadek answered, "Why would you have to leave your parents? I don't have a family. They were all killed. If you marry me, I will have a wife and they will be my family."

Together with Stefania's parents, the newlyweds bought that quiet little place Józef had in mind. Stefania no longer sat on his lap as he told her war stories, but she savored every word. They found healing in nature as they adorned the house in Nottingham with flowers from March to November. The backyard teemed with organic vegetables before organic became the rage. Their trees bore plump fruit on two allotments beyond town. These plots were a wartime source of food for the British. For this family, they were also a hint of Naliboki.

The Love of His Life
They bonded deeply the way only men in battle can fathom.

Used and abused, how did they return to life? The miracle of love – romantic, parental, love of siblings, neighbors, friends, kindness of strangers. The British government, Red Cross, and civilians were preparing food, clothing, housing, and medical care for thousands of military dependents whom they did not know. Kindness of strangers and the gift of friendship.

One friendship touched my own family already living in the United States. It circles back to February 10, 1940, and the abduction of Józef and his family that my brother Henry witnessed. Jan and Zofia Kaniewski and their four sons and daughter were also seized that night. The daughter, my brother's future wife, was a child in one of those cattle cars. Years later, I learned from Roman, one of the four sons, what happened after the family was abducted.

Józef and Jan met in a resettlement camp in England. They bonded deeply the way only men in battle can fathom. They both survived World War I and the 1920 war with Russia. Like Józef, Jan was rewarded with land for helping Poland become independent, then banished years later to Russia for this very reason. Being set free, both families reached the Polish army in Uzbekistan, with the gory battle of Monte Cassino ahead of them. But the Kaniewski's did not stay together.

Jan and Zofia Kaniewski and their five children had crossed the enormous expanse of Russia and Kazakhstan to reach Uzbekistan. With the Polish army ready to lead them out of the Soviet Union, the parents had a dilemma. Zofia worried that the children might not survive crossing Turkmenistan to reach Iran. Jan agreed, "Our children are sick and weak. If we leave Uzbekistan now with the army, our children might not make it, especially the youngest."

Uttering the bravest decision of her life, Zofia said. "Leave without us. Polish men, like you, are joining the British to fight Germany. The children and I are too weak to sit for weeks with little food in crowded trucks across the Turkmenistan desert. Our oldest, Wacek, is fifteen. In a few months, he will leave for Iran to join the fight. Next year, Roman will follow."

Not sure he would see them again, but saying with conviction he would, Jan left his wife and children to join the Second Polish Corps of the British Eighth Army. Wacek and Roman soon joined a military school and trained en route to Iran to replace their fallen elders. As Stefania said, the Russian boys that had helped her mother were on their way to the front to kill and be killed. These Polish boys were on their way to kill and be killed.

Zofia and the three youngest – Regina, Chester, and Eugene – remained in Uzbekistan in a refugee camp. A dangerous place. Zofia contracted typhoid fever and lay dying on a cot. Her children were put in an orphanage. With no one to feed them, some people died of hunger instead of typhoid. But Zofia's lay next to a Jewish woman whose family saved her life. When the woman's family came to feed their mother, they also fed Zofia. They offered her the kindness of strangers.

Both women recovered. Zofia got off the cot, expressed her eternal gratitude to the Jewish family for saving her from starvation. She gathered Chester, Regina, and Eugene from the orphanage and boarded a convoy before Stalin closed the borders. For two years, they lived in camps for military dependents set up by the British in Iran, then Lebanon, and finally in Egypt. The children attended schools staffed by teachers who had been deported to the Soviet Union in mass numbers.

When the war ended in 1945, Jan and Zofia were alive. Their five children were alive. Despite all odds, they found each other. And despite all odds, Henry and Regina also found each other – which takes us from kindness of strangers, friendship, and family love to romantic love.

Uncle Józef wrote my parents that a family in the re-settlement camp in England had become his dear friends. They were leaving for America. When we met them in 1952, Henry shook hands with the four sons, but would rather have kissed Regina. Yet, he had to be content with a long-distance courtship. My brother was named after Henry Mara, and like our uncle, he became an American soldier. After his tour of duty, he came home and married the love of his life.

My brother Henry was a bookworm. He was proud to say that with schools in the camps, and later in England, Regina had earned the equivalent of a two-year college education. When the war was over, Uncle Józef set in motion our two families meeting and becoming close friends. Regina sailed to America, and into Henry's heart. Thank you, Uncle Józef.

Reflections

I don't feel anger or hatred, but mostly sadness.

DC: Can you forgive?

Stefania (Long pause). We are taught to forgive. No one in my family was killed, so it's easier to talk about forgiveness. I'm not bitter because mother found something, cooked something, figured it out. They sold candy for children on St. Nicholas Day, December 6. After long hours in the Russian forest, she stood in line until three in the morning to buy me candy. That's how much she sacrificed for me.

I don't feel anger or hatred, mostly sadness. Why did the Soviet government do this to people? From the misery it caused, it's hard to understand why anyone welcomed communism. Russian villagers were good people. So poor, yet they shared their last piece of bread. The people in power did this and many died an unnatural death, so they had their own kind of punishment.

Father's comrades stayed in England, or went to Canada, United States, South America, Australia. Father had two brothers in America, Henry and your dad Michał, and Jan in Canada, but he was worn out...or maybe being in Europe he was closer to Poland. I'm just grateful to God to be alive.

Stefania Chmara Kuryło was born in Naliboki, Poland on November 27, 1931 and passed away in Nottingham, England in May 2007. Tadeusz Kuryło was born in Poland on May 16, 1921, and passed away in 2010 in Nottingham. He worked for the British Coal Mines for 31 years. They had one daughter who is a social worker with traumatized teenagers, and one granddaughter. Józef was born in Naliboki on November 25, 1898 and passed away in Nottingham on October 2, 1971. Józefa Hodyl Chmara was born in Naliboki on March 3, 1902, and passed away in Nottingham on June 3, 1974.

Stefania (left) with a friend after the war in Africa, 1947.

Endnotes

1 Margaret Macmillan, *Paris 1919. Six Months that Changed the World* (NY: Random, 2001) pp. 207 – 208.

2 Laurence Rees, *Behind Closed Doors* (NY: Pantheon, 2008) p. 47, p. 91.

3 Neal Ascherson, *The Struggles for Poland*, (NY: Random House, 1987) p. 119

4 Marek Tuszynski, interview on February 11, 2009 in Fairfax, Virginia.

5 Tadeusz Piotrowski, ed., *The Polish Deportees of World War II. Recollections of Removal to the Soviet Union and Dispersal Throughout the World* (Jefferson, NC: McFarland & Co., 2004) pp. 10-12

6 Matthew Parker, Monte Cassino, *The Hardest-Fought Battle of World War II* (NY: Doubleday, 2004) p. 289, p. 333.

Chapter 2 Alicja
The Parched Steppe of Kazakhstan

My mother's ability to make friends with people of any age served her well as her contemporaries passed away. Alicja was 30 years younger, and like us, she came from the eastern part of Poland that had been invaded by the Soviet Union in 1939. The European formality of calling each other Mrs. Chmara and Mrs. Pszonka did not lessen the warmth of sewing projects, family photos, and shared food. Such moments helped heal their losses and affirm the ways in which life goes on.

After five miles of traffic and curving country roads, Alicja would arrive at my mother's house in Cranbury, New Jersey, and jump off her bicycle – cheerful and neat. Her subtle toughness began as a two-year-old. Unlike my cousin Stefania who was exiled to Russia with her parents, Alicia's family was thrust into the Soviet Republic of Kazakhstan not knowing what had become of her father.

Alicja was seven when she, her mother, and aunt were liberated and resettled in western Poland. She grew up, married, had a son, then came to the United States in her forties. I knew her as pretty, with thick black hair, a creamy complexion, kind, and a bit formal. While Stefania's family found healing in England, for Alicja's family the war cast a large and enduring shadow.

The Crime: Father Was a Polish Officer

War crushes hopes and ends marriages.

Alicja's parents were ecstatic at her birth in 1938, hoping for a brother or sister one day. But war crushes hope and ends marriages. When Russian tanks rolled into my town of Naliboki in 1939, they also ended a way of life further south in Alicja's village of Worohta (now in Ukraine.) Alicja's grandmother, aunt, and teen-age uncle lived in the nearby Polish village of Rohatyn.

She said, "Mother walked to Rohatyn with me in her arms, but father was never with us. He was a marked man. The Russian secret police, NKVD, labeled us enemies of the revolution because we were an educated family, and my father was a Polish officer. He patrolled the border between Poland and Romania. During a visit to Rohatyn, an NKVD spy could have seen my mother hanging up laundry, so they thought father, mother, and baby were together. Three men burst into the house at midnight. I was clinging to mother as we stood at gunpoint. They searched the house, but father was hiding with relatives. So, they arrested us."

My cousin Stefania's family was deported in February 1940. Alicja's family – three women, a teen-age boy, and two-year-old Alicja – were snared that April as "criminals" to be punished. It was the second of four mass deportations. Alicja said, "If a man was in the military, they punished the family. They hated teachers like my mother and aunt. They grabbed people with some money or a good job."

The "anti-Soviet elements" to be deported included forest keepers, attorneys and judges, engineers, artists, and farmers, Ukrainians, Belorussians, Lithuanians, Jews, and other Polish citizens. I told Alicja, "The Soviets made my Uncle Jan a clerk in the town hall. Alone one day, he found a list of "Anti-Soviet Elements." My family was on that list because my father had served in the Polish army. Then he trained young men in the Polish Rifle Squads. These squads were guardians of Polish independence, so my family was targeted for deportation into the Soviet Union. But with the 1941 German invasion of Eastern Poland, we were deported to Germany instead. My family stayed together, but you were deported while your father was in hiding. Were you ever reunited with him?"

She explained, "We didn't know for years, was he alive or dead? When he returned to us briefly, he told us how the NKVD found him and sent him to a hard labor prison, a *lager*, in Russia.

With Alicja's father lost to them, they were exiled to the far east in cattle cars marked "Polish Transport." No longer pushing toward the Arctic Circle, the crowded trains crossed Asia with many dying of hunger and thirst. The living sat next to the dead until the corpses were thrown out into the

Poland to Kazakhstan, 1940 *(Jan Kostka)*

snowy vastness.   Two months later, they reached the dry tundra of Kazakhstan, then a Soviet republic near China.

A Prison without Walls

It is our own blood and we can't waste it.

Baby Alicja, her mother, grandmother, aunt, and 15-year-old uncle reached Kazakhstan in early summer 1940. Flanked by armed guards, the new arrivals stumbled out of cattle cars that were no longer crowded. But the Grim Reaper was not satisfied with his harvest during the two-month long push into Asia. He decided to stay.

Trudging for miles, the group came to a circle of clay-plastered huts with a well in the middle. Two or three families were crammed into one mud hut the size of two bed-rooms. The huts had no doors, just a chimney-like exit. They slept on tiers of wooden boards that took up most of the space.

The treeless steppe of wild grass offered no relief in temperatures of 120° Fahrenheit. Blinding dust storms tore the scorched grass into clumps. As people died, families of Turkmen, Kazaks, and Uzbeks were brought in. Alicja said, "Like us, they were brought in to do hard labor as some kind of punishment."

I asked, "Why were you being punished?"

"For being Polish. Hitler saw us as an inferior race, and the German and Soviet governments wanted our land. We worked along with Turkmen, Kazaks, and Uzbeks all day under a burning sun, skin raw and blistered. The more children a woman had, the bigger a plot of millet she had to cultivate. I can still see the Russian overseer on a horse yelling, 'Davaj v robotu' – get to work."

They harvested the ripe grain and threshed it by hand. The flour they ground for bread and cereal could have fed them. But it was sent to the Soviet front. Alicja said, "We raised cattle, chickens, and sheep that fed the Soviet army. Men sheared the sheep. Women washed the wool many times in a drafty barn to remove bugs and feces. In winter we spun the clean wool into thread, wove the thread into cloth, and sewed uniforms. Grandmother and I sat in the mud hut knitting our quota of wool socks for Soviet soldiers."

I asked, "What did you eat?"

"Each person got some flour and two pieces of heavy black bread a day. Field workers like my mother also got four 'dumplings,' balls of dirty flour with husks boiled in water that scratched her throat. In summer, we found wild shrubs and grasses, cooked them into a mush, and forced it down. Clever children poured water into one end of a burrow and caught gophers jumping out the other end for a rare taste of meat."

Eating furry gophers seems repulsive to well-fed people, as does an unusual form of personal hygiene. She said, "We had no soap. Mother found a plant that made foam, but nothing was ever really clean. Lice and other vermin infested everything in summer. The hunger was so horrendous that when the Uzbeks and Kazaks cleaned themselves, they ate their own lice."

Alicja paused, regained her composure, and continued, "My mother couldn't stand the sight, so she asked, 'Why do you do this? How can you?' Their earnest answer was, "We have to do this. It is our own blood, and we can't waste it.'"

Eating lice in summer gave way to sub-zero frosts as snowdrifts covered the mud huts. Human contact and prayer were the only warmth within this frigid prison. Alicja said, "Mother held my hand tight as we snuck out to meet secretly in one hut in the late hours. People created their own prayers and songs to the Blessed Mother. We prayed fervently."

With cow dung as their only fuel, one winter they were cut off from the world by a snowstorm. Alicja said, "We had nothing to put to our lips for five days. We lay swollen from hunger. When a food shipment came, it was too late for my grandmother. We lost track of how many people froze or starved to death."

I said, "You were a child when you saw death directly. Did you understand it?"

She spoke haltingly, "We were crammed into that hut with two other families. The worst was watching people die slowly of hunger and cold. I was terrified to see grandmother die this way. I was only two, then three, but I knew it was forever. The huts became less crowded. When we left Kazakhstan...going past the cemetery. A moaning...it rose...it filled the cattle cars. It grew to a pitch...it lasted until the graves were out of sight...completely out of sight. We were all leaving someone...leaving behind someone we loved."

Soviet Crimes Hidden for Decades

If you didn't include historic references, it would be hard to believe these shocking events.

Speaking with Stefania's and Alicja about their childhoods, I wondered why most people know about crimes committed by Nazi Germany, but few, even in academia, know about Soviet atrocities. When I shared these accounts with my former college professor, he told me, "If you hadn't included historic references, it would be hard to believe these shocking events."

Professor Czesław Miłosz addresses the issue of Soviet impunity in Poland after the war in a later chapter. Polish American historian, Marek Tuszynski, explains how the United States and Great Britain created this gap in knowledge due to the urgencies of war. He states that the German and Soviet governments were dictatorships with ideologies of expansion, and they began a war in central and Eastern Europe to implement these ideologies. These ideologies affected my family through the dual invasion of my village Naliboki in 1939 from the east and in 1941 from the west.

From the east, Soviet imperialism was meant to conquer lands that had belonged to Czarist Russia during the
18th and 19th centuries when Poland disappeared from the
map of Europe. Citizens of countries like Poland, especially within leadership ranks, were brutally deported to make
room for Russian settlement. Soviet citizens were then sent
to these countries to impose Russian language, culture, and
rule upon the remaining populations.[7]

From the west, the German *Lebensraum* policy was
behind Hitler's attack on Poland in 1939. It was meant to
eliminate Slavic people and make this area available for German settlement. The Slavic people would be exterminated,
with a few of the strongest remaining as a labor force for
Germany.[8]

Marek Tuszynski explained further that with the Germany invasion of its former ally in June 1941, the Soviet
Union joined forces with Great Britain, the United States,
and other Allied countries. The British and American governments, whose populations were largely unaware of Soviet
crimes, did not want their average citizens to know that their
governments had joined forces with a repressive regime that
had deported and murdered minority populations before and
during the war. This information was withheld because they
needed Soviet manpower to defeat Germany. As the United
States supplied enormous material resources to the Soviet
Union, the Allied war effort benefited from the Soviet military
force against Germany.[9]

Both governments preferred no mention of what British journalist, Neal Ascherson, describes as an attempt at
obliterating the Polish nation. The 21-month Soviet invasion
of Poland during the war "far outdid all the crimes committed against Poland during the century-and-a-quarter of Russian occupation under the Tsars."[10]

The British/American/Soviet alliance lasted until
President Truman allowed the atom bomb to be dropped on
Hiroshima on August 5 and on Nagasaki, Japan on August
9, 1945. When Japan surrendered, Britain and the United
States no longer needed Russian manpower. As the Cold
War began in 1947, Great Britain and the United States
openly criticized the Soviet government.

According to British historian, Lawrence Rees, joining

forces with the Soviet Union did save British and American lives. The difference in the number of losses suffered by the Soviets compared to the Western Allies was huge. He states, "The Americans and British each suffered around 400,000 dead, whilst the Soviet Union endured a death toll of 27 million."[11]

Leaving Kazakhstan

Any remaining survivors and their offspring are still there today.

Polish citizens were deported to the Soviet Union for hard labor between 1940 and 1941 until the 1941 German attack on its Soviet ally gave Stalin another use for these prisoners. He freed some of these men to fight Germany and allowed a Polish army to form in two locations – in Russia and in the former Soviet country of Uzbekistan. Alicja's Uncle was 16 by then and on his way to join the Polish army forming in Uzbekistan, the army that was to lead Stefania's family out of the Soviet Union.

Alicja's father was among the men set free from the *lager*, the hard labor prison, in Russia. Heading south through Kazakhstan, he gave up the protection of his group to search for his wife and daughter. She said, "I don't know how, but he found us. I was afraid of him. I recoiled from this dirty stranger. Nothing like the father who laughed and sang while rocking me to sleep in his arms."

Two years since they had been husband and wife, Alicja's parents had a few days to recognize the beloved faces that had aged decades. Alicja sat with them as they agonized over the next step. Less and less afraid of the stranger who barged into their hut, she saw glimmers of her daddy. Once, she climbed onto his lap and heard him sob as he put his arms around her. Then, she heard talk of leaving. She heard him say, "We must leave quickly to reach the Polish army. They will lead us out of this wretched place. Our teenage nephew has already left to be a soldier. When we get to Iran, the Polish men are joining the British to fight Germany."

Alicja heard her mother say, "That's not possible. You must leave now by yourself. Two frail women and a five-year-

old weak from hunger and work. We don't have the strength
to go across Asia with the Polish army. Alicja might not make
it. We will follow at a slower pace."

He protested, "My child is starting to know me as her
father. You women have been without a man's protection all
these years. I could be killed fighting and never see my wife
and child again. We must go together."

She said, "And we could die of hunger and cold crossing Asia. I think of the life we expected when we married.
The brother or sister Alicja would have had. I could lose my
mind thinking about it."

Alicja's father and his teen-age nephew both reached
the Polish army. It pushed relentlessly out of Uzbekistan before Stalin changed his mind about releasing Polish prisoners. Alicja's mother was right. There were burials along the
way, especially the elderly and children.

Before leaving Kazakhstan, Alicja, mother, and aunt
prayed at the grandmother's grave. No one would ever again
visit her grave as the matriarch's remains would melt into
the Kazak steppe. As they turned their backs to the huts
encircling the well, Alicja hoped to forget them forever. But
these memories resurfaced as nightmares all her life.

Hope of
reuniting with
father and un-
cle tempered the
bleakness as
they moved west
across Asia. But
reaching the
city of Tash-
kent,Uzbekistan
in 1943, they
learned that
Stalin refused
to free any more
prisoners. Stefa-
nia's family had
left in time, but
they were stuck.
With bony backs

Poland in 1945 (Adam Carr)[15]

bent in fields of grain, they again grew food for the Soviet army, tasted the dust and heat of summer, burned cow dung for winter fuel, and swallowed bread that scratched their throats. The one thing the atheistic communist system did not take from them was their faith as they shared rare moments of secret communal prayer. And they outlasted the war.

The war in Europe ended in May 1945. Cattle cars full of skeletal women and sickly children left Uzbekistan and crept toward the Ukrainian city of Lviv (Polish: Lwów) They were the lucky ones. Thousands of other prisoners from the four major deportations were stranded in the Soviet republics forever. Any remaining survivors and their offspring are still there today. New generations may not know about their Polish roots or how their ancestors got there.

When the cattle cars arrived in Ukraine, Polish families took the women and children into their homes. She said, "At age seven, I was surprised to learn that eating was a pleasure. The bread in Kazakhstan was hard to swallow. Our hostess gave me noodles with milk that slid smoothly down my throat. I didn't know food could be soft and pleasant."

I said, "I was seven the first time I remember eating meat, amazed how delicious a sausage could be."

"You and I were the lucky ones to survive as babies. The Polish family in Lwów who took us in brought us back to life. They fed us and let us rest. We talked about what the Soviets did to us without being afraid someone would overhear and report us to the commandant."

Fortified by the kindness of strangers and the warmth of human contact without fear, the two women and child went southwest 90 miles to their former town. An uncle took them in. The familiar landscape, the crisp air and rustle of leaves as they walked in the forest was healing their souls. What joy to have come home. But it was too good to be true.

Free but not Free

The Red Army stayed in Poland against the will of the people for five decades.

My once-Polish town of Naliboki was absorbed into the country of Belarus; Alicja's home further south was an-

nexed to the then Soviet republic of Ukraine. Choosing to be
Polish citizens instead of Soviet subjects, these women were
part of the mass displacement of Polish and German people
who lost their ancestral homes after the war. Yet these two
countries were excluded from a voice in decisions made by
a few men.

British historian Laurence Rees cites archival material made available since the end of the Soviet Union. He
describes a late-night meeting on November 28, 1943 in Te-
heran between Soviet leader Stalin, British Prime Minister
Churchill, and British Foreign Secretary Anthony Eden. "By
the use of similes, metaphors and ultimately props in the
form of matches Churchill and Eden reshaped the boundaries of Poland and Germany – significantly without the presence of representatives from the two countries involved in
this demographic and geographical upheaval...The notes
of the meeting conclude: 'The Prime Minister demonstrated
with the help of three matches [to mark the new borders] his
idea of Poland moving westwards, which pleased Marshal
Stalin'."[12]

During subsequent meetings in Yalta and Potsdam,
the United States and Great Britain accommodated Stalin
by letting eastern Poland become part of the Soviet Union –
displacing Polish people, like Alicja's family and mine. Alicja
said, "Refugees from western Europe were putting the war
behind them and going home. Polish and German people
had their homes taken from them."

American author, Mark Wyman, explains, "...a new
group of refugees appeared – the ethnic Germans or *Volks-
deutschen* – who had resided as their ancestors had in areas
of Poland or other central European countries now freed of
Nazi control, or who lived in regions of Germany transferred
to Polish sovereignty by the Potsdam Agreement. Perhaps 12
million of these "expellees," ... entered Germany in the two
years immediately following the war.[13]

With Eastern Poland in Soviet hands, Alicja's family
felt out of place in their beloved homeland and moved onto
land transferred from Germany to Poland. They settled near
the city of Wrocław (German: Breslau) in southwestern Poland where some of my family from Naliboki now lives.

But not all was well. Poland had new borders and promises of self-determination, promises Stalin never intended to keep. The United States, Great Britain, and the Soviet Union agreed at the conference in Potsdam, Germany in 1945 that free elections were to be held in Poland as soon as possible, and that the Red Army was to leave Polish territory. But, as Alicja said, "The Red Army stayed in Poland against the will of the people for five decades."

Having left their ancestral home to avoid being Soviet subjects, they were now living in a country that was a Soviet satellite and took orders from Moscow. Returning from Kazakhstan in ruined health, Alicja's mother and aunt died young. She grew up, married, and had a son. Despite many warm hours with my mother, she never told her why, when she left for the United States, she came alone.

The war had thrown Stefania and Alicja into the far reaches of the globe. In the next chapter, you will meet my long-lost cousins who lost their country without ever leaving their plot of land.

Reflections

I feel sorrow for people who were capable of such abuse toward their fellow human beings.

DC: *Can you forgive your captors?*

I don't feel anger. I feel sorrow for people who were capable of such abuse toward other human beings. I'm amazed people could behave this way. It was wrong, but they were blinded by that regime.

DC: *Do you think some of them ever understood what they had done?*

The atrocities are coming to light. I think they are embarrassed by what is being revealed. I can't imagine not being ashamed of such behavior. These things are hard to talk about. My mother gave me her bread so I could live. She never talked about it later, but I was old enough to know.

My aunt's heart problems were never treated during our captivity, and she died soon after the war. My mother had a blood clot and pneumonia in her lungs that were ignored. She never regained her health and died in 1969 of lung cancer. Those deaths don't show up in war statistics.

DC: *These memories open old wounds. I am grateful to you for this conversation.*

(Alicja sat quietly for a long time until another memory surfaced.) I heard that the worst torture is the constant dripping of water on the head. It slowly creates such pain that your head feels like it will explode. My aunt was tortured like this. We got a letter in which the common Polish name "Franek" was used, so the communist authorities decided she must be a spy for Francisco Franco.

DC: *They thought she was a spy for the Spanish resistance that tried to overthrow Francisco Franco's dictatorship? (Spanish Civil War of 1936-1939)*

Yes, they accused her of spying for the revolutionaries. What was there to spy on? Dust, lice, and cow dung. My uncle survived the carnage of Monte Cassino. But after my father left to join the Anders army, we never saw him again. He died in 1944 at the Battle of Monte Cassino.

DC: *The last time your parents saw each other was during their brief reunion in that hut with two other families when you were just starting to recognize him as your father.*

Yes. The war ended their marriage.

DC: *Those moments on your father's lap had to last you the rest of your life. The Hoover Institute at Stanford University has thousands of accounts of Soviet deportations. Like you, others have revisited their pain to give witness. Thank you for being so brave.*

War is horrible. An abomination.

Alicja Pszonka was born in March 1938 in the Stanisławów Province of Poland. She was a caretaker for the elderly in the United States. She maintains contact with her son, daughter-in-law, and grandson in Poland. Her account is based on conversations I joined during her visits with my mother.

For More Information. Poland after the War

British journalist, Neal Ascherson, states that in a 1940 broadcast, Winston Churchill told the Polish nation that the end of the war will reward their numerous sacrifices because no nation served the cause of freedom more faithfully than Poland. "They fought Hitler from the first day of the war to the last, on land, at sea and in the air. Polish troops fought in Poland itself, in Russia and North Africa, in Norway, Italy, France and the Low Countries. They were in at the kill in Germany, and Polish troops helped to conquer Berlin. The Polish navy was in action, on the surface and in submarines, through the Battle of the Atlantic, in the North Sea and the English Channel. Poland's airmen took part in the Battle of Britain, in the bombing offensive against Germany, and in the support of the armies over every front. One in five of the entire population of Poland perished..." [14]

Churchill's promises of reward did not materialize. In Yalta, Ukraine, on February 11, 1945, Churchill and Roosevelt allowed Stalin to absorb the Polish lands invaded in 1939 into the Soviet republics of Belarus and Ukraine. The Lublin committee, a puppet of the Soviet government, came to power, and the London-based Polish government-in-exile was dismissed. Before the war, Poland was an independent country. After the war, it was ruined economically and run by a communist system unacceptable to most of the Polish people.

Endnotes

7 Marek Tuszynski, extensive conversations in February 2009 in Fairfax, Virginia.

8 Ibid

9 Ibid

10 Neal Ascherson, *The Struggles for Poland* (NY: Random House, 1987) p. 94

11 Laurence Rees, *World War II: Behind Closed Doors. Stalin, The Nazis, and the West* (NY: Pantheon Books, 2008) p. 406.

12 Ibid, pp. 221

13 Mark Wyman, *DP's. Europe's Displaced Persons, 1945-1951* (Ithaca: Cornell UP, 1998) pp. 19-20.

14 Neal Ascherson, *The Struggles for Poland* (NY: Random House, 1987) pp. 115-116.

15 The Curzon Line refers to the Polish/Soviet border proposed after World War I. It became the Polish/Soviet border after World War II.

Chapter 3 Janusz
Not Enough Strong Backs

Stefania hobbled around in the frozen Arctic wearing two different size shoes. Alicja was banished to the parched Kazakhstan steppe where rationed bread scratched her throat. Janusz and Stanisław Chmara never left home. The invader came to them, took their property, nationality, religion, even their names, and made them Soviet subjects.

These two brothers are my long-lost cousins. In Biblical terms, great-grandfather Florian begat my grandfather Stefan and their grandfather Konstantin. Stefan begat my father Michał and Konstantin begat their father Józik. Then Janusz and Stanisław and I appear. Clans lived and worked nearby for generations. I was 10 weeks old, and they were boys when we were pushed into the same cattle car going to Germany in 1943. On the way, our destinies diverged.

We met 52 years later when my husband Henry and I went to Naliboki in 1994 for the consecration of the church that was begun in 1936. Returning in 2000, we stayed with Janusz and wife Jadwiga. His name was Russified to "Ivan," but to me he was still Janusz. His slightly slanted eyes, like mine when I first awake, trace back to Tartar invasions starting in the 13th century. Removing his cap with large, calloused hands, his white forehead and ruddy face told me this auto mechanic was also a farmer.

Janusz had the serenity of a Zen monk free of ego. Henry enjoyed a good-natured friendship with him based on pointing, mime, and some Polish words, followed by hearty back-slapping. We lost him two years later the same way my father and uncles had left us. A sudden heart attack took him from this world. I am grateful to have shared bread at his table and laughed at his jokes.

After leaving Naliboki, we visited my mother's cousin Maria Baszuro whose family, like mine, had been deported to Germany. When the boundaries of Poland and Germany shifted after the war, our ancestral lands in Eastern Poland were absorbed into the Soviet Union. Refusing to be Soviet subjects, Maria's family resettled in the medieval city of Prusice in Western Poland that had been part of Germany before the war.

Maria and her daughter Irena lived in a substantial house. The walls were covered with oil paintings by Maria's late husband Bernard and Irena's late husband Stanisław's hunting trophies. He had built a cottage in the back yard to hold a precious memento of his army career: a United Nations banner commemorating the 1988 Nobel Peace Prize awarded to the Middle East peacekeeping mission in which he had participated. The German family who left with the change of borders sometimes returns to inspect their former home. Maria wondered if this means hopes of returning someday.

Maria Baszuro was an adult when nine-year-old Janusz witnessed the May 1943 massacre in Naliboki. I include her eye-witness account to validate his recollections.

The First Invader
People I loved were gone in one day.

Janusz lived in a small house in the town center. He said, "My parents Józik and Wercia had five children. There was my brother Stanisław, my three sisters, me and grandmother. My father's brother Edward had a wife and daughter. They lived with us too."

I said, "With ten of your family in one house, I guess you're never alone."

"Father also had a twin brother Bernard, and two sisters Józefa and Hanna, a minute's walk from us."

I said, "Didn't it ever feel like too much of a good thing?"

"We needed each other. We helped with plowing, borrowed horses, shared food. We sat together in the same pews in church, the way our ancestors did, before the communists came."

I said, "When I visit Naliboki, I love to sit with your wife and other women relatives in the Chmara pew where I belong."

Before my father helped build the large brick church they now use, the priest led them in prayer in a snug wooden chapel with a few pews. Janusz said, "We loved Father Bajko. He opened an electric power station, a sawmill for lumber, a furnace for making bricks, and electricity by 1939. Life was getting easier."

Another improvement before the war was the consolidation of farmland by the Polish government. Janusz explained, "We had seven strips in seven places, near your mother's family going south, near your father's family going north. We loaded the wagon with manure, tools and seed each time. Lost time plowing, planting and harvesting in so many faraway locations. If Naliboki stayed as part of Poland after the war, farming would have become more efficient."[16]

Instead of more efficient land distribution, the 1939 Soviet invasion meant confiscation of property and deportations. Aunt Hanna and her husband, the ones who lived a minute from Janusz, were deported to the Soviet Union. I asked, "Why? They weren't involved in politics."

Shaking his head, he said, "Her husband was a policeman. That's why. If you were a landowner, teacher, policeman, forest warden, had four cows, even two, they said you were rich, a *kulak*. They said you exploit the working class. They took their land and sent them to Siberia. People I loved were gone in one day. Forest warden Szerbik boarded with us. He would take my hand, and we explored the forest with his big gray dog. The Russians came to our house for Szerbik. His dog followed. Winter 1940 was bitter cold. Poor dog showed up weeks later shivering. We fed him. He headed for the stove and slept. The next day he left for good, looking for his master."

The Second Invader
Taking sides was dangerous, staying neutral was dangerous.

Janusz witnessed the Soviet invasion at age nine and heard the march of German boots at age 11. Thrusting eastward to seize fertile farmland, Germany invaded its former Soviet ally in 1941. During this surprise attack, German soldiers pushed the Russian soldiers out of our town. Planning to stay, they set up headquarters in the town of Iwieniec, 11 miles northeast of Naliboki.

The Russians also expected to stay. Janusz said, "Germans pushed them out of town, but the Russian soldiers turned into fierce partisans, guerrilla fighters. That thick forest I explored with Szerbik and his gray dog was full of wildlife. Those hungry partisans hid in that primeval forest, the *Nalibocka Puszcza*. They stole food from farmers like us living on the edge of the forest."

I said, "Two years earlier, Germany and Russia were allies and attacked Poland from two directions."

Janusz said, "Germany had helpers. Ukraine, Latvia, Lithuania, and Estonia were on their side."

Polish American historian, Tadeusz Piotrowski, explains why the local Ukrainian government helped Germany. "Between 1929 and 1934, during Stalin's unrelenting war against the Ukrainian peasantry, twenty million farms were collectivized, and fifteen million people perished...In 1932-33 alone, the years of the artificially induced Ukrainian famine, six million people starved to death. (Some estimates say ten million)"[17]

According to Piotrowski, another reason was distrust between Polish and Ukrainian people. When Poland regained independence after World War I, Ukrainian majorities lived in provinces ruled by Poland. Long-standing animosities grew as the Polish minority treated the Ukrainian majority with discrimination regarding land distribution, politics, education, and religion. In addition, Ukraine expected Germany to help it become independent from the Soviet Union. [18]

American historian, Mark Wyman, adds that in Latvia, Lithuania, and Estonia, "The Communists ended religious instruction, brought in Soviet textbooks, and planted spies among the pupils...the secret police began deporting...much of the intellectual and administrative leadership of the Baltic countries...to Siberia, Kazakhstan, or other areas of the Soviet hinterland..." [19]

Wyman continues, "Some 200,000 Jews were killed or deported in Lithuania alone; thousands of young people were recruited throughout the three nations for *Arbeitsdienst* (work service) in Germany; 40,000 Balts were placed in concentration camps; and German troops massacred hundreds in reprisal raids... For the Baltic peoples, growing hopes for the end of the war included no realistic expectation of independence [from Soviet control]." [20]

Janusz and Maria Baszuro watched the German soldiers and Russian partisans lock horns. When the partisans circled Naliboki to carry out food raids, the Germans and their collaborators tried to repel them. Janusz said, "The Russian partisans who stole our food were a powerful force against the Germans, together with the Lithuanian and Latvian fighters who wanted the food for themselves."

Maria agreed, "Partisans hiding in the forest became mean and strong against the Germans. It was a mix of Russian, Jewish, Belarussian partisans. And while they robbed and killed us, they demanded our loyalty."

Janusz said, "Taking sides was dangerous, staying neutral was dangerous. Some people were so terrified they betrayed neighbors. Someone told the Germans that a family was baking bread for the Russians. The soldiers came and ordered, 'Dig a hole!' Stood the family by the pit, shot them for helping the Russians, got in their car, and left."

Such demands for loyalty came to a blazing end for most of the Christians in 1943. But the German invasion in 1941 meant immediate disaster for the Jewish minority living in the town center, called the *miasteczko*, where the synagogue stood. Before we see how differently the German army treated the Christians and Jews, let us get a feel for how they lived together for decades.

Janusz said, "We lived in our part of the *miasteczko*, they lived in theirs, north up the road toward your home in what we called Kamionka. We were private farmers. We sold animals and produce to the Jews. They owned small shops, sold vodka and cucumbers in the tavern. People bargained and could buy on credit. The elderly woman Golda walked up and down the street selling buns. I bartered eggs with her for buns. We knew each other, got along. Some people were friends, went to each other's houses. But we could not marry each other."

Polish historian Eva Hoffman describes how Christians and Jews coexisted. She states that "...pluralism was experienced not as an ideology but as ordinary life. Jews trading horses in a small market town, speaking in haphazard Polish...Poles gradually picking up a few words of Yiddish and bits of Jewish lore...Jewish bands playing at Polish weddings and local aristocrats getting financial advice and loans from their Jewish stewards – all that went into the making of the distinctive mulchy mix that was shtetl culture. This was where both prejudices and bonds were most palpably enacted – where a Polish peasant might develop a genuine affection for his Jewish neighbor despite negative stereotyping and, conversely, where an act of unfairness or betrayal could be most wounding because it came from a familiar. [21]

This way of life ended in April 1942 when German soldiers surrounded the Jewish part of Naliboki. Janusz said, "They forced them out onto the street. The rabbi walked in front, people behind. They wore yellow patches on their backs and fronts. We came out on the street. They pointed guns at us. We couldn't get near them. Someone tried to give them bread. Soldiers whacked him with a rifle butt and threw down the bread. Oh, the terror! The way they cried! The only person I knew who got away was the policemen Honek. He hid in the woods."

The Jewish minority that had lived in Naliboki since the 1800's was brutally eliminated. Janusz said, "The German soldiers took the Jews to a forest near [the city of] Nowogródek. Made them dig a large pit. Stood them on the edge. Then the soldiers shot them."

An Avalanche of Armed Angry Men
On that day, one mother lost three sons.

The Jews of Naliboki died in the pit they were forced to dig. The Christians became pawns between German soldiers and Soviet partisans. When a German soldier was shot, his commander wanted revenge. He had some local people herded into a barn to set it on fire. A German woman married to a Polish man stepped forward. She insisted that these people did not kill his soldier. Bullets unleashed by Russian partisans had killed him. The people locked in the barn stood in anguish, expecting a painful death. But speaking his own language, she was persuasive.

With a crowd of agonized onlookers watching from a distance, the commander told his men not to set the barn on fire. The traumatized men and women heard the lock open, saw the barn door move. As they pushed their way into the fresh air, a teen-age boy fainted. Revived by the fresh air, the disoriented boy walked home with his parents.

The German commander relented, but he insisted the local men must prove they are not aiding the Russian partisans. Before his troops left temporarily for the front, he demanded that the *samoobrona*, the self-defense group, accept German guns to fight the partisans. The men took the few guns and scant ammunition forced upon them, but it was not enough to repel an avalanche of well-armed angry partisans fighting for the territory taken from them by the German army.

The boy Janusz stood frozen at his window on May 8, 1943. He said, "We lived in the center of town, across the street from the church. Russian partisans poured in from the woods, shooting and burning. They went into houses, dragged men outside, and 'Boom!' They killed our friends – three Łukaszewicz men, three Makowskis, one of the Sobols, two Korzenkos, and wounded others.

Also living in the town center, that blood-red day unfolded for Maria before she could say her morning prayers. She said, "I saw them come running and shooting at dawn. One of them threw burning straw into a house. He watched it burn and laughed. They burned houses, barns, the two schools your father built, the power plant, lumber mill, and the German garrison in Iwieniec."

She added, "On that day, one mother lost three sons. Russian partisans lined up our men along with my neighbor's three sons. They sent one of them home for cigarettes. The parents pleaded for him not to go back. The bewildered boy said they would kill his brothers. He went back. They took the cigarettes and killed all the men but one. He lay under the pile of bodies they were kicking. He heard them saying, 'The bitch's son is dead.'"

Janusz said, "The massacre went beyond the town center where I lived. The self-defense group didn't have enough guns or ammunition or men to save us but they wounded the Russian commander. The dying man ordered his men to kill anyone wearing trousers. So they spread out into every corner of Naliboki, taking with them every life and house they could destroy."

I said, "During this massacre, I was sleeping in my mother's womb. Twenty days before I was born, 128 people lay dead."

Summer was usually a time of harvest, devotions at tiny roadside chapels, and young people dancing and falling in love. But my first weeks on earth, the living had just buried fathers, mothers, wives and husbands, sons and daughters. They were rushing to build shelter, harvest grain, and store food before the early frost – unaware of the next human tsunami coming their way.

On August 7, 1943, German soldiers returned to finish the May destruction set loose by Russian partisans. Janusz said, "We had framed shelters for the winter, harvested the ripe grain, put our rye in sheaves. Then it was all burning – our hard-earned grain, our houses. They said to take wagons, livestock, all we could carry. They said they were moving us for safety from the partisans."

Not Enough Strong Backs

A sick father, five children, and a grandmother were useless for labor.

As Naliboki burns, Janusz's 42-year-old father Józik sits in bed, sick and unshaven, his five children by his side. A Russian partisan barges in, sees the helpless man, and steals clothes from the wardrobe. Józik's brother Edward runs in and blurts out that the old and sick who are too weak to walk are being shot. He forces Józik out of bed. Edward's wife helps Janusz's mother Wercia pack what food they can carry. With children and grandmother in tow, they leave the house they will never see again.

They walked 25 miles in three days, slept in fields at night. They met up with my own family at the Stołpce train station. We waited together in a cattle car, my mother cradling her ten-week-old Danusia, as I was called then. Our livestock was on its way to feed the German army, and we were not relocated for safety from the partisans.

Our two families were separated in the occupied Polish city of Białystok. After guards sprayed my family with the insecticide DDT, we were on the way to work in Germany unless we first died from exhaustion and hunger. Janusz and his family remained in barracks enclosed by barbed wire and surrounded by guards. He said, "After they sent you to Germany, we stood in line holding a coupon for a bowl of soup and sliver of bread. A kettle of turnips, beet tops, bean pods, but no beans – they called that soup. A guard stood on the top floor of a house. He waved a loaf of bread at us. He threw it down and began shooting it with his rifle. When he stopped, whoever grabbed the bread ate it right on the spot. He looked down, his round belly shaking with laughter."

Janusz's family waited seven weeks for the *Arbeitsamt* to decide how to use them. This agency set working conditions for Germans, voluntary foreign workers, and forced laborers. As German men fought on the front, this agency

The author in one of the many *ziemiankas,* dugouts, remaining in the Naliboki Forest, the *Nalibocka Puszcza.* 2017

assigned foreigners to replace them on farms and in factories. It sent Józik's brother Edward, wife, and daughter to work on a farm where the harvest helped feed the German army. But a sick father, five children, and a grandmother were useless for labor. Guards put them into a cattle car heading for the Stołpce train station. I asked, "That's about 25 miles from Naliboki. How did you get home?

Janusz said, "We walked all day. Took almost a week. Sometimes we got a wagon ride."

I asked, "What did you do for food? Eight people, including five children and a grandmother."

"We walked past villages. Farmers saw our ragged group. My parents went house to house asking for anything they could spare. People gave us potatoes, bread. An apple or pear. Before it got dark, my parents would pick a field to build an open fire. We cooked the potatoes, and it warmed us during the cold night. My parents fed us, and we fell asleep exhausted in the open field."

When they reached Naliboki, Janusz gasped at the corpse of his beloved town. Pastel colored houses circled by flowering yards and green fields had turned into ash. All that remained of their thriving farm was a barn with a partial roof. Janusz said, "At least we still had a barn. We found a tin container of salt in what used to be our kitchen, the only thing from our house that didn't burn. Aunt Hanna and her husband were in Siberia, but we didn't know what happened to father's twin brother Bernard and his sister Józefa."

The Reincarnation of Naliboki

A hole in the ground would have to be home the first winter.

Word of their return reached Józik's twin brother Bernard. He came to help. He and their sister Józefa had escaped into the primeval forest, the *Nalibocka Puszcza,* with their families during the August deportations to Germany. When the Germans left, they came out of the forest. Walking back to their farm, they found the house the two families shared burned to the ground. To hunker down for the winter, they set up a sturdy tent in Kamionka, the north part of Naliboki.

Janusz said, "Frost can come as early as September. A neighbor who hid in the forest from the Germans showed us how to make a clay stove for heating and cooking. Father and I worked with him making the stove while Uncle Bernard searched abandoned fields. He came back with wood scraps to cover the barn roof and a pile of bent metal bed frames. We cleaned and evened them out. Towns away from the forest did not get burned. Those farmers gave us straw and we made mattresses."

The parents, five children, and grandmother lived this way for five years until they built a house in 1949. In the new house, they had real mattresses, sheets, and pillowcases.

Having secured shelter, the brothers helped families who had nothing left to repair. The first step was to dig out a small cellar, find boards to support the earthen walls, fashion a floor and ceiling, and insulate the wooden roof with moss, leaves, and soil. An iron or clay stove with an exhaust pipe heated these dugouts, called *ziemianki*. A hole in the ground would have to be home the first winter.

More families returned. According to articles compiled by Valentina Buniak, the Naliboki Head Librarian, some 40 households had escaped into the forest during the deportations to Germany. With the German army gone, they left the forest and survived the first winter in such holes in the ground. Then life began to stir.[22]

Winter 1943. Men dug holes and built *ziemianki*. Women gathered potatoes, beets, cabbage, and onions from abandoned fields to survive the winter.

Spring 1944. Men ploughed fields. Women seeded the rich soil. Janusz said, "Szemioty, Bukraby families, Józefa Klimowicz never left and lived in *ziemianki*. They had cows and gave us milk.

Summer 1944. They savored the crunch of fresh vegetables. Janusz said, "The partisans got orders to leave us alone. They were going past with 15 cows and gave us a cow. Now we had our own milk."

Fall 1944. They harvested grain, threshed it with a flail to remove husks, ground the grain into flour. Janusz said, "We finally had flour to bake bread."

After clawing to survive, families were allowed to leave for Poland between 1945 and 1946. Many decided to stay on their beloved ancestral lands. (Far from Naliboki and generations removed, my family still grows a tomato or petunia on any bit of soil we can nurture.) But the final blow came when the land they loved was taken from them to form communal farms. Between 1956 and 1958, many left for Western Poland to start, again, on land that had been part of Germany before the war.

Janusz said, "To my father Józik, Poland with its new borders was not really Poland. He was afraid the Germans would attack again. How my mother wanted to go! We packed. Our neighbor took us to the train station on his horse and wagon. Father was restless. Walked back to check on things.

Janusz Chmara with wife Jadwiga and son Viktor. Nabliboki in the 1960's. *(Author's collection)*

He returned. Mother saw the look on his face. We quietly took our things and walked back. My father didn't trust it would be forever Poland."

By then, my Uncle Józef Chmara and his family had become British citizens. My Uncle Jan Chmara and his family were Canadian Citizens. My Uncle Henry Mara, and my father Michał Chmara and their families were American citizens. Janusz and his family were Soviet subjects. Janusz said, "Instead of moving to Poland, I was drafted into the Soviet army for three years."

I asked, "Do you wish your family had gone to Poland?"

"I was a child. It was out of my control. Our friend who settled in Western Poland comes back to visit. He said every year the former owner comes to see if the buildings are kept in good condition. They are, but why is he so interested?"

Reflections

The German people living today did not cause the war.

The warm bond with my distant cousins showed up in the use of names. The first day, I was Pani (Mrs.) Chmara. Then for a day or two, I was formally Danuta. Eating at the kitchen table, I became casually Danusia. Laughing and making jokes, I became affectionately Danka as we connected over our family nickname. Yes, families had nicknames as I had learned from my brother, Henry.

DC: We were scattered all over the globe, but your immediate family helped rebuild Naliboki.

Families that rebuilt Naliboki died away. Their children moved to Minsk. Only a few stayed whose roots go back for generations like yours and mine. It's a different place now.

We didn't know who was alive. Aunt Hanna was set free from the Russian *Lager* and moved to Poland. When she came to visit, she said that Uncle Edward and his family were with you in the displaced persons camp in Germany. Then they went to England. Like us, your father's sisters, Józefa and Maria, were never deported to Germany. They are now living in Western Poland. The four Chmara brothers were alive – Józef in England, Jan in Canada, Henry and Michał in America.

DC: Do you feel anger toward anyone?

Why should I? I like all types of people. The German side caused the war. Hitler kept pushing and pushing until the politicians got out of his way. Nobody would stand up to him.* But the German people living today didn't cause the war. When German soldiers retreated, they asked for food. If we had a potato, we gave it to them. They said they were forced to fight. If I was in the army, I would fight or they would kill me. If America attacked us, I would have to shoot at the Americans.

DC: But now your American cousin is sitting and eating at your table.

Why keep grudges? Blame the government. Don't blame the people. Why not sit and eat together? We're part of the same family. Do you know about family nicknames?

DC: I do. It goes back to great grandfather Florian.

Yes. We Chmaras were called Śienty because that's how he said the word for 'holy,' which is 'święty.' So, Danka, how could I turn you away? We are both Śienty. You're one of us!"

DC: My brother Henry explained how some people were known by family nicknames more than by their legal names. He said they didn't say it to their faces because some were downright ridiculous. One nickname was padpalka, "arsonist" in

Belarussian. Imagine being proud of that? And a man labeled "Kundaczka" hated his nickname. Henry didn't know what it meant. One day, the man stopped by and sister Mary asked, 'Hey dziadżka, are you Kundaczka?' Dziadżka was okay. It was like calling him uncle. But grandmother's face turned red when Mary said the nickname. And when an older man stopped by, father wanted to be polite. As soon as he said, "Please sit down, Mr. Miadzwiodka," he began apologizing. The nickname meant "bear cub" in Belarussian. Henry called it a funny custom.

Yes, we knew families by those nicknames. So, Danka, our legal last name is Chmara, but we are all Śienty here at this table, including you.

DC: *What joy to find you, eat your bread, laugh at your jokes, sit in church with the women where I belong. And see your faces that look like people I have known all my life.*

We were squeezed in together in that cattle car on the way to Germany. Your mother held her baby, trying to keep you alive. And here you are 51 years later back with us in Naliboki. It's a blessing.

Janusz Chmara was born on December 10, 1930 and passed away on July 12, 2003. He is survived by Jadwiga, their two sons, and three grandchildren. Maria Baszuro was born on October 10, 1910, and passed away on April 3, 2003. She and husband Bernard Baszuro had three children and five grandchildren. Irena Brzezinska was born on July 19, 1933 and passed away in 2017. She and husband Stanisław had a daughter and son, and four grandchildren.

*On September 29, 1938, British, French, German, and Italian leaders signed the Munich Agreement giving into Hitler's demands by allowing him to invade and annex part of Czechoslovakia called the Sudetenland. Despite the British Prime Minister Neville Chamberlain's declaration that this will bring "peace in our time," this agreement emboldened Hitler to invade Poland from the west the following September, followed by the Soviet invasion from the east two weeks later.

Endnotes

16 In many European countries and Eastern Europe as well, not all land owned by a farmer was contiguous. Plots might be in different areas.

17 Tadeusz Piotrowski, *Vengeance of the Swallows* (Jefferson, NC: McFarland, 1995) pp. 39-41.

18 Ibid.

19 Mark Wyman, *DP's: Europe's Displaced Persons, 1945-1951* (Ithaca: Cornell UP, 1998) pp. 32-33.

20 Ibid.

21 Eva Hoffman, *Shtetl: The Life and Death of a Small Town and the World of Polish Jews* (NY: Public Affairs, Perseus Books Group, 2007) pp. 12-13.

22 Based on author's meeting in 2017 with Naliboki Head Librarian Valentina Buniak, this information was compiled from articles written after 1991 in Promień, the Stołpce newspaper

Chapter 4 Stanisław
Always a Sorrow

On our first trip to Naliboki in 1994, my husband Henry and I stayed in the south end of town with my mother's childhood neighbor, Karol Sazanowicz and wife Halina. Across the street lived Stanisław (Staś) Chmara, the younger brother of Janusz. As we sat for our first breakfast, Staś walked into their house, prodding jovially, "Where is she? Where's my American kin."

"You must be Staś Chmara. I'm thousands of miles from home, and someone walks in looking like the other men in my family."

He chirped, "Welcome to Naliboki Pani Mrs. Chmara."

"I'm no pani to you. I'm your cousin. That blond hair, pink cheeks, and round face of yours. I could be looking at Uncle Jan in Canada or his sons."

He laughed, "We're one family scattered around the world."

As we joked, his round body shook with contagious laughter. But when Henry and I returned in 2000, our loveable Staś was a changed man. This time, we stayed with his brother Janusz and wife Jadwiga in the town center. A brisk half-hour walk took us to see Staś and his wife Maryla. He was feeding chickens in the front yard. She was propping up tomatoes in a garden full of happy-looking flowers.

They ran to embrace us vigorously and led us into what felt like a cozy hunting cabin with sofa, easy chair, television, and small table. Deer antlers hung on one wall, a forest tapestry on the other. We exchanged gifts – American towels and coffee, Belarussian linens and chocolates. Seven-year-old grandson, Juri, positioned himself between Henry and me to hear every word about America.

Dinner was then served on a round wooden table in a spacious dining room. I commented on the table being a piece of perfection. It must have been made by Chmara hands. With muted pride, Staś said, "I did all the wood furniture and tools in the house and garden. But please, I hope you like our food. You came so far to be with us."

An array of vegetables and salads on their best dishes looked five-star. A choice of meats was a luxury saved for special guests. Even the scarlet geraniums on sunny windowsills seemed glad to see us.

Parkinson's disease caused the tremor in Staś's hand, but the flat voice and wounded eyes came from deep sorrow. I was told that their only son and offspring Juri had died tragically at age 33, but they did not want to talk about it. The little boy sitting next to us was Juri's child. Staś couldn't voice his pain, so words of consolation sat stuck in my throat. As the day turned to dusk, he spun out local lore with the energy of the man we first knew. Had we grown up together, we would have been friends.

A day later, Henry and I sat at another table laden with food and looked at old photos with my father's goddaughter, Lodzia Okulicz. She and her brothers Janek and Walek, and sister Jadzia looked robust enough in those photos to produce abundant harvests. Now Lodzia's sharp mind lived inside a body bent over from years of labor. Her words echo Staś's childhood memories of two invasions.

Run for Your Life

The dying man told his men to kill everyone wearing trousers.

His parents tried to shield five-year-old Staś from seeing what happens during a massacre. Staś said, "My first memory was people killing each other. You don't see it written that partisans were killing us, people running wild to save themselves. The old people tell it like this: Women wore skirts. The men in our self-defense group shot the Russian commander, so the dying man told his men to kill everyone wearing trousers. He said they were helping Germans. The Germans took our food. The partisans stole chickens and cows to cook in the woods. Our people just wanted to live."

A month after the May 8, 1943 massacre by Russian partisans, Staś saw something else he should not have seen – truckloads of single young people being kidnapped for forced labor in Germany. He saw fear on their young faces, and he heard the parents' anguish.

Lodzia's brothers, Janek and Walek, had avoided these roundups. Their mother had put meat, bread, and warm clothes into a cloth sack. On a moonless night, they snuck out of Naliboki, going west to join the Polish Army fighting Germany under Allied command. Their sister Jadzia was married, and Lodzia was at home with her parents. Strong and tall, she was a prime target for kidnapping.

During our visit, Lodzia took us to a broad tree stump, still solidly in place, where she and her father were chopping wood that day in June 1943. From the corner of her eye, the specter of German soldiers swooped onto the property. She was wearing trousers, unusual for a woman. Having studied some German in school, she thought they said, "There's a strong boy. Let's grab him."

She threw the ax, bolted toward the house. Once inside, she ran to the back, dove out an open window. Dropping on all fours, she crawled on her belly through thick vegetation. Reaching the pasture, her feet flew as bullets whizzed past until the forest embraced her. If she had not risked the bullets, she may have stood next to someone dear to me on one of the trucks of young people that Staś should not have seen on their way to Germany. We'll hear from my godmother in a later chapter.

Lodzia said, "I had no food or water, and nights in the forest get cold. Just before it got dark, I heard footsteps. I stood ready to run from a German soldier or Russian partisan. Or fight back. Then I heard my father's whistle. I chirped back like a bird. He knew my sound."

The stone in her stomach melted with relief as her parents appeared. Her father said, "We didn't find your body, so we knew you hid in your favorite clump of trees where you watch the wild animals roaming free."

"Did they beat you because I ran away from them?"

The father said, "No. They went to the neighboring farm to fill those trucks."

Her mother said, "We brought food and water, warm clothes. We have a long wait until they leave."

It was a bad year. First, the massacre by Soviet partisans, then the abduction of young people for labor in Germany. By August 1943, German soldiers were burning villages, throwing explosives into the forest to smoke out the Russian partisans, and deporting people to Germany. Fleeing into the forest for the second time, Lodzia and her parents heard and smelled the explosives, but again, they were nestled in deeply among the trees that Lodzia knew like a friend one visits in time of need.

Staś told me that, "Russian partisans stole food from farmers living near the forest. The Germans burned towns near the forest so partisans wouldn't have places to steal food. The soldiers had a map where to burn. Naliboki, Kleciszcze, Rudnia Nalibocka, Prudy, Derewno, and many others. The sky was orange from so many villages burning. Then for two days, the Germans herded hundreds of people from those villages onto a pasture with no shelter. To make it worse, the sky burst open with a torrential downpour."

According to Polish ethnographer Dagnoslaw Demski, the August 1943 the arson included 26 villages located near the forest.[23]

When Will it End?

The anticipation almost felt like happiness

The next morning, a mass of humanity from 26 villages was forced to leave the pasture and walk for days to reach the train station where they were loaded onto cattle cars. After the cattle cars and soldiers left, people hiding in the forest came out. I said to Staś, "So Lodzia and her parents were caught in that downpour as they hid in the forest. It was days before they could come out."

Staś said, "Yes. Lodzia will tell you tomorrow what they found when they got home."

The next day, Lodzia described for us the shock of returning to their homestead. She stood with her parents in silent mourning at the ashes of their house, barns, furniture, clothes, and animal enclosures. Livestock was dead or had run away. At least, the shovels were left. They got to work. They dug a hole in the ground to hollow out the kind of *ziemianka* that Janusz had described. Living through the winter in a hole in the ground was bleak, but hope made it bearable. They hoped their sons Janek and Walek would come home. They hoped daughter Jadzia would soon walk through the door.

Staś and his family could not hide in the forest like Lodzia. The five children, a sick father, and grandmother were heading for Germany in the same cattle car as my parents and six children. Stopping in the occupied Polish city of Białystok, Staś said, "They did not even feed us beans, but husks of beans and a bit of potato. Mother pressed on my swollen stomach, and it caved in. Then they said, 'Get out.' What idiot was going to feed a family who couldn't work?"

As my own family was taken further west into exile, Staś's family were headed home. Reaching the train station in the town of Stołpce, eight people walked for days to reach Naliboki. Like his older brother Janusz, Staś said, "We walked past villages away from the forest. They were not burned. My parents asked farmers for bread or potatoes. Father made an open fire in a field. We cooked the potatoes, ate them, and fell asleep. The next day was the same until we returned home."

While Staś was walking back to Naliboki, the work of restoring the farm seemed lighter to Lodzia and her parents. They had received a letter from sons Janek and Walek. It was dated May 5, 1945, three days before Germany capitulated on the western front. They read that letter over and over. Janek wrote, "I am writing to you sitting on the stump of a tree. Tomorrow is our last fight for Berlin. May we live to see you again."

Homecoming preparations began. Lodzia and her mother gathered root vegetables in abandoned fields for their hungry boys. The father picked out two pieces of land. He and his sons would build two houses for Janek and Walek's future wives and children. They asked everyone they knew for news of Jadzia, but she had disappeared. Lodzia said, "Mother would say, if my daughter is alive, she'll come home along with our sons."

The anticipation almost felt like happiness.

One day the parents received an official-looking letter. They knew it would either bring joy or break their hearts. The words cut like a knife. Janek and Walek were killed on the last day of the war, two days after they had written home. All they had left of their sons was the last hopeful letter Janek had written while sitting on the stump of a tree. The family then learned that the married daughter Jadzia had gone to the United States and vowed never to return. She had seen enough violence.

What's Yours is Mine

They were told what to plant, to harvest, how to marry, how to raise their children.

People were caught in the crossfire of German and Russian hostilities until the region fell under Soviet control and remains so today. Staś said, "Russians freed Belarus from the Germans on July 3, 1944. When we had nothing left, the partisans got orders to leave us alone. They even gave us a cow. When we heard a "thud," a cow's head lay in the doorway from the partisans. Mother made what you call *galareta* in Polish [meat gelatin or head cheese.] Then they left the forest and went to the front as soldiers."

Farmers living away from the forest grew food and raised livestock during and after the war. They gave what food they could spare to people returning from deportations that first winter. In the spring, they shared some of their seed. Staś said, "My mother's mother gave us a kilo of seed [2.2 pounds] to plant our own food. The next year we planted more. Slowly, we were coming back to life until our land was taken from us."

They had witnessed the 1939 Soviet invasion and 1940 deportations, the 1941 German invasion, killing of the Jewish minority in 1942, the 1943 May massacre, roundups of young people in June 1943, burning of villages and deportations to Germany in August 1943.

Then another calamity encroached upon their lives. As we saw in Alicja's chapter, a few men in power caused upheaval for millions of Polish and German people. Poland had been a parliamentary democracy. After the war, its pre1939 boundaries were declared void, making Eastern Poland, including Naliboki, part of the communist country of Belarus within the Soviet Union. Land reform to benefit farmers had begun when Naliboki was part of Poland. After the war, the Soviet government had other plans for the land and farmers. It waited until families, adults and children had restored the devastated land. These hardy souls cleared the land, plowed

Young Stanisław Chmara drafted into the Soviet military. Kaliningrad in the 1950's.

acres, walked those acres planting seed, built houses, barns, animal enclosures, bought and raised livestock.

Then in the 1950's, the land they had restored no longer belonged to them. The government declared that no one would own private property. Staś said, "We were getting on our feet. Then they took our land, the horse, and even some of our seed. They left us the house we built, one cow, room for a garden, and a potato patch in the field. Everything else went into the *kolkhoz*."[24]

Families like mine had been private farmers for generations. They decided how to work and live. The communal farm, the *kolkhoz*, theoretically belonged to the people, but Moscow controlled their lives. In the new system, they were told what to plant, to harvest, how to marry, how to raise their children."

The two-building school my father helped build had gone up in flames in 1943, so Staś attended the one-building school put up after the war. Then, with an engineering degree from Pinsk Technical School, he supervised land management, water drainage, and canal construction. Staś said, "I took correspondence courses to improve my skills. But working in the *kolkhoz* and growing our own food on what was left of our land were two full-time jobs. I had no time left for courses."

I thought, "No time or energy left for education, creative pursuits, or political dissent."

When Staś and Janusz got married, the men in the family built a house for each of them. Staś said, "Maryla and I had good jobs. We didn't want to lose them, so we did not marry in church. We were married in a civil ceremony. When our son Juri was born, we had him secretly baptized. We had to teach Juri not to talk about his Polish roots in school."

I said, "No doubt, his classmates were told the same in their homes."

With the 1990 fall of the Soviet Union, decades of forced atheism melted like a child's sandcastle at high tide. My cousin Irena had met Adam Sieniakiewicz when he was sent to be the school principal in Naliboki. He boarded with Irena's parents and got himself a wife in the bargain. The reward for denying religion was an education for their two sons, one a high-ranking officer in the Soviet military. Like Staś and Maryla, Irena and Adam took vows in church after 40 years of a shared life.

The *kolkhoz* system collapsed after decades of denying the right to private property. Businesses now rent land from the government and hire local people to raise livestock. Households got back small parcels and could buy back more of the land that was taken from them if they would farm it. Staś said, "Some of us have died. Some are sick. What's the point of buying back our own land? Who is strong enough to take up the horse and plow again?"

Reflections

Danka, without the war, you would be living here in Naliboki with us.

DC: Do you feel anger over all that was taken from you?

Staś: It was war. What will anger accomplish?

Maryla: It was happiness just to have enough to eat. I led a team that grew vegetables on the communal farm. We are retired but still grow our own food. Everyone here grows their own food on little plots of land. You couldn't live on what they have at the store in town.

Staś: Maybe it was better if they made us stay in Germany like your family, maybe worse. Only God knows. When I was young, a piece of bread made me happy.

DC: If they kept you for work in Germany, you may have gone to Poland after the war.

Staś: If we went to Poland, I would have been a Polish soldier. But my brother Janusz and I did three years in the Soviet army. They sent me to Kaliningrad. That land isn't connected to mainland Russia. Sits between Poland and Lithuania.

DC: You were guarding it against Poland.

Staś: But I could have been a soldier on the other side guarding Poland from Russia. At least we have enough food now, if only we had some money. I knew hunger, cold, fear, people being killed. That was my childhood. Now I have horrible stomachaches, maybe because of the war. And who is to blame for the war? I don't even know myself.

Maryla: The Germans are absolutely to blame, but our life was just as hard after the war.

Staś: Who is to blame? What do you think?

DC: Both governments were evil, driven by blind power, with no concern for human life.

Staś: There you have it. And, Danka, without the war, you would be living here in Naliboki with us. When Jadwiga said you were coming, I went to see where you were born. My mother and sister used to sow rye on our strip of land north of town, near your land. My sister remembers stopping in, where do you suppose? To see the Chmaras in Kamionka. That was you!

But who am I supposed to be mad at? Hitler started the war. Maybe Stalin was up to some devilry that made Hitler attack him. It's not for us to figure out, true? Who wanted all this to be burned? Do we want to be having war now? Who are we supposed to be angry at now?

They fought in Afghanistan, Viet Nam, Korea, Serbia. They are fighting in Africa, Russia, Chechnya. The

Soviets took boys from all the republics. How many from Belarus, from Naliboki died in Afghanistan? Your cousin here, Irena Sienkiewicz. Her son was in Afghanistan two years, lieutenant colonel in the Soviet army. Fighting never stops. Look at us. We lived under Polish rule, German rule, Russian rule – and never left Naliboki!

Deep green woods and fertile yellow fields surround the church cemetery where Janusz, Jadwiga, Lodzia, and I visited our ancestors. We prayed at the well-tended graves of my grandparents Stefan and Emilja Chmara, the area where my grandfather Justin Byczkiewicz is buried, and at the monument to the 128 victims of the May 8, 1943 massacre. Our procession from grave to grave became a meditation as Lodzia talked about a season for everything, all things in nature knowing what to do, and when to do it. She was still seeing her 78th autumn with awe, as did Janusz and Jadwiga.

We returned to the house as visitors came with gifts and farewell embraces. Staś gave us dried mushrooms and a bottle of moonshine. I told him I visited and prayed at his son Juri's grave. His eyes softened and, finally, we sat on the garden bench and talked about bearing the unbearable.

Stanisław Chmara was born in Naliboki on May 25, 1938 and passed away in Naliboki in September 2015. Maryla Chmara was born on June 17, 1940 in Minsk. They had one son, and they have one grandson, Juri. Lodzia Okulicz was born on August 24, 1929 and passed away in January 2018. She and her husband Franciszek had a daughter and two sons. Her husband and one son predeceased her.

Endnotes

23 Dagnosław Demski, *Naliboki I Puszcza Nalibocka – Zarys Dziejów I Problematyki* (Etnografia Polska, t.XXXVIII: 1994, z. 1-2, PL ISSN 0071-1861) p. 62.

24 A collective farm

Chapter 5 Jadwiga
Between God and Party

Jadwiga walks a tightrope, and beneath her benign smile lives a woman skilled in the art of survival. The government political and ethnic registry lists comrade Jadwiga as a Belarussian communist. After a three-year program in animal husbandry at an agriculture college in the town of Golshany, she was assigned to Naliboki where she met my cousin Janusz. Although her parents took a brave stand against the abolition of private farms, she became an official in the system that took from them the land they loved.

Jadwiga is also a Roman Catholic of Polish parents, so walking this tightrope took balance. To protect her career, she married my cousin Janusz in a civil ceremony. To make peace with God, she had their two sons baptized in the middle of the night by a sleepy priest in a distant village. With a sharp mind and quick words, she covered her tracks from agents who roamed villages to sniff out Christmas and Easter preparations. She taught her sons not to speak of these home celebrations with other children who had their own secrets to keep.

Even today, Jadwiga's loyalties still hang in the balance. She favors private farms and religious freedom. She enjoys conveniences unknown to our ancestors – telephone, television, refrigerator, propane stove, freezer, canned and packaged foods. But like many who were secure in the old system, she supports the current Soviet-style dictator. She said, "After the Soviet collapse, old people weren't getting their pensions. Our president got them for us, and we're still getting them."

After our stay with Jadwiga and Janusz, my husband Henry and I had to catch a 5 a.m. bus to Lithuania. Jadwiga sat us in a circle in the cold drizzly predawn, knees almost touching. Did they used to pray like this, secretly, in the dark? Taking out an *opłatek*, a sacred wafer shared on Christmas Eve, she said, "Danuś, we'll share this *opłatek* as you leave your home again and go into the world."

We shared the wafer and stood up to leave. After long tearful embraces with Jadwiga and Janusz, their son Viktor held my shoulders steady to walk me out the door.

Early Lessons of Survival

That'll be a secret between you and mommy.

When Poland was partitioned in 1795 by its three neighbors, Russia, Prussia, and Austria-Hungary, our area fell under the Russian partition. Jan Glinski, a Polish man, resented being conscripted into the czar's army that had invaded his homeland. Much to his satisfaction, when he returned from World War I, he came home to what was again part of Poland. (Poland was an independent country between 1918 – 1939.) Ready to take a wife, Jan chose well when he married Maria Łynsza.

Jadwiga said, "My parents worked years farming an estate for a wealthy nobleman. They allowed themselves no luxuries until they saved enough to buy 12 acres near Pershai, north of Naliboki. As private farmers, they were determined my brother Stanisław and I would own our own land, be our own boss."

Jan and Maria cultivated their land lovingly during those happy years of marriage until World War II brought new masters. At age two, Jadwiga did not remember the 1939 Soviet invasion of Pershai. But two years later, during a German food raid, she saw her mother put a barrel over a basket of eggs and sit on it. The soldiers barged in saying they would shoot "mother" if she was hiding food. Jadwiga heard her mother say, "My children are hungry. I don't have any food to hide from you."

They poked around with a long sword, then said, "There's nothing to eat here. Looks like mother told the truth. Let's see what her neighbor has to offer."

They left. Maria got off the barrel. She took out the eggs and told Stanisław, age nine, and Jadwiga, age four, "This is our supper. If any of them come back, don't say anything about the eggs. That'll be a secret between you and mommy."

Maria Glinska needed her wits even more when such raids left the cupboard bare. She entered a pen of cattle confiscated from farmers. She told the guard, "I need to milk my cow to feed my children."

He laughed and insisted she couldn't recognize her own cow. She replied, "Sure I can. We live closely with our animals. We know them well."

He shrugged his shoulders and said, "What do I care? They're going to the front to feed our men."

Maria saw a cow with heavy udders that needed badly to be milked. She made up a name and called the cow to her. It began mooing. Maria came closer. It began licking her hand. She patted her head, spoke gently to her, then milked the cow. Her children had milk that day. Jadwiga was learning early in life from her mother how to make the best of what should not be.

Good and Bad Partisans

The long line of women and children stood paralyzed to face their death, a guard pointing a rifle from each end.

German soldiers and Russian partisans both demanded loyalty. Some people chose sides, others tried to be invisible. To Jan and Maria, Russian partisans were a salvation from German soldiers. Years later, Jadwiga still had an affinity for the Soviets. She said, "During the 1941 invasion, our Russian partisans were running from the Germans, and warned us the Germans were coming after us. People packed food, harnessed horses, tied cows to their wagons, and headed for the forest."

As people of Pershai were setting up shelter, bombs began swooping down on them. Maria and Jan ran deeper into the forest with Jadwiga and Stanisław on their backs. They got stuck in a muddy bog. The German soldiers caught up with the group and separated the men from the women and children.

They marched the men to the German garrison in Iwieniec and locked them in a barn. At night, Jan Glinski began counting the interval between steps as the guard walked back and forth. Jan calculated when he could loosen some stones along the wall of the barn without the guard noticing. As the sleepy guard's steps became less frequent, Jan crawled out. Two men followed. Jan had a way with horses and found one roaming free to take him home. The remaining men were shot the next day, suspected of helping the Russian partisans.

Back in the forest, the German commander lined up the women and children. He did not believe their pleas that they were not helping the Russians. Grasping her mother's leg, the four-year-old heard a piercing wail ripple through the group. Some of the women had understood the commander yelling to one of his men, "Shoot all of them. They are helping the partisans."

During our visit, Jadwiga became a terrified child again as she spoke haltingly, "The German soldier sank down. Beneath a big tree. He began to cry. Held his rifle tight. He said he is a husband, a father. He has a wife. His children look like these children. How can he kill them?"

She continued, "The commander looked angry and yelled something at him we did not understand. The soldier stopped crying, got up, adjusted his uniform. He walked over to his commander."

The two men spoke. The long line of women and children stood paralyzed to face their death, a guard pointing a rifle at each end. Their conversation may have been minutes, but it seemed endless for those about to die. A woman fainted. Sobbing children wrapped themselves around their mothers. Some lost control of their bodily functions. A shrill moaning saturated the forest of mothers and children wanting desperately to live and praying for God's mercy.

The young man with a wife and children returned to the line, walking with exaggerated authority, and clutching his rifle. He tried to look like a soldier. Made himself stand straight. But he did not point the rifle at them. He cleared his throat, then spoke with a forced bravado. He told them in a gruff voice they better not be caught helping the partisans. And they could leave.

The German soldier convinced his commander that the women and children had done nothing wrong. There was no reason to kill them. In agreeing with his subordinate, the commander made the wrong decision in terms of the brutal strategies of war. Some were aiding the Soviet partisans. But he made the right decision as a human being. Not all were helping the partisans, and I doubt the children, like four-year-old Jadwiga, knew whom to help. That moment is forever locked in her body and soul. She tells me about it with the same urgency as if she were still in the forest each time I visit Naliboki.

Having been spared, Maria Glinska walked back to Pershai with her two children. When Jan returned, they repaired the gaping hole inflicted on the kitchen during the German incursion. Expecting the partisans to help keep their home, Maria carried messages between Soviet encampments. She passed German checkpoints by hiding the messages inside the bun twisted on top of her head.

Maria's sister-in-law also helped the partisans. They brought bags of flour to bake bread for them. A German soldier walked in and wanted to know why she was baking so much. She insisted she had a large family. All they had left to eat is bread. He dumped the dough on the ground, soiled it with tobacco, and said, "Stop feeding the partisans."

When Jadwiga's son, Viktor, and his wife Kira stayed with my husband Henry and me in 2002, we talked about loyalties. But first, let me describe these first members of the Naliboki Chmara clan to visit the United States.

Viktor resembled my father as a young man – strong jaw, straight dark hair, eyes alert, and strikingly handsome. Like many Chmara men, Viktor speaks little, works hard, puts family first, and defers to his wife on important matters. Like many European women, Kira leaves the house coiffed, made up, and nicely dressed. A pair of sweats will not do. They were amazed by our casual dress in public, and the huge platters served in American restaurants. They were impressed by our extensive facilities for handicapped access, and people of all ages taking classes or attending college.

Back to the issue of loyalties. Viktor said, "My grandmother, Maria Glinska, told me this story to show there were good and bad partisans. A Russian partisan came on his horse to a cluster of six houses near the village of Pershai where my grandparents lived. He entered a house. He shot the husband in front of the wife and children and took all the food. The widow reported the murder to the man's commander and identified her husband's killer. The commander gathered the people along with his men, and said, 'If any of these men harm you, I will do to them what I will now do to the man who killed this woman's husband.' The killer begged the widow to forgive him. She did not. Her children were fatherless, so he should die."

To this widow, the Russian partisans were killers. To Maria Glinska, who got a cow from them that provided milk for her children, they were protectors. She carried messages for them at great risk. She could more easily identify with the Slavic rather than with the German invader, and loyalty can be based on need and fear rather on a shared ideology.

The Price of Independence

I felt embarrassed, like something was wrong with me for being left out.

Peace at last. Then came the betrayal from the Slavic brethren for whom Maria had risked her life.

After years of austerity, Jan and Maria had bought their own farm. They loved this land almost as much as they loved each other. Before the war their sweat and muscle had built a house and barns, bought and raised livestock, plowed fields, planted seed, and harvested food for winter.

They did it again after the war, but they were older. Putting the devastated farm back to working order was harder. Then in the 1950's the Soviet government said they no longer owned their land. It would be part of a communal farm, the *kolkhoz* system. Jan and Maria refused to give up their land for a theoretical utopia in a distant future.

The government punished Jan and Maria for their independence in two ways. First, through the children. Jadwiga and her brother were excluded from youth groups to which their friends belonged. Jadwiga said, "We were kept from activities with the other children. Youth groups had projects and trips by age. At age ten, they were part of the *Pioneri Group*. At 16, they joined the *Komsomol*, and by the time they became young adults, they were communists."

I said, "It must have been hard at that age to be excluded from what the other children were doing."

"Oh, yes. When the children in school talked with excitement about trips and projects, I could only listen. (Long silence.) I felt embarrassed, like something was wrong with me for being left out. When father couldn't hold out any longer, he lost everything. I could then join a youth group."

The second punishment was economic. Jadwiga said, "My parents raised crops and livestock to sell, and the government kept raising taxes on all they earned. Not able to keep up with more and more taxes, their land went into the *kolkhoz*. Mother kept the property deed, hoping the area would return to Poland and they would get back their land. She didn't live long enough to see the system disbanded five decades later, and farmers could buy back land that was taken from them."

Jadwiga learned the price of independence by watching her parents' defeat. Years later, she became a leader in the *kolkhoz* system that contained her confiscated inheritance. But the woman walking the tightrope constantly balanced career with her parents' heritage.

When Jadwiga's son Viktor and his wife Kira stayed in our home in 2002, they were in their mid-30's. Married 13 years prior in a civil ceremony, they wanted a church wedding. Kira is Russian Orthodox, but as a Roman Catholic, Viktor had to receive First Holy Communion before taking marriage vows. Our English lessons gave way to prepare him for this sacrament. That is when I learned that Jadwiga had secretly taught her children the customs and prayers of their religion.

Viktor and Kira took marriage vows in Holy Trinity Church in Helmetta, New Jersey. We celebrated their wedding dinner in our home. They called their mothers with the news. Despite her leadership in the atheistic system that harmed her parents, Jadwiga had asked her son to take this step to bind him to the heritage of his Polish Catholic grandparents, Jan and Maria Glinski.

Reflections

At my level, I knew when to keep the rules and when to bend them.

My father was a fearless man. When he was in the czar's army, he escaped his Romanian captors. Then he escaped the Germans from that barn in Iwieniec. And when the Soviets tried to take the land from my parents, they held on until they couldn't keep up with the taxes and lost everything.

*DC: This was re-
venge for their indepen-
dent thinking, which
in the Soviet system
involves the whole fa-
mily. Yet you became
a high ranking member
of the system that cru-
shed your parents.*

You have to
make the best of
things, Danusia. Peo-
ple knew when to keep
the rules and when
to bend them. All
Saints and All Souls
Day were big holidays.
Huge processions
walked into the ceme-
tery singing hymns for
our dead and stopped
to pray at graves of our
ancestors. This was
forbidden in the com-

First visit to the United States from the author's family in Belarus. Son of Janusz and
Jadwiga Chmara, Viktor and his wife Kira
arrive at Newark Airport, 2000.

munist days. We had to work on those holidays. By the
time people got out, how were they going to stumble around
that cemetery in the cold dark November night? So we all
pretended this was an ordinary day. But the higher ups let
our workers slip out early. Officially, the farming operations
stayed open until closing time. When we got a call from central administration, nothing was mentioned.

DC: You were taking a big risk with your career.

It was dangerous, but it never got back to the authorities.

DC: They could have had their own secrets to keep.

The system was good in many ways. Everyone had a
job, everyone ate. I worked hard and I was rewarded. Our

potato field was plowed for us. The firewood was chopped
and sent to our barn. I got the Order of Lenin for my work
and loyalty. (Jadwiga shows me the medal, beaming with
pride.) Now that I'm retired, our two sons come in from
Minsk to plant in the spring and dig potatoes in the fall. I
don't know how else we would manage.

*DC: Poland is a democracy. Belarus still has the old Soviet
system. Should that change?*

I don't want our president put out of office. He is good
for the country. He made sure the old people got their pensions. We are grateful to him.

DC: And you are experiencing new freedoms.

Janusz and I were married in church and we started
going regularly. But now, with my legs hurting so much, I
only walk to church or special occasions.

DC: And I couldn't visit you before.

Oh, no. Most visas only allowed foreigners to stay in
hotels. If someone wanted to visit, agents came to see if the
house was fancy enough for foreigners. They didn't want
people to think we were poor. Now with the breakup of the
kolkhoz, young people can own their own farms but they
don't want to stay. They want to work in Minsk and live in
apartments.

*DC: You walked a tightrope to have a good job
in the communist system and a clear conscience
in your parents' world. There were many like you.*

Jadwiga Glinska Chmara was born in Pershai in 1937.
Jan Glinski was born near Derewno in 1893 and passed
away in Pershai in 1982. Maria Łynsza Glinska was born
in 1901 and passed away in Pershai in 1990. Viktor Chmara was born in Naliboki on November 1, 1966. After his
Soviet military service, he had two years of medical training,
then supervised medical services for a government compa-

ny. Viktor is now a physical therapist in Minsk. Kira is a computer programmer for a private company. Their son Arthur is a classical pianist and professor of music.

Chapter 6 Weronika
Beware the Enemy, Beware the Ally

Weronika Buraczewska is tall and matronly, with several threads of narrative running through her vibrant mind. As a baby, she was a free Polish citizen; as a grandmother, she is a free Polish citizen. In-between, for five decades, she had maneuvered two oppressive regimes.

We met after Sunday Mass at Holy Trinity Church, which was founded by Polish immigrants in 1911 in Helmetta, New Jersey. She stood outside taking in the view with cool vigilance. But when her daughter told her I was born in Naliboki, a mere handshake would not capture her joy at our connection to the same soil. She enveloped me in her ample arms, singing, "Moja Naliboczanka – my Naliboki girl." Lost in her embrace, I knew this was a woman two oppressive regimes could not destroy.

During our visits, she spoke like an actor in an ancient Greek chorus, voice and body unfolding a drama of epic proportions. First, she set the stage, "My father Bolesław Łukaszewicz was a farmer. My mother Dominika was from the Farbotko family. I was the youngest of two boys and four girls. We took the sickle, cut down rye in the hot sun all day, threshed it with a flail. We worked hard, earned little. Who thought they would take us far away and tear our family apart?"

A Frenzy of Hatred

People were yanked from their houses in a winter so cold their eyelids stuck together.

Women found the parish priest attractive, but the robust man in his 30's with blond wavy hair and boyish features was a comfort to all. He preached that man does not live by bread alone, and saw being able to afford the bread as a human right. He was also an engineer who set up a brick factory, a lumber mill that began offering paid employment, and the force behind installation of electricity. Children no longer did homework by candlelight. Adults did not stumble in the dark.

Monsignor Józef Bajko was a window onto his parishioners' world. In August 1939, eight-year-old Weronika heard him say at Mass that two years earlier the German army had invaded Sudetenland – the part of Czechoslovakia bordering Germany, and France and Britain did not stop them. He was now hearing from Warsaw that Hitler had his eyes on Poland. His people should secure their houses, harvest their crops, hide their valuables. There may be war! He was right.

Monsignor Józef Bajko, beloved priest and leader of Naliboki, 1930's.

Germany invaded Western Poland on September 1, 1939, and its Soviet ally invaded Eastern Poland on September 17, 1939. Weronika said, "Word reached our tiny village of Terebejna that Naliboki was swarming with Russian soldiers, so my family ran into town. We saw some Jewish residents welcoming the Soviets and telling them to free them from Polish oppression."

The welcome turned sour for both Jews and Christians. Zionist organizations were banned. Hebrew and Polish were banned. Religious schools were closed. Businesses were disrupted. Anyone above the poverty line was labeled an exploiter of the people and deported to the Soviet Union. She said, "People were yanked from their houses in a winter so cold that their eyelids stuck together."

During this first invasion from the east, Weronika lived within a cluster of 20 houses with her parents, grandmother, single sister Stasia, and single brothers Kazimierz and Stanisław. Living next door was sister Maria, her husband Władysław, and their three children. Completing the family cluster of 17 were Weronika's sister Jadzia, husband Adam, and their three children.

Within this multicultural region, the Catholic church was the tallest building in Naliboki. The Eastern Orthodox house of worship, a *cerkiew*, was about 25 miles away across the Niemen River where the Belarussians lived. Rather than walk or harness the horse and wagon, the Belarusian family in this hamlet attended the Catholic church and joined in the wedding celebrations.

Weronika's neighbors were a forest warden, his wife, and two sons. The warden had a good job and income. She said, "The Russians drove up to the forest warden's yard. Father was working in the field, saw them from a distance. People who weren't dirt poor were carted off to Russia and Siberia. Father ran home. Grabbed a bed sheet, filled it with bread, ham, fatback. Tied it up. Father threw the food for them onto the wagon. The family walked out barehanded. It happened so fast, we found raw bread dough sitting on their kitchen table. The bewildered look on my two playmates scared me. We had large tracts of land. We could be next. But we stayed until the Germans came."

Weronika was hurt in a less dramatic but enduring way. Her formal education ended with the Soviet invasion. Russian became the language in school, and some Polish teachers were fired. To continue her education in Polish, Weronika's father brought sacks of potatoes, meat, and flour for two teachers who had lost their jobs. Weronika walked every day to study with the wife, while the husband did carpentry jobs to survive. The wife had kidney disease, so Weronika also helped with their two children until the second invader appeared in 1941.

When Weronika was ten, German soldiers pushed the Russians out of Naliboki. These men retreated into the primeval forest, the *Nalibocka Puszcza*, and became fierce guerrilla fighters. This second invasion doomed the Jewish people. As my cousin Janusz described earlier, the Jewish residents of Naliboki were marched out of town and killed by the German army.

After this tragedy, the Naliboki residents lost the man who had devoted his life to them. German soldiers took Father Bajko from the rectory and killed him in the forest south of Naliboki. Persecution of priests was part of Hitler's goal to tolerate Christianity until Germany won the war. Hitler would then eliminate all religion. He and the Nazi party would be deified in its place. (We will explore this in Father Hyacinth's chapter.) Older people I see on my visits to Naliboki still remember Father Bajko lovingly, the young know him by reputation. Today's priest, Father Marian, told me that Father Bajko remains his role model of pastoral care.

Tragedy consumed Naliboki: Soviet invasion 1939, German invasion 1941, Jewish residents killed 1942, Monsignor Bajko murdered, Soviets massacre 128 residents May 8, 1943, young people kidnapped for forced labor in Germany June 1943. Yet before the final arson on August 7, 1943, a little sweetness comes into Weronika's family.

A New Life Flickers

Bring me a light. My baby is cold.

Seven weeks after the loss of 128 lives, Weronika's sister, Jadzia, and husband Adam held a feisty little girl, their fourth child. Half the town was burned during the massacre, but the extended family, now 18 people, never expected to leave. Preparing food and shelter was urgent before the sting of September frost. Even 12-year-old Weronika had a job.

Weronika saw the two family cows as her pets and took them out to pasture each day. The twitter of birds and bees in the sunny meadow of yellow flowers were a relief from all those strange men in town. Her peaceful moments ended as her mother came running and screaming, "Run home, child. We don't know what will become of us."

She said, "I ran home. Soldiers were pouring water on beehives, tearing out honeycombs. Father yelled for my brothers, Kazimierz and Stanisław, to save the sheaves of winter rye and hay for the animals into the barn. Kazik moved slowly, kidneys damaged in a fight with partisans. They lit the barn so fast nothing was left to save. My sister Stasia was pulling precious family photos from the walls in the house. A soldier grabbed them, smashed them with his boot, set the house on fire."

She added, "Another soldier lit the second house we had just built for my brothers and their future wives. At night, the sky was red from entire villages burning: Naliboki,

Kleciszcze, Terebejna, Prudy, Jankowicze, Rudnia, and other places."

Operation Hermann had arrived to finish off the Russian partisans hiding in the forest, and to provide Germany with a workforce to replace its own men at war. Hundreds were herded onto a pasture near the town of Jankowicze, three miles south of Naliboki. Latvian, Lithuanian, and Ukrainian soldiers were helping the Germans, hoping to become free of Soviet domination. Weronika said, "Out in the open field, some of Germany's helpers got drunk and began raping the women. A soldier tried to drag Stasia away. My brother Stanisław tried to save her. They beat him."

She added, "The Germans came, fired shots in the air, and stopped the screaming frenzy. Then the downpour began. A woman gave birth in the deafening thunder and lightning. By morning, we were wet. Our food was wet. We looked like a horde of muddy ducks. German officers and their helpers were pushing us onto the dirt road."

With children crying and livestock to prod, they walked for days and slept in fields until they reached the train station in the town of Stołpce 25 miles away. The animals were put into one yard, people into another. Weronika said, "One day I snuck out to find my two pet cows. I found one, took her by the neck, stroked her, and cried. They stayed with me all my life. When I dream about them, we get money or the children do well on exams in school."

Weronika's pet cows were on the way to feed the German army. Her family of 18 was packed into a cattle car heading toward the occupied Polish city of Białystok to be disinfected with DDT before entering Germany. Weronika's sister, Jadzia, held her seven-week-old baby as my mother had held me when I was ten weeks old. One night, as Jadzia tried to nurse the infant, she sensed what she most dreaded. She said, "Bring me a light, my baby is cold."

The light revealed the vacant serenity of her dead baby's face.

Jadzia enveloped the little body and wept quietly until the train stopped. Doors unlocked. Guards yelled to hurry and squat under the train as a toilet. Anyone not back on time was crushed by the train starting up again. Jadzia did not move. A guard saw her sitting in the cattle car, cradling the baby in her arms. He felt the baby's body. It was cold. He told the translator that the mother had to leave the dead infant. She must place her little girl next to the tracks. And hurry. The train is about to leave.

Her parents tugged Jadzia gently out of the cattle car. She stood paralyzed, clutching her baby. The family surrounded her. They tugged the baby out of her arms. They put the tiny body on the ground. They lifted Jadzia by her arms and legs back into the cattle car and jumped on as the doors slammed. Unable to look at each other, they were leaving the newest member of their clan with no proper burial.

Weronika added, "Adults died too, but Danusia, you were about the same age as Jadzia's baby. Those tiny bodies of babies like you died from hunger, thirst, and heat."

I said, "We don't know how many babies died or if they show up in statistics of wartime deaths."

She said, "I don't think so. You were lucky to live."

Reaching Pirmasens, a city in southwestern Germany near France, 500 prisoners harvested potatoes to feed the German Army. Weronika's family was then trucked to a large estate where Polish and Russian workers replaced German men who were called up to fight on the war front. An aged commandant, driven around by a bodyguard wielding a gun, made sure everyone worked. Having left the tiny body along the railroad track, they were 17 people, still together, until brother Stanisław was sent to work in a bomb factory.

The grandmother cooked for six Polish families that worked in the field. With damaged kidneys, her brother Kazimierz (Kazik) often passed out. To hide his inability to work, the grandmother replaced him in the field and 12-year-old Weronika took over the kitchen. When informers told the commandant, he punished the family by separating them further. Weronika and her parents stayed. The grandmother, sister Stasia, and brother Kazik were sent to a factory in Berlin. The two married sisters and their families went to two separate farms 12 miles away.

A week before Christmas 1943, Kazik died in Berlin from kidney failure at age 23. When she found out, Weronika's mother Dominika lay down and refused to do her job of chopping wood. The commandant walked in briskly, tall and erect in his crisp uniform. Behind him trailed the translator and a policeman with a rubber club. Dominika glared at them like a wounded caged animal. The commandant left abruptly with his entourage.

No Celebrations for Some

These Germans committed suicide rather than face the wrath of the victorious Red Army.

The war ended with singing, hugging, and laughing in the streets. But not for everyone.

With Germany's surrender on May 8, 1945, the Allies created four military occupation zones. France held the southwest, Britain the northwest, United States the south, and the Soviet Union held the eastern part of Germany. As a reward, "Stalin gave orders allowing the Red Army for three days to rape, plunder, and even murder the population living in the German territories that now comprise western Poland and until 1945 had been part of the Third Reich. The Soviets, having Stalin's permission, made no distinction whether the people were German, Polish, or Czech." [25]

Weronika said, "We were in the Soviet zone. I was almost 15. For three days, we hid in the closet from drunk soldiers raping Polish women, German women, anyone. That was the end of the war for us. Germans living in that zone ran from the Red Army with scooters and carts, cripples and soldiers in rags with one shoe, running for that protection in the American zone."

She added, "My single sister, Stasia, left in a cattle car going to Poland to avoid being in the Russian zone. Jadzia, Adam, and their three children did the same. The rest of us gathered for survival. Stanisław left the bomb factory and found my parents and me. We walked to the estate where Maria and husband Władek [Władysław] had been working. Władek's two brothers were also there. The other foreign workers had run away. The German owners were so terrified of torture by the Red Army, the wife had shot her two children. She shot her husband. Then she shot herself."

Against this grotesque backdrop, the men built wooden huts to put on top of two horse-drawn wagons. The women prepared food, clothes, and blankets for 12 people: Weronika, her parents, grandmother, Staś, Maria and Władek with their three children, and Władek's two brothers.

With firearms and bicycles from the farm, they planned to escape the Soviet-controlled zone of Germany and enter Poland. But finding a place where the rule of law prevailed was as elusive as looking for the Wizard of Oz. They slept one night in an abandoned school. A drunk Russian soldier slid in through an open window. Maria was awakened by the weight of his body. Her screaming awoke the others, and Władek used his gun to stop the imminent rape.

When they left in the morning, Russian soldiers on horseback ambushed the caravan. They gulped down the food as they stole it, took all their identification documents, and left. By afternoon, the family found a resort near a lake where a Russian Orthodox priest, wife, two children, and two Russian women were hiding. They all huddled in the corner of what was once a dance hall filled with music and laughter. The men took turns standing guard at night.

At dawn, a piercing cry brought them to their feet. Maria had fainted at the sight of a German soldier who hanged himself during the night. They roused her, then cut down his body and carried him past abandoned gardens toward the lake. The stench of rotting flesh led to a pile of bodies in the lake. These Germans had committed suicide rather than face the wrath of the victorious Red Army. The dead soldier was placed with his people, safe from the enemy's vengence.

The family was forced to wear the letter "P" in Germany. Now they thought it might be safer to wear red ribbons in the Soviet zone identifying them as Russian. The Russian priest told the two women with no male protection to stay with his family. Then he led them in prayer for Weronika's family and their big gamble. Leaving the Russians they had befriended, Weronika's brother Stanisław, Maria's husband Władek, and his older brother, went ahead on bicycles wearing red ribbons. The women and children, Weronika's father, and Władek's younger brother trailed behind.

The gamble backfired. A woman in uniform and beret stopped them at a crossroad. She ordered, "'Reds' go left. 'White and reds' go right."

Maria protested, "We are Polish."

The guard snapped, "The men with red ribbons are Russian."

"But that's my husband," Maria said.

The guard yelled with an amused look on her face, "There's nothing to discuss, but you can follow," and waved them forward. Their clunky wagons rattled through rutted fields toward a dilapidated house. Then, the shock. Stanisław, Władek, and his older brother, walked out ashamed. They wore Soviet uniforms, Red Star on the lapel. Weronika gasped, "Our men turned into Russian soldiers!"

Władek told Maria, "Don't look at me. Leave now. Your family will shelter you until I return."

Losing their three strongest men, they faced the next cruelty. Weronika said, "Germans had radios. We didn't know Germany lost until Stanisław escaped the bomb factory and found us on the farm. Damn it, if we left sooner, we might have escaped the drudgery waiting for us. We were in the Soviet Zone in Germany, and they made us go home. But Naliboki was no longer part of Poland. We were going back to that cursed communism. We fell into the bear's claws and it said, 'You are mine.'"

They were put on a train going to the city of Minsk, in the Soviet country of Belarus. Weronika said, "The authorities promised to help us get resettled. Then they dumped us out into the frozen darkness of the Minsk train station, hours away from Naliboki. At least, they gave us quilts for the children. People were roaming around to steal anything they could sell for food. We heard of a woman bundled up against the cold. A man grabbed her suitcase and ran. When she came home in tears, the father realized he had robbed his own daughter."

She continued, "We had two men left, my father Bolesław and Władek's younger brother. Father found a wooden dresser in an abandoned building. He made a fire. Maria wrapped her children in the quilts. As we waited out the night, three men approached. They asked if they could dry their socks by the fire. Just as father nodded, "Yes," they grabbed one of the quilts. Hearing the child inside scream, they dropped the quilt and ran.

At daylight, Bolesław heard of a clothing store being looted. He joined the free-for-all and grabbed two fur coats and a bolt of fabric. He used the fabric to pay a man to drive them to the platform for the Stołpce train station. Weronika said, "My father and Władek's younger brother had axes to protect us. When we reached the station, the train did not stop. It moved at a crawl to stop robbers from jumping on to attack passengers for their luggage. We tossed out everything over a kilometer, even the children and grandmother had to jump off the moving train. We were amazed to be alive. A higher power was protecting us."

An uncle came to the station to return them to the scorched earth of Naliboki as year 1945 was ending.

Out of the Ashes: A Different Naliboki
We had to vote, whether we wanted to or not.

Weronika's aunt and uncle lived in a *ziemianka*, a hole in the ground. After the arson of so many towns and villages, families who had escaped deportation to Germany survived the winter in such dugouts. She said, "Boards covered the earthen walls, a roof kept the wooden floor dry. A small door gave the feel of a room. An iron stove is warm as hell. Next time you're in Naliboki, see for yourself. The partisans – Polish, Jewish, Russian, Gypsy, men on the run – had villages of *ziemianki*. They sit abandoned on the way to the village of Kleciszcze."

Like seedlings after a forest fire, little houses were sprouting up to replace the *ziemianki*. Weronika's family of 18 had been deported, nine returned: Weronika, her parents, grandmother, Maria's husband's younger brother, and Maria with her three children who had last glimpsed their father in a dusty field wearing an ill-fitting Russian uniform. This family of nine lived in a small house with another family, sleeping on the floor until they improvised cots.

Howling wolves at night reminded Weronika that six years of war gave them ample flesh to eat, but humans survived on cabbage, beets, and potatoes. She said, "I stayed with my aunt the first winter. We took sauerkraut from the barrel, added raw onion. We baked potatoes. That was our dinner. Somehow my aunt fed the hungry beggars too, orphans of Russian men and women killed on the front. She would give each child in rags a potato. They slept outside until orphanages were built."

When the ground thawed, Weronika went home to help with the planting. The colt they bought was not yet strong enough to plow. They dug the field by hand without their three strongest men still in the Soviet army. She said, "The first year was the worst. You know how youngsters are. Someone plays a guitar, we dance. A boy took my hand and said, 'Wow, your hands have blisters on blisters.'"

Their three men returned to a budding economy. Farmers set up markets to sell milk, butter, and eggs. Houses replaced holes in the ground. A hospital was built in the nearby town of Derewno, and a first aid station with a nurse was set up in Naliboki. But it had a different feel. For centuries, people strolled up the gentle hill to church. They prayed, shared their joys, and sought comfort in sorrow. Now the town hall, the *Sielsoviet*, was run by an atheistic government as the center of activity. Familiar bonds of mutual aid and trust were unraveling.

Weronika paced back and forth, and said, "When I was a child, we weren't afraid, talked openly. It changed with the *kolkhoz*. Workers trucked in from God knows where. People kept to themselves. This one's a communist, this one's a spy, this one a party leader, damn it, who knows what this one's up to? Robbers knew that people returning from Germany brought back valuables. Two boys came to our house with guns. Stood us against the wall. Took clothes, an alarm clock, and the two fur coats from Minsk."

Peddling fur coats is not like selling eggs. News of the robbery spread quickly. The next day, a boy came running from Nowogródek, about 34 miles away, to report two young men selling fur coats at the market. Weronika's father, cousin, and a policeman caught up with them. She said, "They were Polish boys, near Derewno, but we didn't know them or their families. The general secretary in the *Sielsoviet* said, 'If one of you was smart enough to marry this young lady, you would have a fur coat and a beautiful wife.' They were embarrassed, eyes lowered."

The Stołpce court gave them ten years in jail. The fur coats were gone, so the family got a horse as compensation. Weronika said, "Huh! We had a local election. Father was assigned to hitch the horse to a sled and take the ballot urn to snowed-in areas. The horse got cold, legs swelled, dropped, and never got up. We had no vets. You get sick, you die, right?"

The horse perished for an election with foregone conclusions. Weronika said, "We had elections. We had to vote, whether we wanted to or not. The party chose the person, organized a dance with an orchestra, young people had fun, and voted. It was prearranged. Without television, we didn't hear what went on and not everyone had a radio."

Party faithful provided the official version of news, ran collective farms, and rigged elections. Occupiers and occupied worked, intermarried, and formed a community. Weronika said, "The policeman was Ściopa, Russian. Dywonis, ran the *Sielsoviet*, Polish. Józef Huber was general secretary. We played together as kids. Flora and her father ran the post office. They go back generations. My aunt's son was in the Soviet Secret Police and carried a firearm."

Right before Our Eyes

Those girls danced in their flared skirts like they were possessed.

Between 1945 and 1946, Polish families were allowed to leave with their livestock and whatever they could carry. With one exception. The Soviet army claimed their sons. Weronika said, "Boys were smuggled into Poland. My cousin didn't want to leave his Belarussian girlfriend, but they hid him in a wagon loaded with hay. Must have been scary crossing the border. He's now married to a Polish girl, and they have three children."

Weronika's parents stayed. She spoke the now familiar refrain, "We plowed fields, planted crops, built houses, bought and raised livestock, rebuilt the town. We toiled for five years, then they took it from us. They left us a vegetable garden and potato patch."

As a child, Weronika learned about the coming war from Father Bajko. Now another priest delivered bad news. She said, "We were walking to Derewno on the feast day of Saint Bartholomew. The priest stood up looking nervous. He said our private farms that we rebuilt will be taken from us.

Naliboki would become a *solkhoz*. Jankowicz, Terebejan, and Prudy would be a *kolkhoz*. This happened in Russia, but we didn't think of ourselves as Russian. The women walked back sobbing and said, 'Why did God punish us again?'"

The *solkhoz* and *kolkhoz* were two types of communal farms with little difference. Harold Leich, Russian area specialist at the United States Library of Congress, told me that a *solkhoz* was a state farm managed directly out of Moscow, with no pretense of participatory management. The *kolkhoz* had, in theory, councils of member representatives making decisions regarding running the collective farm. But at the practical, day-to-day level, the two institutions were similar and since the farmers were forced into collective and state farms in Russia between the late 1920's and early 1930's, neither institution had a voluntary, democratic origin.[26]

The family returned to Naliboki when Weronika was fifteen. The nearest high school would require boarding out, an expense few could afford. Weronika worked with a group of girls stooping over barrels to remove the oozing sweet syrup from 3,000 trees. Then at age 20, she married Marian Buraczewski. When they had a son and two daughters, born at home, she changed jobs. She said, "Field and forest workers got measly pay. The money was in livestock. Marian worked with horses. I tended two hundred pigs. I lay down to sleep and couldn't feel my hands from lifting heavy pails of feed. But I wanted the best for my children."

As private farms disappeared, Polish names were changed to Russian. Weronika Buraczewska became Vera Burak. To further transform a Polish town into a *solkhoz*, the Soviets brought in a tractor and two truckloads of Belarussian and Russian girls. They ate in a kitchen open to the outside with a roof, long tables, and benches. They slept in tents by the lake until wooden houses and a recreation hall were built. Then two more truckloads of workers arrived, including men.

Weronika said, "We watched in amazement. Those girls plowed fields, planted tomatoes, cabbage, corn. As poor as we were, they were surprised we had kasha and wheat flour. All they had was soy flour. They heard the bell and went to that cauldron to get their fill of soup. They didn't want to leave, so they were obedient. Otherwise, they would have been sent back to Minsk."

The girls from Minsk worked hard, but when evening came, male workers arrived with accordions and moonshine. Weronika said, "Those girls danced in their flared skirts like they were possessed. Our boys said, 'Look how strong those girls are.' Things got mixed up. Well, we were decent girls, ambitious. Here in America, girls call and come for the boy. I taught my children differently. So, our boys went to see the dancing. Next thing, she's pregnant and he's terrified. She's Russian Orthodox and doesn't want to go into the Catholic Church. Well, they married those girls and divorced them."

Some marriages lasted. Some of the girls whose dancing enchanted the boys are now stooped over with arthritic knees, still growing vegetables in Naliboki.

Faith vs. Career
The ones afraid of nothing and no one, they were free!

In Weronika's youth, the mayor ran the town, while Monsignor Bajko's judgment went undisputed. This balance between world and spirit ended when Naliboki was tossed into communist hands. Walking around the cemetery with my cousin Janusz's son, Viktor, he told me, "We became part of Belarus after the war. The authorities wanted to turn our brick church, which your father helped build, into a dance hall. But they got the message no one would party next to graves where their ancestors slept. So, they made it a warehouse. Even so, we cleared a space in the church for holidays, and to mourn our dead. By the 1950's we had no priest to say Mass."

Brave souls like Weronika spoke with their feet. Sundays, she walked six miles to the church in Derewno that remained open. Some walked 12 miles to the wooden white church in the town of Rubieżewicze. But the red brick church, 11 miles away in Iwieniec, was turned into a factory. She said, "Young people with good jobs stood outside the church in Derewno under trees, in the shadows. Workers like me who worked in fields and stables, we didn't have a party booklet and we went to church. The ones afraid of nothing and no one, they were free!"

People who worked in offices or schools were punished for going to church. As role models, teachers were required to patrol crossroads to prevent students from reaching the church. Clever children snuck in through dirt paths and fields. Priests could not baptize, lead pilgrimages, or pray in the cemetery. Mourners carried the casket to the grave and completed the burial ritual. Weronika added, "They started expelling children of laborers from school for going to church. No one knew when the priest got them ready for First Holy Communion. Babies were baptized secretly and far away."

The further away the better. Weronika came often with fellow pilgrims to the wooden white church in Rubieżewicze. One time, they saw parked cars full of children. Weronika said, "A Russian woman approached me and asked if I was one of the faithful. I said I am. We walked all night on pilgrimage without food or drink to get here."

"We also came far. We heard this church is open. How can we get our children baptized?"

"We have to see the priest. I'll take you to him."

Many of the Russian Orthodox *cerkwy*, which were architecturally different from Catholic churches, were shut. But the Russians had also travelled far to protect their jobs, to not be recognized. The nervous priest had a toothache, and now, this. He was afraid, but this rite receives the child into the community of faithful. How could he deny them that?

Children poured out of cars parked in the shadows. He baptized them all. They prayed together, the Russian parents, their children, and the Polish pilgrims. The Russians then left in their big cars as if this had never happened. Weronika said, "It was dangerous for them and for the priest. This was the Soviet military brass, the ones with hefty government salaries and pensions. They tried to give the priest money but he refused. He said it could be a trap. Well, who knows?"

Join the Army or Die
See that? He's back from the army!

Russia, Prussia, and Austria-Hungary carved up Poland in 1795, and Naliboki fell under Russian rule for 123 years. Polish men forced into the Russian army resented defending the country that had occupied their land. My Uncle Józef Chmara was such a man. He left the czar's army during World War I to help put Poland back on the map of Europe. But newly independent Poland lasted only 21 years (1918-1939). After World War II, my eastern lands were back into Soviet hands, and Polish men were again forced into the Soviet army.

After some Naliboki boys were killed during the Soviet occupation of Afghanistan (1979 – 1992), the boys at home hid in the forest to avoid conscription. Unlike my uncle Józef Chmara, whose loyalty to Poland trapped him some 25 years later, the punishment was immediate. Weronkia said, "Russian soldiers surrounded the forest. Not one of our boys walked out alive. I was in town when they brought in their bodies. They told me to round up the mothers. I told the first mother, 'Listen, Ignatz and Józek are lying there.' She cut me off and went to see for herself. Then each family buried their sons."

After more boys were killed in Afghanistan, resistance grew stronger and enforcement grew more brutal. Weronika said, "My sister-in-law was in a hospital from complications of childbirth. Her husband left the baby with his parents and ran away to avoid conscription. Russian soldiers caught him, shot him repeatedly in the stomach. They brought the body to his parents' house and threw it on the porch. When they came out, the soldiers shouted, 'See that? He's back from the army!'"

A more effective way to enforce conscription was by building loyalty in children. After Weronika and her family moved to Poland in 1957, she returned to Naliboki to visit her sister Maria and husband Władek. It was in the 1980's, when Gorbachev and Solidarity appeared on the world stage. Maria picked up a newspaper and said, "See her carrying a palm? They made an example of what happens if a teacher goes to church on Palm Sunday. She no longer has a job."

Weronika explained to her sister that, with Poland being controlled by the Soviets, people in high positions go to church secretly. But everybody else celebrates holidays like they did when she was a child. Maria complained, "All we have is that bald devil Lenin. It's all according to Lenin. He ruined everything for us."

Maria's grandson, who attended kindergarten, was playing in the room. Pinned on his shirt was a picture of Lenin inside a Red Star. He tugged at his grandmother and said, "Granny, are you allowed to talk such nonsense? One more word and I will report you."

Weronika laughed at a six-year-old putting his grandmother in jail. The child said, "Why are you laughing so stupidly?"

Weronika shouted, "I'm laughing at you for praising that idiot Lenin."

He stood erect, head high, and said, "If you want your dear Poland, be quiet before they lock you up."

Weronika said, "This is what they teach children. Soon there will be no trace of their Polish heritage."

Before returning to Poland, Weronika and a childhood friend visited the church that had been turned into a warehouse. She said, "Men and women dug the foundation for a beautiful church. Now it had a birch tree five meters tall [16 feet] growing out of the wall. My friend asked if we dare hope to get back our church someday. I said I'm hoping, so let's protect our building. Let's cut down that birch. A strong wind could knock it over and tear out half the wall."

Without asking permission, the two women came back with tools and cut down the tree. No repercussions, no punishment. Perhaps no one noticed. Perhaps someone did and was secretly pleased. And their hopes came true. "See that! We saved the wall, the Soviet Union fell, we got back our church," intoned Weronika as if she knew all along this would happen.

Out of the Bear's Claws

When we get out, we'll give them back their booklet and they can kiss our...

Weronika's sister Jadzia, husband Adam, and their three children were living in Poland after the war. Jadzia was broken in body and spirit long after the ink had dried on peace treaties. Her spirit died the day she left the spent body of her baby girl wrapped in a bit of cloth along the railroad tracks, without even a proper burial. Her own body gave out when she was thirty-eight.

Weronika's sister, Stasia, also returned to Poland and married a man who had worked as a forced laborer in Germany. When they visited Naliboki in the early 1950's, the first television was being unveiled in the community center. Weronika had received first prize for productivity and expected her prize money during the gathering. But nothing happened.

The next day, Weronika ran over to the town hall, the *Sielsoviet*, to collect her money. The nervous clerk shuffled some papers than blurted out that he could not pay her. She demanded an explanation. He did not know. Getting louder, she said, "How could you not know?"

Unable to look her in the face, he stuttered, "I don't know."

"I want to see the director."

The director appeared and insisted, "Vera, we can't pay you. You earned more than I did."

Standing firmly, hands on hips, Weronika created a scene loud enough for everyone in the building to hear. She shouted, "You can't pay me? You need more money than I do for all your women? The two hundred pigs under my care don't die. If you don't pay me, I will take care of twenty. The rest will die."

After he paid her in full, Weronika told her sister Stasia, "We must leave this place. I saw enough of their Red Army when they were chasing us in Germany. I will carry my son on foot to Poland, but he will never wear the Red Star. If I can't leave, I will die."

Returning to Poland, Stasia made a pilgrimage to pray for them at the nation's spiritual center, the Shrine of Częstochowa. She then sent an official invitation to start the immigration process. The red tape to leave was slow, so Marian decided to put a roof over their barn. He cut down wood in the forest and brought it home. Weronika said, "The forest warden saw it. He was a Naliboki man from his roots but acted like a dog bit him. We knew each other as children, but it was different now. We would finish the barn and he would have a few extra *rubles* in his pocket. But he told the director."

The next day, the director knocked on the door and asked what all this wood was doing in their yard.

She shot back, "Looks like rafters to me. The cow is under the open sky. We need to cover the barn."

The director wanted to see her husband at the town hall. There, the director told him he could finish the barn for a fine of 3,000 *rubles*. But if he and Weronika join the party, all would be forgiven.

Weronika stood up and blurted out, "We could buy a house for 3,000 *rubles*! Okay, we'll join the party. When we get out, we'll give them back their booklet and they can kiss our... Damn, how life improved. We got free firewood, chopped. But when papers came to leave, they fired Marian and I quit. If pigs died, they would blame me. I was paid all that prize money, we had milk, eggs, and a garden. What else do you need, right?"

A party leader from Minsk came to see these two hard workers. Weronika said, "He asked what is this foolishness about leaving? You don't understand where you are going. Everything, even bread, costs more in Poland. I shot back at him. You throw our bread on this wall and it will stick. This piece of bread my sister Stasia brought from Poland, even dry, you will want to eat it."

Agitated, the party leader told the director, *"Vypuscit i odvisci ich jeszcze na vakzał potomu, szto ana nye vernulas.* Let her out, even take her to the train, just so she never comes back."

Leaving their ancestral land, but taking their children, their Polish names, and their religion, they began a life as Polish citizens in the town of Szlichtingowa in Western Poland as Weronika and Marian Buraczewski.

Reflections

You got a letter today, but tomorrow you pretend it never arrived.

DC: Do you feel anger or hatred toward the Germans or Russians?

I don't hate anyone. Absolutely not. The worst was the partisans fighting each other in Naliboki – Gypsy, Jewish,

Polish, Russian, Ukrainian, Lord knows what else. As one left, the others came. Some stole our food along with the pot.

I told my son he must take me back to Germany, or I won't die peacefully. We went 60 years later to the towns of Rostock, Schwaan, Guestrow, Beutzow, Schwerin. We even went to the estate where we worked. I thought of how we prayed there, even said some version of the Mass together.

DC: But when you returned to Naliboki after the war spies were watching everyone.

They were. You got a letter today, but tomorrow you pretend it never arrived. Flora was a sweet Polish woman who ran the post office. She kept her mouth shut. We had a sense of who got things, but God forbid talking about it. After the war, Poland danced to the tune played by Russians. Now it dances to the tune played by Americans. It needs that NATO protection from Russia.

For me, communists didn't exist. People were waiting for the region to return to Poland, some are still waiting. I went on with my life. I worked, sang, and danced at weddings with orchestras. Everyone respected me. When we left in 1957, it was the same in Poland. I served on committees although I only finished grade two. Someone even asked me to run for mayor. I'll think about it.

Weronika Lukaszewicz Buraczewska was born in Naliboki on January 28, 1931. Marian was born in Naliboki on April 13, 1931 and passed away on September 21, 2008 in Łódz, Poland. One daughter is deceased. The other daughter owns a travel and real estate agency in New Jersey. Their son is a businessman in Luebeck, Germany. They have seven grandchildren. We spoke between 2001 and 2009 in her daughter and son-in-law's home in Princeton Junction, NJ.

Endnotes

25 Włodzimierz Knap, Interview with Piotr Kolakowski, Mogło to zrobić NKWD, Nowy Dziennik (NY: Outwater Media Group) December 5, 2003, p. 14

26 Harold M. Leich, Russian Area Specialist, European Division, The Library of Congress, Washington, D.C., interview on January 24, 2005.

Part Two: From the West: The Master Race Brings Fire 1941

Those with Many Children, Few Workers

Those with Few Children, Many Workers

Those Who Were Single

Chapter 7 Helena and Michał
Homeless but Alive

We now transition from the Soviet to the German deportations, and the people who kept me alive. We were discarded in a starvation camp, but my father's carpentry skills got us moved to a labor camp where mother used all her wits to find food. My older brothers and sisters, themselves still children, also helped feed the youngest ones – Mary, Van, and myself – by begging for food.

Coming to America after the war, mother fed the hungry, clothed the poor, visited the sick, and comforted the grieving. Her Biblical values still guide me like the North Star. In poverty or prosperity, my parents did not preach right or wrong. They taught by example. After the Statue of Liberty welcomed us, mother worked as a seamstress in a clothing factory. She also created a welcoming home, grew a garden, sewed, canned, and kept us fed. She made us a real family by putting everyone to work. By age fourteen, I was cooking supper after school. I felt valued and needed.

My mother was a self-educated woman who read Polish, Russian, and English. After watching the evening news and the game show "Wheel of Fortune" to learn English, she would curl up with a Polish novel or Dostoyevsky's *Brothers Karamazov* in Russian. When she turned eighty, mother complained about fatigue after weeding the garden and painting the outdoor furniture. Her doctor hoped to have such energy when he reached her age. And what a traveler! After a trip to Hawaii, she held court in bed while her children visited her, exhausted but happy to have seen Kilauea Volcano.

Father was a man of few words, happy to stay home. He took pride in building houses for a living. Having lost our house and land, we cherished the home he built for us in America. He loved our back-yard picnics, and mother's chicken dinners on Sunday after church. Mother led us girls to the front pews on the right, father took my brothers toward the back on the left. Those days men and women sat apart. As I sit there now, his deep voice lingers in song behind me. Father is my idea of what a man should be.

The day before father left us at age 76, he secured all the windows and doors in our house. Did he know something? Like many Chmara men, he was a thinker and doer until the moment his heart stopped. The day before mother left us at 89, she asked me for graph paper to sketch some arts and crafts ideas. The paper remains blank, but her life was full. She was my best teacher.

My Parents' Courtship

Until they stood at the altar together and said, "I do," my parents had never been alone.

Michał felt Cupid's arrow when he saw her in church, and at 24, it was time to find a wife. She lived in the south end of town; he lived in the north end. With few cars and no phones in 1927, he wore out a pair of shoes walking two and a half miles each way to court Helena. He sat upright in his best clothes talking with her parents. Anna and Justin Byczkiewicz liked him, but she sat aloof, observing. In fact, until they stood at the altar together and said "I do," my parents had never been alone.

Her "I do" saved him the next pair of shoes. As was custom, mother moved in with Michał's mother, sister, two brothers, their wives, and children – 11 people in one house, one kitchen, one stove, one general room, and one outhouse in the field. The expected squabbles ended a year later when father finished the house he was building for his bride.

My parents were married 50 years. In the sweetness of the first thirteen, they created a home, raised a family, and made sure no one went hungry. We lived on the *kresy*, the borderlands between Western and Eastern Europe at times under Russian rule, at times under Polish rule, and briefly under German rule. My parents married during the Polish times, and had three boys and three girls: Heniek, Czesiek, Janina, Marysia, Wacek, and I was Danuta, the youngest.

Two invasions put an end to the sweetness of home. The Soviet Union invaded in 1939, the German army invaded in 1941, destroyed the Jewish minority in 1942, burned our town in 1943, and deported us to Germany. Yet we were blessed. No one was killed or maimed. After two years in a Nazi forced labor camp, followed by five homeless years, we found deliverance in America. We became Henry, Chester, Janka, Mary, Van, and Donna.

Within the Grip of Two Neighbors

The 1941 German invasion saved my family from eating dog meat.

Fussing in her American kitchen years after the war, mother deflected her own losses and spoke of the Iraqi Kurds and Iranian Shi'ites whose homes were destroyed during the 1990 Persian Gulf War. She broke two eggs into a bowl and said, "They have it worse wandering around those mountains. What will become of them? The Germans chased us from our country, but at least the Americans saved us."

She paused, then asked, "Remind me. What is the word the Russians call Americans?"

I answered, "Capitalists."

"Right. Communists hated capitalists or anyone not poor. We shared a two-family house with your Uncle Józef, wife Józefa, and little Stefania when the Russians came for them. They grabbed people to build roads, clear trees, put up buildings. Oh, the hunger. I knew a priest sent to Siberia. He forced himself to eat dog meat. And my friend, Mrs. Suchocka, saw a dog running way ahead of a rich Russian woman. She grabbed the dog, choked it by the throat, and sat on it with her big skirt. When the woman came looking for her little pet, my friend knew nothing. The family ate dog that night."

The 1941 German invasion saved my family from eating dog meat. When the Soviet army of Russian soldiers invaded in 1939, father's brother, Jan Chmara, was made a clerk in the town hall. He came upon a list of "Criminals and Enemies." Staring at him like neon lights were Michał Chmara, wife Helena, and children! My father's patriotism was to be punished. He had served in the Polish army and had trained young men in the Rifle Squads. The Soviets targeted these guardians of Poland's independence for elimination. My family was to be deported to the Soviet Union in July 1941. But they were one month too late.

Germany betrayed its Soviet ally and invaded Eastern Europe in June of 1941. The list of "Criminals and Enemies" got trampled by some dusty boots as the Russians fled for the forest and became lethal fighters against the German army and its Latvian, Lithuanian, and Ukrainian auxiliaries. The second invader was trespassing upon a way of life marked by growing seasons and communal worship which was the spiritual and social glue of rural life. Mother said,

"So beautiful, the processions stopped at little chapels. We built them secretly at night when we were under the Russian partition. Once it went up, it stayed up. I was nursing your brother Wacek [Van]. I put on my good dress and carried him to church with me. Corpus Christi was a big holiday. We decorated banners with flowers and lined up for procession. We walked together for days through town and fields singing hymns."

This time, when mother arrived, all she saw was father's cousin, Zofia Wolan, washing the bodies of some dead Lithuanian auxiliaries. These German allies were killed trying to stop a food raid by Russian partisans. The German soldiers put them in rows near the lake and had local women prepare them for burial.

Mother said, "Living up north, we didn't hear about every fight. But they found us. Germans come daytime, complain we feed the partisans. Russians come at night and say we feed the Germans. We didn't want to help either devil. The meadows were far away. Our men went for a week to mow and bundle winter hay for the animals. Partisans attacked them in the meadows, tore shoes off their feet. You went to church, returned barefoot. They stole the pitcher of eggs I was saving for your baptism."

That stolen pitcher of eggs lives in memory because the place of baptism remains one's spiritual anchor. I was baptized quietly, with a celebration 51 years later. Learning I was baptized in Naliboki, Father Marian had shy blond-haired children welcome me home with flowers and songs. I sang with them from some deep place in my heart. I still belong to that parish.

Operation Hermann

A woman gave birth in the field, in the cold rain, in the thunder and lightning.

With both German soldiers and Russian partisans demanding loyalty and food, mother told father, "What if the partisans force you into their guerrilla units? I work in the field, take care of the children, the house, the livestock; and a horse on top of that! You've got to sell it."

Father sold the horse as Operation Hermann was unleashed. Local resident and eyewitness, Hanna Regulska-Ślusarczyk, describes two attempts by the German army to wipe out the Soviet partisans in the Naliboki Forest. "The first attempt at liquidating the partisans in the Naliboki Forest Region was conducted in 1942 with the help of the Latvian and Ukrainian police and collaborative units... [And by August 1943] approximately 20,000 people had been deported. Train after train thrust itself through the helpless Polish countryside, making its way into the heart of Germany to change a free people living off the land into a slave work force."[27]

During the August 1943 deportations, the old and infirm who could not walk were shot. What about children, useless for work? With six, ranging from 12-years-old to me at ten weeks, mother stopped two German soldiers, stood firm, looked them in the eye, and said, "Do you plan to shoot us?"

One of them stuttered the standard lie in Polish, "You will be moved for protection from Soviet partisans. You will need your livestock on the new farms."

As German officers and their allies on horseback continued to herd us onto a meadow near the village of Jankowicze, a fierce rainstorm swooped down upon people from 26 villages who had been made homeless overnight. The guards put mother and other women with babies into a shed with a dirt floor. Father put the four older children under a wagon. This offered some protection. Nearby, a woman gave birth in the field, in the cold rain, in the thunder and lightning.

In the morning, our neighbor put mother, me, and Wacek (Van) on his wagon. Van was two; I was ten weeks old. The four older children walked with father. We were together with his brother Jan, wife Antonina, and their seven children. The Stołpce train station was 25 miles away. Mother said, "Four adults and thirteen children walked for days, slept in fields. No place to wash. We go in the bushes. Your little body was red from the heat. Your sister Janka's hair was so matted I couldn't comb out the lice."

We were not moved for safety. Our livestock went to feed the German army. We waited for days in crammed cattle cars, food and water gone. As the train started up, a family friend, Mr. Kuziomko, was squatting under the train as a toilet. My grandmother told me that the moving train cut him in half. The pitch of the speeding train muffled the plaintive sound of prayers and hymns sung in desperation.

Reaching the occupied Polish city of Białystok, we were herded into a building and told to undress. Our clothes were taken to be disinfected. Father took Henry, Chester, and Van. I clung to mother's naked body. Janka and Mary walked beside her. We were sprayed with DDT, a pesticide now banned in the United States. Brother Henry told me, "Later in America, I was spraying our vegetable garden. Father yelled at me, 'That's the poison they used on us. Get that garbage out of my sight!'"

Two Rooms – 21 People

We were put on display for farmers to choose the strongest.

With DDT invading our bodies, we put on our clothes and got back into the cattle cars. We stopped at the town of Kirchhellen, in the Westphalia region, near the Belgian border. We were put on display for farmers to choose the strongest. The rest were sent to a labor camp, but my family and Uncle Jan's family, with many children and few workers, were discarded in the starvation camp. The men were trucked daily to the labor camp to build military housing, dig bunkers, or were rented out to farmers.

Women stayed with the children. Mother prayed for a miracle as her children were fading on a daily bowl of soup and piece of bread. Weeks later, mother and Uncle Jan's wife Antonina were told to board a truck with the children. They drove in silence. Reaching the labor camp, they saw father bent over sawing boards, Uncle Jan was mixing cement. The *Lagerfuehrer* got good work from these two brothers and decided to rescue their families from the starvation camp. That was the miracle!

My family of eight lived with two other families, 21 people in two medium-sized rooms. The five Sobols were a husband and wife with two boys and a grandmother. The eight Makowskis, were a husband and wife with two single daughters, a single son, and a married son with wife and child. The crowding was hard on children. Mother said, "Our Mary was curious, got into everything. She was outside kicking up the wooden shoes we got to see how high they would go. She kicked it high. It flew through an open window into the soup of a couple about to eat. My God! They get it once a day and a shoe land's in their soup. The German officer, Willi, grabbed her before I could hit her."

My oldest brothers, twelve and eleven, worked in factories or for farmers. Mother said, "Blessed Mother! I went to the office. Told the interpreter they were too frail for men's work. The *Lagerfuehrer* was sitting at a table. He grabbed a heavy bowl filled with fresh fruit and heaved it at me. That was his answer."

Mother knew his wrath again as she walked to the town of Gladbeck, three miles away, to look for food. He rode by on his bicycle. She said, "He was inhuman, damn him. He didn't hit me but screamed because I went without permission. I ran back, gave you to Mrs. Makowska through the window, threw off my scarf not to recognize me, and walked into the barrack looking innocent."

The *Lagerfuehrer* demanded a lineup. Prisoners stood erect in rows as his boots broke the silence. He stopped and stared at mother. She stared past him stone-faced. If he recognizes her, she won't get that turnip soup. He walked up and down, glaring at her, until she heard, "Disperse!"

Being denied the daily bowl of soup was mild punishment. A Russian boy did not step off the sidewalk, take off his hat, and let the Germans pass. For this, the *Lagerfuehrer* had the guards take him aside and shoot him. Mother's voice quivered as she added, "So you see what we lived through. But when I look at those people in Iraq. We were rescued. Their suffering has no end in sight."

Will My Children Eat Today?

Once they gave out big portions of lard. It had a human smell.

The Nazi system poisoned the soul, but the high-ranking German officer, Willi, rejected the venom. He wore the Iron Cross for military service, a war hero. He paid for this honor with one hand blown off on the Russian front. Mother said, "He supervised the kitchen but, eh, what sort of kitchen? We went with our bowls for turnip soup once a day. A worm might be floating on top. You and Wacek [Van] each got a cup of milk. At five, Marysia [Mary] didn't get a drop. The devil knows what they ate, but the Germans had their own kitchen with real food."

Women in other camps had to work while their babies lay bundled flat all day. Willi let women in our camp stay to care for their babies. He ignored the starvation level food rationing system he was supposed to implement. British journalist, Neal Ascherson, explains that the law allowed "2,613 calories a day to a German, but a mere 699 to a Pole... Like the Jews, but on a slower time scale, the Poles had been designated as an inferior, vermin-race to be eliminated from physical existence."[28]

West Europeans were seen as having value as human beings, so Italian and French prisoners of war in the camp were given larger food rations. East Europeans were seen as only having value as laborers, so Slavic workers – Polish, Russian, and Ukrainian – got smaller food rations. Other groups who were not valued as human beings wore colored triangles: brown for Romani, red for political prisoners, pink for homosexuals, purple for Jehovah's Witnesses. Mother said, "Jews wore the Star of David, whoever was still alive, they were killed quickly. We were to work and die slowly."

Mother cringed, "To get our daily ration, Polish people wore the letter "P." Once they tried to give out big portions of lard. It had a human smell. Maybe from the ovens where they burned people. As hungry as we were, no one took it."

Refusing the lard, the three families living in two rooms shared their meager resources on Christmas Eve, *Wigilia*, the holiest night of the year for Polish Christians. In normal times using the best linens and dishes, a place is set for a hungry stranger who may appear, and to remember absent loved ones. Straw under a plate recalls Christ's birth in a stable. After the first star, we share a wafer called *opłatek*, eat a meatless meal, and sing Christmas carols.

On our *Wigilia* in exile, we ate turnip soup from tin bowls and spoons marked with swastikas. Mother found pea pods outside the German kitchen. The children picked out the moldy ones; she washed and cooked the rest. Mrs. Makowska cooked wheat instead of traditional barley. Her husband ground chunks of salt with his mortar and pestle from home. Mrs. Sobal's piece of white bread replaced the *opłatek* wafer.

This *Wigilia* fed us spiritually, but the German officer, Willi, understood physical hunger. Mother said, "I volunteer in the kitchen. Peel some potatoes, stuff potatoes and peels into my sleeves, and leave. That was our supper. Once Willi walked into our two rooms as I was unloading my sleeves."

I said, "He was supposed to enforce the 699-calorie limit per day for Polish people."

"Yes. But he saw, and not a word. He left. No report. No punishment."

Besides potatoes up her sleeve, mother put ration cards to good use. Americans dropped them from airplanes. They looked like 50/50 raffle tickets, or larger on a roll of white paper. Some French prisoners found them and buried them in front of our barrack window. After dark, Henry and Chester dug up what resembled a ball of yarn the size of a human head and hid it.

Mother used them during a budding romance. She said, "A fine boy from Warsaw, Rogalski, was sent to work in Essen but came to see Janina Makowska some Sundays. They went someplace to get their picture taken. A stunning couple! I gave him ration cards to use in Essen. We couldn't go in stores, but he got a German to shop by sharing some cards. He then sent me packages of bread. The women gossiped about me getting mail from Rogalski. Huh! If the Germans knew, they would shoot us all."

We needed the *Lagerfuehrer's* permission to leave the camp. My mother and my brothers risked punishment each time they left to find food, otherwise, none of us would have survived. Mother picked berries and mushrooms in the forest and would carry me along with a bucket of plump blackberries to the town of Gladbeck. Once, as she handed the pail to the bakery owner, one of Hitler's elites killing squad, the *Schutzstaffel*, walked in. The woman signaled with her eyes to leave. Mother said, "I wasn't supposed to even be in the same room with this higher up. Walking back empty-handed, I heard a bicycle. Was the SS man coming after me? I turned around and a man from the bakery pushed two loaves of bread into my hands, one white, one rye, and left quickly.

Mother added, "Some Germans were decent that way. Some women on bicycles threw down ration cards. When Henry and Chester were out begging for food, the bombs began. I was wild with worry. But the German women let them into their safer bunkers."

The *Lebensborn*

We had no rights, not even to our own children.

The three oldest, Henry, Chester, and Janka went to school in the camp run by a German couple who taught German and Russian. Mother thought the real purpose was to promote Hitler's philosophy. She made sure we knew who we were, but some children lost their identities. Mother said, "A couple from Jankowicze had their baby taken from them. They never knew what happened to it. We had no rights, not even to our own children. When a woman from Naliboki gave birth, the *Lagerfuehrer,* said, "I have many children and they all manage somehow. Let this one stay."

I asked if it was his child. Mother said, "His, but she couldn't do anything if they took it from her."

American historian Jackson J. Spielvogel explains that, "Hitler and the Nazis, as in so many areas of life, offered conflicting attitudes toward sex and morality. Official sex education promoted strict rules calling for self-control... yet numerous Nazis, including Hitler, scornfully rejected the old "bourgeois morality" and castigated it as "prudish hypoc- risy." Hitler encouraged 'wholesome delight in existence' and argued that one must not attempt to restrain robust males, especially in wartime."[29]

German soldiers were encouraged to sire children outside of marriage, and the state set up facilities for these births. Polish American historian, Richard Lukas, tells us that, "established in 1935 to provide maternity facilities for the wives and girl friends of the SS and police establishment, *Lebensborn* [Well of Life] broadened its activities to include the Germanization of kidnapped children." [30]

"Abduction and Germanization of Polish children was a major part of the Nazi program aimed at the biological re- duction of the Polish nation and the corresponding increase in the strength of Germany....The Germans subjected the children to racial, medical, and psychological tests to deter- mine the candidate's suitability..."[31]

"Children considered unfit for Germanization found their way to Majdanek and Auschwitz where they died...200,000 Polish children were deported for Germaniza- tion... only 15-20 percent of the children kidnapped by the Germans were recovered at war's end. Some parents and relatives are still looking for their children."[32]

I could have been among them, but my story has a charitable twist. Mother walked to Gladbeck and chose a prosperous-looking house. She knocked on the door. The woman who opened the door looked well-fed, so chances of getting food were good. From the woman's perspective, in- stead of a young woman basking in the joy of motherhood, there stood a beggar in rags holding her hungry baby in a thin piece of cloth. That was me. The homeowner looked long at the babe in mother's arms. She then called over her Pol- ish-speaking neighbor to ask why there were so many for- eigners in the area. Their government said we were gypsies roaming freely. They were surprised that we came by force. The woman gave mother food and told her to come back. Mother had something the woman wanted.

(Left) The Chmara family after liberation, front row: Janka, Mary. Back row: Henry, Van, Chester. (Right) Mother holding Donna, the baby she refused to give away. Germany 1948

Each time mother returned, the woman had questions. She learned that mother had five more hungry mouths to feed at the labor camp. In time, she asked mother into the house. Mother knew enough German by then for basic conversation as the woman rocked me in her arms. Once, after cradling me a long time and humming German songs, she asked my name. Mother said, "Danuta."

"Why doesn't she have a nice German name?"

"I would like to know, what are some nice German names?"

"Maria, Heidi. But if she was my baby, I would call her Heidi."

Mother knew from then on, when asking for food, I had a nice German name Heidi. But her time with the two women ended abruptly. One day, the Polish-speaking neighbor joined them in the garden as the German woman cradled me in her arms. After some words between the two women that mother did not understand, the neighbor voiced an urgent plea: "This. Woman. Wants. Your. Baby."

Mother stiffened and her heart was racing. The neighbor coaxed her gently, "Give her this little girl. She and her husband have no children. For you, six is a hardship. You may be saving her life."

The German woman had decided on a name for me. Trying to reassure mother sitting wide-eyed in stunned silence, she said, "This baby will have every advantage, my little Heidi."

Mother struggled, "No, my baby. Give away my baby girl! No, no. That's not possible."

"It will be easier for you and your family with one less child to feed."

"But she is my family, part of me and my husband. Whatever happens, will happen to the whole family. Give her away? No. We cannot be separated."

Mother yanked me out of her arms and held me tightly. She told me, "My God, Danusia, how she wanted you! Both women pleaded with me. I held you tighter and started to leave."

The woman told mother to wait while she went inside. Babies were taken from parents, would there be trouble? But she returned with bread, grain, and sugar for the family. Eager to be a mother, she had laid out baby clothes. She gave mother little outfits, booties, and blankets meant for her new baby Heidi. She kissed me tenderly, lingered to touch my cheek, and walked into the house with effort. Had mother placed me in her arms, I would someday be a German tourist named Heidi visiting Poland.

The Darkest Hours

We stood in bunkers beneath the fury of German and Allied air battles.

When the bomb blew him to pieces, it could have been us. Once, a bomb landed on a bunker just as my father stepped out. But this bomb chose the first commandant, the *Lagerfuehrer*. Was it karma, the Buddhist idea of consequences for all we do? Did this atone for his hatred of helpless people?

The new *Lagerfuehrer* was not disdainful. Mother said, "When Chester bent over with stomach pain, he drove me and your brother to a hospital. And he loved your brother Wacek. We hear the siren, race for the bunker – a trench covered with boards and soil. Little protection from bombs coming at us. The new *Lagerfuehrer* would come into the bunker to make sure your brother was warm. Wacek figured out that saying *"Heil Hitler,"* made the man beam with delight."

I said, "Van was only four but was already doing his part to protect the family."

The bombing escalated when the city of Cologne (German:Koln) fell to General Hodges' First Army on March 6, 1945. Germany was losing the war. We stood in bunkers

Chmara family photographed two years after liberation in a displaced person's camp. Sitting: Mother Helena, Donna, Father Michał. Standing: Mary, Janka, Henry, Chester, Van. Germany 1947

beneath the fury of German and Allied air battles. Mother said, "They aimed at each other. When they missed, the bombs fell on us. My friend's little boy was killed that way."

Mother befriended a Russian family with seven children, plus one whose parents were killed by a bomb. The Russian family took the forlorn little tyke into their family. Mother said, "We slept in our clothes and shoes so we could rush our children into the bunker during an air raid. Hearing the bombs, Mrs. Samochin would say to me, 'My dear Yelenushka, we must keep our babies alive.'"

When the new *Lagerfeuhrer's* visits to check on Van stopped, Henry and Chester saw guards kill a calf, bury the bones, take the meat, and run for their lives. Mother said, "Mrs. Makowska and I dug up the bones, washed them in the river. We made soup with the bones between air raids in Makowski's large pot from home. So good, not like that foul turnip soup with the worm on top."

When Henry and Chester's begging for food was successful, mother would give us each a piece of bread, dry the rest, and put it in a cloth bag. In case it got worse. Yes, it got worse. Palm Sunday 1945, officers and guards were running away but Willi stayed to lead us to a safer German bunker. Mother said, "On the last three days, we stood shoulder to shoulder. No room to sit. Your father stepped out, got water from a bomb crater. I wet the dried bread and fed you children and Willi."

She added, "You were suffocating, dying. I pushed through. Someone yelled to step aside, the child is dead. I got you outside. You were lifeless. I was shaking your limp body and breathing into you. I was praying, please God, let my baby live."

I said, "I was slipping from you into that long tunnel, you were yanking me back."

"You twitched, grunted, and gasped for air. A little breath. Then another. No bombs coming at us."

On that last day of the war, rescue came from strangers across an ocean. American soldiers found a bunker full of humanoid creatures about to die from working too hard and eating too little. The soldiers helped us crawl out of the ground, pausing to vomit from the stench of human waste as they carried out the weakest. They pulled out lifeless brother, Van, and rushed him to Saint Barbara's hospital in Kirchhellen. On one of mother's visits, Van was again a normal child, playing "horsie" on the back of an American soldier. "Heil Hitler" was no longer needed to save the family, so Van asked mother, "What should I say now?"

Mother added, "Janka was also in a hospital for her kidneys, but you and your brother, Henry, nothing could mow you down."

Are We Still Human?

Mother gathered food and clothes and sent Henry and Chester to find Willi.

We trudged for hours led by American soldiers and staring at death, so Halloween playfulness doesn't feel amusing to me. My eyes turn away from skeletal figures and tombstones on people's front lawns. Mother said, "My God, my God! We walked through bloody cobblestone streets, fields, and bombed forests full of dead people, dead animals."

I told mother, "I saw the cobblestone streets. The dead soldiers. The burned-out forests."

"That's not possible. You were a child. Two years old."

Until I sought therapy, I always felt cold when I talked about the war. So, I told mother, "Let me describe what I remember. A man is carrying me. The cobblestone streets are splattered with blood. A dead soldier lies mangled on the ground. His horse lies next to him, its guts spilling out. We walk through scorched woods and try not to touch the dead bodies. I see this again and again."

Mother said, "Heavens, yes. What you remember is what we saw for hours walking away from the bunker. The man carrying you was your father, and Henry and Chester. Even your sisters. I was so weak; I could barely walk. So, they took turns carrying you and Wacek. We reached an old church, then collapsed into the pews and slept."

American soldiers rescued us on Holy Thursday, the day of the Last Supper. On Good Friday, they led us to empty German houses and told us to eat, wash, and dress. On Easter Sunday, April 1, 1945, we were free. Free and homeless. In five years, we lived in five displaced persons camps: Muelheim Ruhr, Raderhorst, Rekenfeld, Emmerich, and Essen. Our lifeline in those camps, again strangers across an ocean, was the United Nations Relief and Rehabilitation Administration, UNRRA.

"Between 1944 and 1947 the UNRRA rushed food, clothing, and medical supplies to war-torn nations....The United States took responsibility for most of the cost of UNRRA aid. The aid went to both allies and former enemies. Grain, mainly from American farms, was shipped to Europe and Asia. Tractors and plows were sent to hundreds of farms. Pumps and pipes restored Greece's water systems. Missouri mules found new homes on Yugoslavian farms. In its race against starvation and chaos, the UNRRA distributed some 22 million tons (20 million metric tons) of supplies."[33]

We got eight UNRRA packages a month for two years. Mother asked around until she heard where Willi might be hiding. Unlike dried bread crusts in the bunker, she gathered food and clothes from the packages and sent Henry and Chester to find Willi. Walking through rubble, they found a dilapidated building. They knocked on the door of an apartment that could be habitable. No answer. They banged loudly. Nothing. They yelled, "Willi, we are the Chmara boys. We have food for you."

Silence. More banging. Silence. Turning to leave, they heard a click of the lock, a door squeak. Willi peered through the crack. He seemed disoriented and whispered, "You really are the Chmara boys, alive. Come. Before anyone sees you. Come in."

He laughed, he cried, he hugged them fiercely. How different he looked. No uniform. No club. No Iron Cross to make that uniform even more important. An ordinary man. But he was not an ordinary man. He was a man with the

Studio photo of the author's parents Helena and Michał Chmara. Germany 1948

courage to be kind when kindness was a punishable offense. He said, "I hide from my government. They could punish me for being good to people in the camp."

Speaking German by then, my brothers said, "That government doesn't exist anymore. Our mother thanks you. For your kindness. For those potatoes she stole from the kitchen. We even ate the peels."

Willi opened the packages. Seeing real food, he cried. They visited him several more times until he felt safe enough to leave his hideout to look for his wife and children.

Reuniting families was next. Mrs. Kowalewska was missing her husband and daughter. The four Rosinski sisters knew nothing of their mother and brother. Mother told them that her Michał was leaving to look for her brother and sister and would also try to find their families. During his search, father got off at train stops to read "Lost Persons" notices on municipal buildings. Mother beamed with pride when he returned with Aunt Eleanor and Uncle Józef, and their missing family members.

The bond between mother and her Russian friend, Mrs. Samochin, had made the nights in the bunker bearable as they watched over their children. And being on the front did not stop Janina and Rogalski from falling in love. I asked if they got married. Mother said, "They lost contact during air raids. He came to say good-bye, already married to a Ukrainian woman, but took the picture of him and Janina. She never spoke of him again."

Of the twenty-one people in two rooms, the Sobols returned to Poland. Some Makowskis went to Australia, others to England where Janina met a new love. Father was rebuilding the city of Essen and his employers wanted him to stay. But we left when President Harry Truman signed legislation allowing a quota of refugees to enter the United States. Our path had been paved by father's brother, Henry, who had promised years ago to take care of his family from far away.

*1913. Father's oldest brother Henryk Chmara left Nali-
boki to find peace and prosperity in America. Twenty-one and
gutsy.*

*1917. Now called Henry Mara, he served with the
American Expeditionary Forces in France during World War I.
Twenty-five and ready for battle.*

*1925. A married man with a successful farm in Cran-
bury, New Jersey. Hard-working.*

*1950. Father of two, he took in eight people to house
and feed. Generous. So very generous.*

The USS General Ballou left Bremerhaven in November 1950 and headed for New York. Henry and Chester worked in the kitchen as a hurricane tossed us up and
down the Atlantic. I was in the medical ward, too nauseous
to walk. A kind nurse helped me draw flowers, but I wanted
my parents. Mother said, "The boys were with your father
in the men's section, the girls were with me together with a
rabbi's wife and children. He looked after everyone, not just
his wife. That rabbi helped us all."

Life before the Cattle Cars

**...our teacher could be sent to Siberia for teaching us
Polish.**

Mother was born in 1909, the first child of Anna
and Justyn Byczkiewicz when Naliboki was under the Russian partition. Mother said, "Your grandfather's stepmother
taught Polish in our house. An older boy stood watch. If he
yelled, "*Urjadnik* is coming, we hid under the bed or stove
where we kept the chickens. Who the devil was he? Some
Russian official patrolling houses. If he saw a lot of children
it might be a secret school. The older children knew to hide.
I was too young. It was an exciting game for me. I learned
later that our teacher could be sent to Siberia for teaching
us Polish."

I said, "Amazing that after 123 years, people still had
a sense of their own identity and culture."

Anna and Justyn's second child, Franek, died in infancy from whooping cough. The third, Józef, was born in
1914. He was seven weeks old when Justyn was drafted to

Roadside chapel near Naliboki large enough for three people, much like the ones Helena Chmara mentions in her chapter. Belarus 1994

fight in the czar's army against Germany in World War I. Mother said, "Father was gone four years. Mother took care of me, baby Józef, the house, a garden and orchard for food, the livestock, and gathered firewood in the forest."

With the men at war, women could not plow fields and plant grain on top of everything else they did. Grandmother Anna baked coarse bread from lilac heather, wheatgrass, animal fodder, and rye. It fell apart. They couldn't eat it. When World War I reached Naliboki, Russian soldiers paid people to bring their own shovel and dig trenches for fighting the Germans. Anna even dug trenches to buy my mother and baby Józef real bread.

When World War I ended in 1918, the surviving men came home to a famine, prepared the land with horse and plow, planted grain, and started families. My grandparents had three more daughters. Bronisława died of whooping cough, but you will meet Eleanor and Mania who survived. The men also came home to the newly independent country of Poland. Children no longer hid with the chickens to learn Polish. But, she said, "My teachers, Albert and Karol Chmara, came to the house. They told my father to keep me in school. They said I learned quickly. I could make something of myself. I loved school but had to quit after grade five."

Anna and Justyn were not cruel parents, just poor. Anna's once robust husband returned from war with chronic asthma. Mother was needed to tend geese and to help plant potatoes, linen, barley, and rye on their 15 acres of land. When mother grew up, a Jewish family hired her and some friends to clear brush on their land nine miles away. They worked eight days and kept returning to get paid. Shoes were expensive, so on a warm spring day, they went barefoot and were told to wait another day. They slept in the forest. Mother said, "We finally got some fabric, but snow fell, and we walked home barefoot. They didn't have the money. That was our life. It got better when I married your father. He built houses, a school with two buildings, and he was working on the new church."

Mother was no longer poor, but like her mother Anna, she mowed fields with a scythe, threshed grain, prepared hay, and walked to the forest for firewood. Mother said, "How I worked! Your grandfather Stefan was gone, but your Grandmother Emilja lived with us. I wanted help with the children, but your father said his mother worked hard all her life and it was time for her to rest."

Child mortality was high. When Mary and Van had pneumonia, mother watched over them day and night in the infirmary. Her sister Eleanor prepared the fields and planted the potatoes. The current priest, Father Marian, told me that potatoes are still the second bread that gets a family through winter.

Reflections

How could I give you away?

DC: How did you and my father meet and get married?

Young people knew who they wanted, but families had to approve. They had a go-between, a *swat*, to get agreement, settle a dowry, pick a date. The wedding party was a way to show off young people for marriage. Mothers made sure their daughters got invited to be bridesmaids. Church was a place to see who was single. Your father saw me in church. Once the families agreed, the priest announced the marriage. I didn't know Michał went and told the priest to announce our marriage bans for all to hear. My parents liked him. He knew they would agree. He came to tell us, and I somehow agreed.

DC: He never proposed to you! Well, did you like him? We children loved him.

Not much at first (laughter together.) I was twenty-one, he was twenty-six He was a good man, but jealous. *(Mother surprised me at his funeral when, seeing him in the coffin, she said, "Even now, you are so handsome to me.")* We had a fine wedding. Six bridesmaids. Cousin Maria Baszuro was maid of honor. My parents borrowed money for the wedding from Stefczyk's money lending. Each year, the best they could do was scrape up the interest.

Naliboki was beautiful, cobblestone streets, green fields. The forest began at our doorstep and ran for miles to the Niemen River. We worked hard, but we were happy. It hurt to see it burning – our home, our grain, the two schools your father built. Those schools meant a lot to him. Father Bajko came to our house often. He sat with your father and together they planned the new schools and new church.

I walked barefoot to church in Germany and cried in the pew. Sometimes I still cry. Your father and I didn't eat for days and gave our rations to you children (voice cracks). Sometimes we had nothing to give you. God forbid, if Germany won. Saturday was payday. Your father got a notice he owes money. They charged room and board for eight people, the bare wooden boards and vile turnip soup.

At least, the Americans saved us. When I look at those people in Iraq, I could give away everything. But whatever is brought in, the fastest grab it. The weak get nothing. Women and children suffer, the hunger goes on. The fighting never ends.

DC: You kept your Danuta. I didn't become Heidi. Could I have been taken from you?

It's possible but more likely if you were born in Germany. You were born in Naliboki ten weeks before we were deported. I breast-fed you until I went deaf. I lost taste of bitter or sweet, sour or salty. The women in the camp said I will leave the others orphaned if you suck the life out of me. When I stopped breast-feeding, you went crazy at first until you calmed down.

DC: I grew up in a large loving family. Thank you for keeping me.

How could I give you away?

    Michał Chmara was born in Naliboki on November 1, 1903 and passed away on February 7, 1979 in Cranbury, NJ. He had been a sergeant in the Fourth Artillery Regiment of the Polish Army in Suwalki, Poland. He was a carpenter and mason for Thompson Park in Jamesburg, NJ. **Helena Byczkiewicz Chmara** was born in Naliboki on March 15, 1909 and passed away on March 20, 1998 in Princeton, NJ. She worked as a seamstress in South River, New Jersey. My parents had six children and thirteen grandchildren.

134 *Surviving Genocide*

Endnotes

27 Hanna Regulska-Ślusarczyk, *Ziemia Mickiewicza* (Newcastle, Australia: 1999) p. 33, p. 35.

28 Neal Ascherson, *Struggles for Poland* (NY: Random, 1987) p. 99.

29 Jackson J. Spielvogel, *Hitler and Nazi Germany* (Englewood Cliffs, NJ: Prentice Hall, 1988) p. 184.

30 Richard C. Lukas, *Did the Children Cry? Hitler's War Against Jewish and Polish Children* (NY: Hippocrene, 1994) p. 116.

31 Lukas, *The Forgotten Holocaust: The Poles under German Occupation 1939-1944* (NY: Hippocrene, 1986) pp. 25-26.

32 Lukas, *Did the Children Cry?*, pp.109 – 121.

33 Clifton Daniel, ed. *Addison-Wesley US History* (Menlo Park, CA: Addison-Wesley, 86) p. 605.

Chapter 8 Six Children
From Abduction to Freedom

Henry: American Soldier

In my brother Henry's world, children worked as soon as they could hold a pitchfork, lift a bale, or supervise a cow. By age eight, he was tending livestock in the pasture after school. By 11, he was defending Naliboki. By 12, he was begging for food to feed our family.

After the war, Henry, Chester, and my sister Janka boarded out at a high school, called a Gymnasium, in Lippstadt, Germany. With a roof over his head and food in his stomach, Henry absorbed new ideas, formed friendships, and finished a university preparatory course.

In 1950, father's brother Henry Mara, wife Minnie, son Walter, and daughter Eleanor took eight people into their home in Cranbury, New Jersey. They gave us three quarters of an acre to create our own homestead. Father built houses. Mother, Henry, Chester, and Janka worked in factories. Mary, Van, and I went to school. Each Friday, they all handed their wages to mother. She gave them pocket change, set aside grocery money, and father bought building materials with the rest. Riding past some summer evening or weekend, you would see mother churning cement, father cutting boards, Henry and Chester nailing up walls. A year later, we moved into our first real home since 1943.

Paths to Staying Alive

Finding bread in dead soldiers' pockets, my brothers gobbled it up crouching next to them.

Forty-five years after building that home, Father, Chester, and Janka were already with the angels, but with my immediate family, in-laws, and grandchildren, our 1997 Easter celebration meant two long tables for thirty. Mother dyed the eggs dusty red and rich brown with onion skins she had been saving for months. Henry shredded the pungent horseradish, tears biting his eyes like raw onions.

Unlike tin plates decorated with swastikas in Germany, we ate on mother's best china with a rose petal design on tables covered with crisply ironed white linens.

Our chatter stopped as she said the blessing. We then dove into ham, kielbasa, meat gelatin, mashed potatoes, salads, pierogi, cookies, cakes, babka, pies, fruit, and nuts. But the Easter lamb shaped from butter stood untouched and admired.

Food, glorious food, took Henry back to the lean days and the paths to survival. One path was begging for food. We were on the war front, but near towns and farms. Finding bread in dead soldiers' pockets, my brothers gobbled it up crouching next to them. But when they begged for food, Henry said, "Many German farmers had lost sons on the Russian front. They were angry and chased us with axes and shotguns. We ran like rabbits. Thank God, I didn't have my creaky arthritis then."

Another path was hard work. He said, "The commandant of the starvation camp, big fat guy, kept our measly pay. When we were moved to the labor camp, father and I were rented out on a farm. German and Polish people were forbidden to eat together, but we worked hard and the farmer welcomed us at his table. After eating, he went, "Hrrrrr," let out big fart, which meant the food was satisfying."

Mother's sense of people's egos was a path to survival. Henry said, "Mother snuck out to clean house for a German woman. The woman cried for her dear Hitler's safety. Mother tried to look sad, too. Her dear Hitler was trying to kill us, so I asked how mother could look sad in front of that woman. She said, "Who do you think gave me the bread you're eating? But mother refused when a German woman begged her to give you away. That woman wanted you badly."

The 17-year-old Russian boy Ivan did not understand ego. He drove the *Lagerfuehrer* to town in a three-wheel car. It broke down. His boss could not repair it. Ivan fixed it. Returning from shopping, the man beat the boy with a bat for showing him up. Henry said, "That *Lagerfuehrer* was killed by a bomb. He was so cruel, people danced when they learned he was dead. With the new *Lagerfuehrer*, four-year-old Van had his own way of protecting the family. He smiled, gave a Nazi salute, and said, '*Heil Hitler*.' The man showed off this blond and blue-eyed child to visiting dignitaries."

And it helped to know when to disappear. Henry and Chester swam with other boys in a bomb crater full of rainwater the size of a house. The German boys tried to push them out. Henry said, "Russian kids cut the German kids with knives. The Gestapo made an uproar. Chester hid in the woods, I came back. Father took a whip and beat the shit out of me. He said if guards saw me with those boys, I could get us all killed. By the time Chester came back, father had calmed down."

Henry's son, Staś, said, "You were somewhere you shouldn't be. You were putting the whole family in danger, so grandfather had to make an impression on you. Those guards were brutal."

Henry said. "Yes. Some wore black uniforms, boots, hats with skull and bones, and big belts with 'God is with us' on the buckle. When Chester and I snuck out to church, even the altar boys clicked their heels turning around right there on the altar! Click, turn. Click, turn. Hitler was their hero."

Friendship blunted the brutality. Henry worked on a farm with a Russian boy Misha. Finishing his own work, Henry helped Misha with the huge job of milking cows. Misha would then hand Henry the pail. The warm white milk gliding down Henry's throat felt a bit like sharing Communion. And when some Italian prisoners of war found an old accordion, people gathered for Saturday night dances to their music. Until the bombing began, a bit of wounded humanity in a forced labor camp came to life.

Sin in the Garden of Eden

Grandfather's stepmother Maryśka taught Polish secretly in her home.

As we lingered over Easter dinner, Henry described a happy childhood. Naliboki was part of Poland. Mother took care of six children, the house, and farm. Father earned money building houses. The older children went to school. Henry sat spellbound as his teacher Dremza described how Poland was carved up (1795 – 1918) by its neighbors, Prussia, Austria-Hungary, and Russia. Henry said, "Naliboki became part of Russia for 123 years, and teaching Polish was forbidden. But people like grandfather's stepmother Maryśka taught Polish secretly in her home."

This land grab ended in 1918 after World War I. Naliboki briefly became part of Poland again. Henry said, "We went back and forth between Polish and Russian rule, but our parents always told us who we were. When the Russians invaded in 1939, I knew not to talk in school about Maryśka

or that we were Polish. She risked her life to pass down
our mother tongue. In your video of the Naliboki church
consecration in 1994, children sing and speak Polish with a
Belarussian accent."

I said, "Naliboki was a Polish settlement since the
Middle Ages. It fell under Russian rule in 1795, but people
were still trying to learn their language secretly in the
1900's."

The Polish history lessons ended with the 1939
Soviet invasion. Father's brother Józef Chmara, wife Józefa,
and daughter Stefania disappeared. Mayor Gregorcewicz,
policeman Dubicki, teacher Dremza, forest warden Szczerbik
disappeared. And hundreds more. The Russians made
father's brother, Uncle Jan, a clerk in the town hall. Henry
said, "Uncle Jan noticed that the officer in charge locked
his office door at the end of each day. He peeked through
the keyhole. This leader in the atheistic communist system,
large in boots and uniform, was small and humble kneeling
in prayer."

Soviet atheism may explain hatred toward the town
priest, Monsignor Bajko. When the Russian partisans came
for him, townspeople rescued him with pitchforks and axes.
A man who rarely attended church, embarrassed by his
old clothes, led the charge to save their beloved leader. The
priest hid, grew a beard, and tended livestock on a farm.
Expecting to be safer with the 1941 German invasion, he
returned to the church.

Monsignor Bajko had admired German culture. He
set up an electric power plant, sawmill, and brick factory
with machinery from Germany. But the second invader sent
the machinery back to Germany and demanded moonshine.
Parishioners helped until they ran out of grain to meet the
demand. The next evil is still remembered in Naliboki. The
German soldiers who drank moonshine took the beloved
leader into the lush primeval forest and murdered him. It
had been a Garden of Eden for Henry and Chester with its
deer, moose, bear, raccoon, wild boar, and beaver roaming
freely until the priest's brutal death, and a strange encounter
following the murder.

Exploring their magical forest, Henry and Chester came
upon a clearing with six men talking among themselves. As
my brothers crept away, the strangers heard the rustling of
shrubs and began walking toward them. Henry said, "Some
of them were tall. They asked us something about finding
guns. We ran as fast as our legs could carry us. Years later,

Studio photo of the Chmara family in America. Sitting: Father Michał, Donna, Mother Helena. Standing: Chester, Janka, Van, Henry, Mary. South River, NJ 1951

I read about the Bielski brothers, Jewish partisans who saved Jewish lives in local forests from the German army. I saw their photographs, and remembered a face. He was one of the men that Chester and I ran away from that day."

According to American historian Timothy Snyder, "After the German invasion of the Soviet Union in June 1941, [Tuvia] Bielski tried to defend Jews from mass murder. He and his brothers established a family camp in the Naliboki Forest early in 1942. Like other family camps, this was a Jewish initiative; but, as elsewhere, the leaders had to come to an arrangement with the Soviet partisans."[34]

Their Garden of Eden became a place to avoid as children became soldiers. Tending livestock, the boys found weapons and ammunition. Henry said, "We were thrilled to fire the big Russian rifles with lots of kick. Three boys held a rifle and aimed at Germans in the distance. A boy pulled the trigger, we ran like crazy. I didn't dare tell mother and father, but we had to defend Naliboki."

Disposable People

All my life I tried to forget seeing our home in flames. But I can't.

Christians and Jews were connected economically, and by a mix of distrust, prejudice, mutual aid, and

Author's sisters Janka and Mary wearing outfits sewn by mother Helena. South River, NJ 1951

friendship. Henry said, "Father sometimes gave us a few coins to stop after school at Skniut's café. He was father's friend. When we walked in, Skniut would sing with affection, 'Here come Michał's boys.' We had tea and he always gave us extra sugar. We loved going there."

When German soldiers rounded up the Jews for extermination in 1942, this small-town familiarity meant wrenching decisions about "your life or mine." He said, "They hid in the forest or in Polish homes. When father's Jewish friends tapped on the window at night, we didn't have much after being robbed by Germans, Russians, and at times Jewish partisans. But father fed Skniut and others and let them sleep in the barn. Mother said the Germans would kill us for helping. I was terrified. But father would say they are people like us, and think of the children."

He added, "I can't forget old Leiman. One of the first to perish. For a small fee, he watched people's livestock. If he lost a sheep to the wolves, he cried like it was his own. We never found out if Skniut and his son made it into the forest or what happened to the Jewish girl that Uncle Jan hid in his attic."

After marching the Jewish residents to their death, German soldiers were forcing Polish men to fight the Russians, and the Russians were forcing Polish men to fight the Germans. Mother was eight months pregnant with me when three partisans barged into our house on May 7, 1943, to force father to join them. With rifles aimed at him, sister Janka shrieked like a child possessed. Our neighbor Franek Chmara came spinning a tale of father being pals with their commander. Franek said, "The other night your commander was at this man's house. They drank vodka and sang Russian songs till morning."

One of the partisans barked back, "What is the name of our great leader?"

Franek said, "I don't know. I am a simple man. The others called him *Tovarish kamandir.*"

No commander had visited, no vodka was consumed, no Russian songs were sung. Franek had gambled that the ragged partisans might fear infuriating some dignitary laden down with medals on his fancy uniform. One of them kicked father in the behind and yelled, "You son of a bitch," and left.

Unable to repel the Russian partisans, the Germans ordered local men between ages 18 and 40 to form self-defense units to fight them. Henry said, "It was dangerous to refuse. Our men belonged to the Home Army, the military arm of the Underground Resistance. They asked for direction. The Army reluctantly agreed, but the Germans didn't leave enough arms or ammunition to stop the massacre.

Deep in the night of May 8, 1943, Russian soldiers were airdropped to aid the partisans on the ground. At dawn, the partisans and official military entered Naliboki. Henry said, "There was some question about the German presence. The Russians attacked in a large cavalry formation, not sneaking up behind buildings. This suggests that, at that point, there was no German garrison in town."

The self-defense units were like a feather in a tornado. By nightfall, 128 people lay dead and part of Naliboki was burned. Ten weeks later, August 7, 1943, Operation Hermann marched in with five German SS divisions and several tank battalions with Estonian, Lithuanian, Latvian, and Ukrainian SS units to crush the Soviets and to deport us to Germany. Henry said, "A soldier lit straw and threw it into our house. I was 12. All my life I tried to forget seeing our home in flames. But I can't."

We remained in the forced labor camp for two years until Henry saw guards packing up food. Germany was losing the war, but they had to dispose of us before running for their lives. Thanks to the German officer, Willi, we lived to see Easter 1945. The *Lagerfuehrer* announced he was evacuating the camp the next day. Guards would march us across the bridge to a safer German bunker. But Willi knew. All would end in the middle of the bridge. They would blow it up – young, old, babies, families, me. Even the favorite prisoner – my blond blue-eyed brother Van. We were disposable people.

That night, Willi led several hundred people into an abandoned German bunker. Henry said, "Willi was a great human being. The bombing became so fierce, the guards ran away, but Willi stayed to help us. For three days, we stood beneath Allied and German battles in the air. Donna, you were suffocating from the crush of people. People were saying the child is dead, but mother pushed through and got you outside. You began to breathe and came back to life."

On the last day of the war, an American soldier stuck his head into the bunker, and gagged from the stench. He then boomed in Polish, "I am a Polish American from a place called Chicago. We will get you out but don't try to leave yet. I mean it. Some of our guys shoot at anything that moves."

Henry said, "We came out six hours later. Some benevolent hand had guided the bombs away from us. A dead soldier lay there, stinking. The most vile stink is dead human stink. A half-naked black soldier, shining and sweating, was pulling himself out of a tank. It was the all-black 761st Tank Battalion, the Black Panthers. Later as an American soldier, I was trained to be a tanker myself. This was 1945. President Truman ended military segregation in 1948."

Walking 25 miles behind American lines, we found an old church. Henry said, "Some rowdy young Russians carried on all night and went and defecated on the altar. They were praying with us in the bunker. It was their communist upbringing to curse the bourgeois God. Mother and other women cleaned the house of God in disbelief."

My sister Mary's husband Eugene cautioned that there were good Russians, bad Russians. That's true for every group. You can't knock a whole nation because of some people. Henry's son, Staś, agreed.

Reflections

There is no limit to my admiration for the American soldiers who risked their lives to free us.

DC: We lost everything but not each other. No one in our immediate family died during the war.

Peace was tainted with sadness. Russian partisans killed my 16-year-old cousin Edward. His brother

Kazimierz was my teacher, an engineer, and leader in the Naliboki Underground. He was tortured at Bergen-Belsen concentration camp in Germany until one eye hung out of its socket. He died as we were freed. His mother was my father's cousin, Zofia Wolan, the woman mother saw washing the Lithuanians laid out for burial. She wore black the rest of her life.

DC: *You speak to school groups to educate the younger generation about what happened.*

I was having lunch at work with my boss and our two clerks. We saw a news segment about German concentration and labor camps. I said, "I was there." My clerk said, "Henry, all these years I never knew you were Jewish." That hurts, like the war didn't happen to us. I speak to school groups because we need to remember all victims.

DC: *Some five million Polish Christians died from Soviet and German aggression and other groups were targeted. So I want to tell our story. But how did you start a normal life after such trauma?*

Mother and father were our inspirations, gave us their rations. That's love without limits. Father and I were looking for food after liberation. An American soldier caught a German farmer hiding in his barn. He gave father a rifle and said shoot. Father said he'll go hungry before he kills this man. His example kept us going. We were in rags, so when you saw a well-dressed man, you thought it was Hitler. You started hitting him with a stick and saying 'Beat Hitler, beat Hitler.' Mother chastised you for being rude to an older person.

Chester and I worked in a synthetic gasoline factory. Air raids all day, people left at night half crazed from fear. We promised when we got out, we would never go hungry or be afraid of anything again.

DC: *Did it turn out that way?*

The communists and Nazis never broke our spirit. We remained loyal to our loving God who gave us many blessings. We are loyal to our new country and try to pay back all we received. Despite all we lost, our family has many successful people. There's no limit to my admiration for the American soldiers who risked their lives to free us. My military service was a tribute to them. I ran into the captain of the USS *General Ballou*, the army ship that brought us here. We spoke, both of us proud that I had become an American soldier.

DC: You were the second person in our family to serve as an American soldier.

Uncle Henry, who came to America at 21, did not mean to change his name from "Chmara." The immigration clerk heard "Mara" and wrote it on the forms. It stuck when Uncle Henry went into the American army. He became a successful farmer. When he sponsored us to come to America, he "sold" us a piece of land, 100 x 300 feet for one dollar. Every Friday, we gave our pay to mother for food and building materials. In one year, we had a house and no mortgage. We had beautiful traditions, Sunday picnics, praying the rosary, holiday dinners, and our favorite – *Wigilia*, Christmas Eve. We were a happy family, and father walked among us like a proud peacock.

Mother said that father could be jealous. She never gave him cause, but he was so in love with her. Mother was beautiful and looked young, so when the family was out socially, our friends would ask Chester and me to introduce our "sister."

DC: Have you grasped the American dream?

It was hard, but we came to love it here. I wrote a column about the American dream for the New Jersey Turnpike Authority in the house publication to celebrate Thanksgiving:

"Some people see discrimination and call it America. Some lack appreciation for the material goods they enjoy and the freedoms they were given at the supreme sacrifice of others, and they call that America. Some see generosity and all that is good and call it America. I see a youth landing on these shores long ago, confused and bewildered. He mistrusted his fellow humans caused by the harsh realities of war. Yet, he found personal dignity, was accepted, and was treated with fairness. To him, dignity, freedom, and fairness are America."

DC: Have you found peace through forgiveness?

I try to forgive by remembering those who were kind. I pray for the German, Officer Willi. I pray for Franek Chmara who saved father's life by convincing the partisans that he was friends with their commander. I pray for my teachers at the *Gymnasium*, and the commanding officer who refused to send me to Korea saying, "This boy saw enough of war." I pray for colleagues who supported my work promotions. I pray for our parents who showed us how to love. Mother gave me the rosary father held when he died. He was my hero. When I kiss it, I feel him near me.

When Henry went before the draft board in Newark the first time, he was told to learn more English. The second time, he spoke fluently. He was with the Third Armored Cavalry Regiment during the time of the Korean War. He graduated second of 80 students from warfare school, and taught biological, chemical, and radiological defense to soldiers going to Korea. Scoring high on aptitude tests, he was offered officers' school or helicopter pilots' school. Not wanting a military career, he attended non-commissioned officers' school and graduated third out of 86 candidates.

When stationed at Fort Meade, Maryland, Henry passed tests in Polish, Russian, and German and was offered a career in the intelligence service. But he had enough of life on the run.

Henry Chmara was born on January 1, 1931 in Naliboki and passed away in Neptune, New Jersey on October 29, 2011. He was an administrator with the New Jersey Turnpike Authority. His wife Regina Kaniewska Chmara was born in Puzieniewicze, south of Naliboki. They had four children - a son in manufacturing and a union leader, a deceased son who worked in the trades, a daughter who is an art teacher, and a daughter and son-in-law who own several car dealerships. They had six grandchildren.

Chester: Big Brother

After beating the odds on the front lines, Chester and Janka were mowed down by cancer at ages 43 and 54 respectively. The vignettes below come from my loving memories of them.

A Modern Skill

Cars were rarely seen in Naliboki. In Germany, mother wanted someone in the family to learn to drive a vehicle. When Chester began driving a truck, she beamed that he had learned a modern skill.

The Raggedy Doll

Studio photo of Janka Chmara. South River, NJ 1951

My family of eight lives in one cramped room in a displaced persons camp. I am four and during the day, I cling to a few toys. At night, I cling to my mother until she pries me away. As people find jobs and leave Germany, the refugee camps are consolidated. We move from camp to camp, leaving behind a few bent pots and chipped dishes. Chester is a grown-up in my eyes, all of 16. As we pack for yet another camp, he sees me crying. He asks, "Danusia, what's wrong?"

I can't put into words that the familiar surroundings of this camp were starting to make me feel more secure. I said, "They said we can't take much with us. I don't want to leave my toys."

"Go pick out your favorite one. We'll take it with us. If anyone complains, I'll hide it in my sweater."

Squeezed into a truck, I hold tight a raggedy doll and snuggle up to Chester all the way to the next refugee camp. He makes me feel safe.

The Harmonica

Chester taught himself to play the harmonica while he and Henry and Janka were studying at a German high school, the *Gymnasium*. He radiated joy while playing the harmonica. Imagine what he could have done if he had

access to musical instruments. When we came to the
United States, Chester enjoyed a good party. His young
face lit up when he danced or played the harmonica. Henry
would rather read a book, and Chester would rather make
beautiful music.

Chester Chmara was born in Naliboki on July 23,
1932 and passed away in New Jersey on September 11,
1975. He was a carpenter for the New Jersey Turnpike. He
and his wife Stefania Cierniak Chmara had three children.
He did not live to see them grow up to become an attorney,
a medical doctor, and an accountant nor to know his three
grandchildren.

Janka: Heart of Gold

My sister and confidante, Janka made me clothes,
taught me to cook, and said "Yes" to life. As she was dying,
the hospital staff said they had never seen so many visitors.
Meeting her friends, I told them I had a special relationship
with her. They all said, "So do I." At first, I was jealous to be
among many. But as the years recede, I need more and more
of what I learned from her. That is, when you love profusely
as she did, you have enough love for everyone who appears
on your path in life.

A Striking Part of Her Beauty

Children tended livestock by age seven but leaving
the boys in charge of sister Janka was risky. Father wanted
mother to see Father Bajko about some plans for the new
church they were building. Walking to church with four
children would take all afternoon (Van and I were not yet
born.) Mother took two-year-old Mary and told the boys to
watch four-year-old Janka. They seemed to understand.

When mother returned, she saw a different child.
Who is this boy who came to play with them? But getting
closer, she began to scream, "Heavens, this is my Janka!
What did you do?"

Henry and Chester had cut off Janka's thick blond
hair. With mother so angry, they hid under the large tile
stove. When she calmed down, they climbed out to explain.
Jewish merchants buy hair pulled from pig hides after
slaughter. Janka's beautiful hair must be worth more and

would earn money for the family. Their good intentions melted mother's fury. Janka's thick blond hair grew back to remain a striking part of her beauty well into womanhood.

Her First Holy Communion

Children grew up fast in Naliboki anyway, but in war some had no childhood. If a child died, parents wanted their little girl or boy to leave this world having received First Holy Communion. Normally the congregation would stand as girls and boys marched into church and sat in the first pews for all to see. After the ceremonies, home celebrations with family and friends lasted until evening. The girls in frilly white dresses and boys in dark suits would remember this day forever.

But celebrations had become impossible. Janka said, "Chester and I were at Grandmother Anna's house in the south end of town. It was closer to church than our house north of town, and safer to walk there. Russian partisans were killing Polish men or forcing them into their units and attacked the women, so no one else could go with us. Poor Chester. I was 8, he was 11 when he got the job of getting me to church. He led me across dirt paths and alleys to avoid the partisans."

She continued, "Children received their First Holy Communion and left quickly. Chester and I entered the meadow facing Grandmother Anna's house. He said to stay close to him. Look straight ahead. Don't turn around. See grandmother's house? Keep looking at that. I held onto him and kept telling myself don't turn around. He talked gently, like to calm me. It won't be much longer. We'll soon be at grandmother's house. Then he said, 'That stream ahead. It's narrow enough for us to jump across. When we get there, close your eyes. We'll hold hands and jump across together.'"

Janka took a deep breath and continued, "We walked a few steps. We jumped across the stream together. We started to walk away. I tried to do what he said. But I turned around. I understood what he didn't want me to see. The stream was red with blood of people killed in the May massacre that took 128 lives. On my First Holy Communion, Chester tried to save me from seeing the stream turned red. He didn't want me to see what war looks like."

That day in Janka's life seems Biblical. Against the Angels' warning, Lot's wife looked back at the destruction of Sodom and was turned into a pillar of salt. When Janka looked back against Chester's warning, her heart could have turned into a pillar of stone. But some grace within her rejected cold and hard. Some grace within her embraced warm and kind.

On my trips to Naliboki, I stay with cousin Janusz and wife Jadwiga Chmara. They live across the street from the church property. Beyond their house is the meadow, and beyond the meadow I see the Koniec end of town where Grandparents Anna and Justyn used to live. I can see where their house had stood, where my mother grew up before she got married.

On one visit, their son Victor and I were strolling the meadow. When we reached the stream, a bolt of clarity passed through my body like lightning. I was standing on the spot where Janka and Chester had jumped across so long ago! I thought, "My dear Janka, you were not supposed to see this stream when it was red with blood. My dear Chester, you were just a child yourself as you tried to shield your sister on her special day. Do your spirits visit this meadow? I hope you are at peace. Perhaps you are walking beside me now. It is safe. The stream is now barely a trickle of clear water. I hope my love is reaching you across space and time."

The Orange

My family visited Janka in a hospital after the war where she was treated for her kidneys. We stood around the bed talking, but I could not ignore the orange gleaming like a piece of gold on the plate next to her. I did not know how an orange tasted, but it must be delicious from the way people talked about it. Sick as she was, she saw the craving in my eyes and said, "Please take this orange." This was the first of countless jewels she gave me from her heart.

Feed the Body, Feed the Soul

Janka lived in Spotswood, New Jersey, and often invited her emotionally fragile neighbor to join her for meals. When Janka died, the funeral procession went slowly past her house. My brother Henry saw the neighbor standing in Janka's front yard, crying, "Who will feed me now?"

Our cousin Walter was the son of Henry and Minnie Mara who had rescued us from homelessness. As a bachelor, he had relied on his mother's cooking. I learned years later that after his mother passed away, Janka shared home-cooked meals with him, quietly bringing comfort into his life.

Janina (Janka) Chmara Proszynska was born in Naliboki on May 12, 1935 and passed away in New Jersey on September 20, 1989. She worked in manufacturing for 30 years. She and her late husband Leszek had two children, a son in scientific research and a daughter in the health field, and three grandchildren.

Mary: Beauty and Brains

To my child's mind, my sisters were like glamorous debutantes – gowns with crinolines, dyed shoes, headpieces they wore as bridesmaids, and beauty parlor hairdos. I watched suitors come to court Mary and Janka. I admired Henry and Chester handsome in dark suits, smelling of after-shave. They were escorting their sisters to dances in Bayonne where Henry's future wife Regina lived.

Some families have one child who is an acknowledged beauty. When we walked down the street, Mary got the second looks. At weddings, men took turns dancing with her. In each new outfit, she could have stepped out of a fashion magazine. But Mary created a life based on brains and stamina – like our mother, sister Janka, and Grandmother Anna. These women showed me how to shape a life.

Mary married, raised four children, worked full-time in law enforcement, earned a degree in criminal justice, trained seeing eye dogs, studied karate, kept a home, and sculpted gardens full of waving sunflowers. Like our mother, her vitality was boundless.

We go to America as a family or not at all.

Henry was 12, Chester 11, Janka 8, Mary 5, and Wacek was 2. At ten weeks, I was sleeping as mother told them that German soldiers were burning our home. Mary knew the house well. She said, "Our big white house had a garden and a long path leading to the road. I picked the neighbor's cucumber. Mother made me take it back. The lady washed the cucumber, cut it in half and said, 'For bringing it back, we'll share it.' Mother planted nasturtiums, and to this day, I plant nasturtiums in my garden."

Ten weeks earlier, a woman stood near mother lying in bed. It was odd to see mother in bed during the day. She was working in the field yesterday. Mother did not seem to be in pain, but the blood on the floor startled Mary. Mother told her to stay warm in the cubbyhole above the big tile stove. Mary sat staring at the ceiling until the midwife said, "Look Marysiu, we have a new baby."

The white house, cucumbers, nasturtiums, and my birth are the last of Mary's memories of home. Mary said, "Nothing bad *ever* happened until *that* day when I heard mother say, 'Soldiers are burning our house.' We followed father down the long path and held onto mother. We waited by the road with other families. Father's friend gave us some apples. Mother cut them and fed us."

Mary's next memory is a pail of human excrement. She said, "We used a pail in the cattle car for the bathroom. A man picked up the pail and dumped it on a German policeman. I heard angry screaming and I was scared they would punish us for this."

After the cattle cars, came crowded barracks. Mary said, "Father left for work every morning. We were anxious until he came back at night. I sat next to mother and brushed her hair all the way down her back. At night we were, like, six people to a bed. We stood in line for that watery soup, hoping the kitchen wouldn't run out. I felt bad about my wooden shoe. I was playing and I kicked it through an open window. It fell into the soup of an old couple. They would not get food the rest of the day. I was five but I knew people were dying of hunger. I never got the shoe back, either."

At age seven, she stood in a damp bunker for three days. She said, "Oh God, the images are coming back! At our end people pray the rosary. At the other end, people make fun of us praying. A bomb hit their end and blew them to pieces. I don't remember their nationality. When American soldiers led us out, mother was so weak, father and the rest of us took turns carrying you and Van or pushing you in a baby carriage. We walked for hours through forests. I tried not to let my feet touch the corpses on the ground. Then we came upon an old church and collapsed into the pews."

The next day, American soldiers led us to abandoned German houses. We ate, washed, and put on clean clothes. Our tiny grandmother, *Babunia*, lived with us. She dug trenches during World War I to earn bread money for her children. Another war, and she had grandchildren to walk to church through forests that smelled like Christmas. She taught us to braid wildflowers into wreaths and put on our heads. We danced in the meadow of yellow daisies and blue cornflowers. Mary said, "You were with us, two by then. We were free, giggling, picking flowers. *Babunia* was running, laughing with us."

Six months later, we were moved to a displaced persons camp. Father got a job in construction. After school, we would run barefoot up a grassy hill, then roll down laughing. When father was coming back from work, we sat on the hilltop waiting for him. We got excited when we saw him, carrying his lunch box. But images of disaster sat below the surface. Some girls told Mary that a monster lived in the woods where Henry and Chester picked berries. She prayed for them to return, as she did when they had begged for food. When they snuck out to go swimming, she said, "We thought that river near the camp went around the world, we never saw the end of it. I worried they might drown."

The day of my First Holy Communion, someone had given father a drink to celebrate the festivities as he was returning from work. It went to his head. I stayed dressed up to show him my communion dress. With mother carrying on, he never noticed that I looked like a little bride. Mary said, "I never saw father like that. Mother was yelling at him and he was laughing. Even then, he was nice to us."

I said, "We adored father and we were a bit scared of mother. She was the disciplinarian."

Mary said, "We got United Nations food packages, but father got a job so he could take us to town. On Saturday afternoon, I held onto him in the trolley car with one hand. With the other, I clutched the coins he gave me to buy candy. And once a week, we all walked to a vegetable market. Once I pushed my way into a crowd, and there stood a black American soldier. At first, people were nervous. They never saw a black person. But he gave us chewing gum and slices of bread. I gobbled up that soft white bread. He said something friendly in Polish and made everyone smile."

No longer twenty-one people in two rooms like the war, but the barracks in the camps were crowded. Mary said, "Oh Donna, it's coming back in waves. Saturdays mother made us sweep the cobblestone streets and rake the ground. A man walks by with a piglet in a baby carriage like we pushed you in when we were freed. When American soldiers did inspections, people hid the piglet. We weren't supposed to cook, not to overload the electrical system. The owner later killed the piglet and shared the meat."

She continued, "We ate *szmalec*, lard, on dark bread with salt. Good like whipped cream. The United Nations Relief Agency gave each child an orange and hard candy for Christmas. We had to decide how to eat it. We never had an orange before. Wow! It's coming in waves – someone dumping the bucket on the Gestapo's head, people making fun of us praying, the blue cornflowers, the black soldier, and me teasing Chester about a girl Alina that liked him."

When Henry Mara left his family in 1913 at age 21, he promised to take care of them from far away. He made true on that promise thirty-seven years later. To sponsor us, he had to prove that he could take eight people into his home and provide for us until we found work. We also needed health clearances. An x-ray showed a spot on 12-year-old Mary's lung, possibly tuberculosis. Mother told father, "Take the other children now. Your brother is waiting for you. We'll come when Mary gets cleared."

Father said, "We survived cattle cars and bombs together. In the worst hunger, you did not give away our Danusia. We go to America as a family or not at all."

We were being moved to yet another camp when the spot on Mary's lungs was discovered. She needed to be near the doctor handling her case. At age 11, Chester had taken Janka safely to her First Holy Communion. At age 18, he had another adult job. He stayed behind with Mary as her guardian until she was cleared of tuberculosis. Otherwise, we could not go to America.

Reflections

We have a radio where people talk and you can see them.

DC: Do you remember seeing the Statue of Liberty in New York harbor?

We never left mother's side. She was a good mother, constantly watching over us. If she saw it, I saw it. I tried to eat those hard-boiled eggs in the middle of a violent storm but all I did was throw up on that ship. Everyone looked like ghosts. I don't know why, but I didn't have shoes when we landed.

DC: That's because I was constantly seasick, and accidentally vomited into them.

My only pair. Uncle Henry, Aunt Minnie, and cousin Walter came for us. Riding in the car, we saw a small plane turned over from the hurricane. Aunt Minnie said, "We have a radio where people talk and you can see them." We never saw a television, so I thought Aunt Minnie must be teasing, there's no such thing. The electricity was down, so we didn't see the "radio where people talk" for three days.

The first time I tasted chicken soup, Aunt Minnie put noodles in my bowl and poured broth over the noodles.

Brother Van teaching history at Edison Township School District. Edison, NJ 1980's

So good, that's how I make chicken soup. Cousin Eleanor had a closet full of clothes and six pairs of white socks. Wow, six pairs! Every hour, I ran upstairs to look. Then Aunt Minnie's friends gave us more clothes than I ever saw in my life.

DC: *Do you feel hatred or anger toward anyone?*

(Long pause) Personally, no. I am grateful to one-armed Willi who protected me. And the German owners on the farm where Aunt Eleanor and Uncle Józef worked were good to them. I can't hate the Russians, either. If I was abused, it might be different. A lot of women were. Nobody hurt me physically. Emotionally, yes. It was pure horror, dead bodies and crumbling buildings. I won't go back. I'm afraid they might keep me and I would have to relive the camps, the dirt, the hunger.

My grandchildren, Mary and Jeffrey, sit mesmerized and want to know. But some scars never heal – the fright. Eugene watches the History Channel and war pictures. Do not ask me to see a war film or read a war book. It sets off the worst nightmares. Once the nightmare was so real, I woke up sweating. Even my skin hurt. I was caught and they wouldn't let me out.

DC: *You may have some bad dreams after this conversation. It happens to me. We come from a long line of strong women and I admire the way you have made a rich life for yourself.*

No matter what happens, you must go on with your life. Thank God I did not have tuberculosis. I would feel awful to keep the family from our new life in America with Uncle Henry.

Mary Chmara Wojciechowski was born in Naliboki on December 12, 1938. She is among the first group nationally to earn professional standing as a Certified Municipal Court Administrator, a position she held in Monroe Township, NJ for 40 years. Her husband Eugene served with the New Jersey State Police for 29 years. He passed away on November 24, 2014 in Princeton, New Jersey. They had four children – a daughter who is a homemaker, a daughter in the fashion industry and real estate, a daughter who is a Doctor of Chiropractic, and a son in the trades. They had four grandchildren.

Van: Teacher and Gentleman Farmer

Van had a military bearing, shoulders back, straight posture. To soften the memory of war, he surrounded himself with life and beauty. He and his wife Roseanne raised horses, rabbits, cats, dogs, sheep, ducks, and chickens on four-acres of land. Brilliant sunflowers, zinnias, lavender, and cosmos swaggered in the breeze among rows of luscious vegetables. Birds flocked to bushes thick with blueberries, gooseberries, currants, and raspberries. As with all of us gardners in the family, my brother was the conductor of his own unique symphony.

As a history teacher who knew the refugee experience, Van was a beacon for immigrant children. He managed easily with students from Eastern Europe. If they were from places like Viet Nam or India, he had extra doses of patience to reach them.

Van's open classroom door signaled his open heart. His students asked for him in their moments of crisis. As a soccer coach, he instilled confidence in boys who were learning to be men. A colleague said, "Because of his compassion, both the American and immigrant students loved him, and I mean, loved him! The girls had crushes on him. Visiting graduates checked on Mr. Chmara. The faculty admired his generosity, the garden produce, the fall mums, and Christmas poinsettias."

After he retired, this gentleman farmer loved to stop and smell the roses in his garden.

From German Bunker to American Classroom

When the second *Lagerfuehrer* showed off his favorite prisoner to visiting dignitaries, Van greeted them in German. These words, and his Nordic looks, might save the family. He said, "Sirens go off. We run like lightning before bombs hit the wooden barracks. I'm the commandant's pet. He always comes into the bunker to check if I'm warm enough. But one time, he doesn't come in. I never see him again. I can't breathe in the damp crowded bunker. Even as a young kid, I knew any moment could be our last. When we came out, the barracks we just left were shattered like toothpicks."

On the last day of the war, American soldiers pulled Van out of a bunker where we had stood for three days. An American-sponsored sanitarium saved his life with medical care, sleep, food, and walks in the woods. When he recovered, an army transport took us to the next displaced person's camp. Thousands from many nationalities had been displaced and lived together in stark rows of barracks. We draped blankets for privacy when we shared one room with a Latvian couple and a child.

Civility replaced fear. Volunteers helped with food preparation and kept order without weapons. Van said, "Father always got a job. We could finally go into stores, and he wanted to buy us things. Others lived off whatever they got. One camp had an outdoor pool full of young people. Father said they could get jobs. After the war I guess they figured they deserved something. Mother didn't let me have a chicken. Pets were not allowed, but other people had chickens. One family kept two sheep. Maybe that's why I got land and raised animals. Our family has a feel for the soil, and I love animals."

Schools in the displaced persons camps offered high quality education and were set up in several languages. Mary, Van, and I attended a Polish school Monday through Friday and Saturday morning. Each teacher taught several subjects. Van said, "We learned about measurements, pacing off outside for the instructor. That same teacher taught literature and history."

Mary completed grade six in Germany, Van grade three, and I finished grade two. Coming to America, we were put back one year because we did not know English. Six months later, Van and I were sitting under Uncle Henry's pear tree and spontaneously started speaking English to each other. And we already knew the math and geography being taught. It was not necessary to put us back. Van said, "We started elementary school in Monroe Township, then Jamesburg High School. Henry, Chester, and Janka worked right away so we could build a house."

In addition to good schools, we prayed openly. Refugees created elaborate altars for All Saints' and All Souls' Days in November and Corpus Christi in June. Each barrack built its own altar and walked in procession through the camp – a mix of devotion, competition, and celebration. Van said, "It was fun, but we wanted to be near Aunt Eleanor and Uncle Józef who were already in Connecticut."

Van continued, "Our friends were the Mieńko family from a village near Naliboki. When their barrack burned down, the parents and son Alfonse put their bed outside our door. Mr. Mieńko was deaf. He had been to America, so we wrote questions about America, and he answered. He joked it's a good thing he didn't stay, or there would be no wife and no Alfonse."

Reflections

...it was so misty and dark, we thought ol' Liberty was Jesus.

DC: What are your first memories of America?

We docked in New York during one of the worst hurricanes in 30 years. With power lines down at Uncle Henry's house, we waited three days to see how a television works. Aunt Minnie gave us sweet corn. We only knew livestock corn. We liked this new kind of corn.

DC: You loved school. In high school, you distinguished yourself athletically and academically. Your classmates thought you were still a cute blond boy because you were chosen prom king.

I was just happy to be here, safe, our own place. After the war, this was a land of milk and honey.

DC: At Monmouth University you were president of the service fraternity, Alpha Psi Omega. As a teacher, you were trusted and loved by your students.

We made a good life here in America.

DC: Did you see the Statue of Liberty as we arrived in New York harbor?

I did. Mr. Mieńko was a deaf old man. I was a kid, but we were friends. He said to look for the Statue of Liberty in the harbor. It was so misty and dark, we thought ol' Liberty was Jesus.

Van Chmara was born in Naliboki on June 1, 1941. He passed away in Princeton, NJ on September 12, 2018. He taught social studies in the Edison Township School District, NJ for twenty-five years. His wife Roseanne Bemben Chmara was a mathematics teacher for 25 years in the same school district.

Donna: The Scribe

The General Brings Us Home

The USS General Ballou left Bremerhaven, Germany in November 1950. It reached New York harbor a week later with a cargo of displaced persons from Eastern Europe. We saw our homes, villages, and towns burnt by the Nazis during World War II before they took us to Germany to work until we perished. This was early 20th century ethnic cleansing. Many of our neighbors, friends, and relatives were dead. We were the survivors.

The boundaries of the town where my Polish Christian family had lived changed with the prevailing politics. Once part of Poland, it is now part of the country of Belarus. Germany invaded Poland from the west on September 1, 1939. My town was invaded 17 days later from the east by the Soviet Union before it fell to the German army in 1941. In 1943, we were herded into cattle cars headed for Germany. The killing of Polish people began with the 1939 invasion of western Poland. By 1942, Jewish people were targets for immediate extermination. Slavic Christians were to die at a slower rate, with the strongest kept for physical labor. I am alive because they did not have time to kill me.

It hurts to see today's refugees on the evening news, especially the babies. That was once me. I was ten weeks old when captured, and two years old when the war ended in 1945. I was seven when, after five homeless years in displaced persons camps, my family left Germany in 1950.

Headed for America, we are grateful to leave a refugee existence. The safe and sturdy army ship, USS General Ballou, has a rough encounter with the high seas. On this journey of hope, an angry hurricane tosses around its traumatized passengers like a toy and motion sickness sets in. We finally have food, but a private spot on the deck offers some dignity when holding it down is not possible.

Feeling like human wreckage, we pull into port on a cold and murky day. Through the drizzling rain, my mother sees a welcoming beacon. "Look, children. Over there! It's a statue of Jesus. In America they greet you at the harbor with a statue of Jesus. This must be a good country." Translation: We have come to a place where we will not be killed for who we are.

As the General inched toward land, mother realized this was not a statue of Jesus. But being met by the immigration authorities did not cramp her style. My parents had their own victory. They did not become bitter. They rose from the ashes like the legendary Phoenix to start a new life built on love.

In one sense, my mother was right. She was looking at the Statue of Liberty on that rainy day in November 1950, but America really is the land of Jesus. It is also the land of Moses, of Krishna, Buddha, Muhammad, and of all the great beings, human or divine, whose best thoughts we celebrate freely in our many cultures and religions. Has there ever been such a place as America? A land where many different people live together, where the goal is equality, where we are all valued? We do not live our ideals perfectly but as long as we reach for them in our laws, our public institutions, and in our personal friendships, then we are on the right track. Ethnic cleansing has been replaced by ethnic diversity. Has there ever been such a place as America?

Four days after arriving we celebrated our first Thanksgiving.

Selected from hundreds of entries, the author's essay, "The General Brings Us Home", was one of 25 "first prize" winners in *The New York Times* Journey Home Contest which was judged based on originality and the ability to inspire.

Endnotes

34 Timothy Snyder, *Black Earth: The Holocaust as History and Warning* (NY: Penguin) Random House LLC, 2015) p. 101.

Chapter 9 Flora
A Quiet Little Corner of the World

Formal photographs of people in their Sunday best were a must in displaced persons camps. Well-groomed and standing upright in a carpeted studio, they were saying, "I look human again, I want this record of my humanity preserved."

Looking at one such photo in my living room, I see cousin Flora and my Aunt Mania pose leaning toward each other and smile demurely. Looking chic in silk stockings, black heels, and knee length dresses, one holds a purse in her right hand, the other in her left hand. The symmetry and feminine charm give no clue that these women had recently worn the letter "P" on their prisoner uniforms.

Flora's thick dark hair, smooth skin, and full lips cover her perfect white teeth. What a knockout! Looking closely at her young face, do I see anger, fear, or strength in her eyes? Or are these the eyes of a woman in love? She remains an enigma. My Mona Lisa. But Flora's girlish days were brief. She soon became a wife, doting mother to four sons, a widow, and a bereaved parent. Within six months, she lost her oldest son John to cancer, then her third son Wally to a heart attack, both in their 50's. Her body shrank with each loss, hurt in a way even war could not hurt her. Parents should not have to bury their children.

We Didn't Feel Poor
They started with us, and they will finish with you.

The four Chmara brothers had once owned their own destiny, worked hard, and slept soundly. They were wed to the soil and the harmonies of the day: roosters crowing at daybreak, horses neighing and wagons rumbling as men left for the fields, the swoosh of women churning butter in wooden casks, laundry fluttering in the wind, children laughing and playing tag, hogs grunting over their swill, cows with full udders mooing to be milked in the afternoon, and wolves howling at night.

These harmonies ended as the four brothers went their separate ways, not always by choice. Henry Mara was growing potatoes on his farm in New Jersey. Józef and family toiled in Russian forests below the Arctic Circle. Flora's father, my father Michał, and their families were heading in the same cattle car to Germany, leaving the ashes of the homes they had shaped lovingly with skilled hands.

Decades later, I sat with cousin Flora in her kitchen in Toronto, Canada as she described a lost way of life. The oldest daughter, she helped her mother Antonina raise the other seven children. She said, "Women rose at dawn, worked till dark, ten o'clock on summer days. No appliances. Who heard of a machine washing clothes? Our fathers were out building houses, demanding work without today's power equipment. But they got paid in money, grain, or hay. We stored enough fuel and food for winter and never went without bread. People said, 'He's a Chmara, he'll always make a living.'"

She added, "We were too far away for most people to get good paying work. They worked all day for one *złoty* of Polish money to buy a pound of sugar. Some did housekeeping or farm work for Jewish people. Young people burned brush, planted trees, and cleared patches of forest."

I said, "One pound of sugar for a day's work! Think of all the groceries you could buy in the US or Canada for one day's work, any kind of work."

Flora said, "But we didn't feel poor, and we were happier than some people today with money. We thought we lived in a quiet little corner of the world. Only big shots from Poland came to hunt in our pristine forest, our *Nalibocka Puszcza*. No one else will look in on us. But they looked in, all right. The Russians came in 1939, robbed our lumber, and sent it to Russia. They were brutal to those who had a little something, a job as a forest warden, a policeman, a teacher. They said we must be evened out. We all must work in the communal farm. Everyone must be the same."

Outsiders looked in again in 1941 when the invader's uniform changed from Russian to German. I told Flora, "Our cousin, Janusz, described how German soldiers rounded up Jewish villagers in 1942, and marched them out of town. A heavyset woman, Bluma, warned prophetically as they took her away, "They started with us, and they will finish with you."

Flora said, "They took Bluma with the others to an open space in the forest. Had them dig a large pit. Made them jump. Shot them as they fell in. A few were kept to cover the pit with soil. It was moving from people beneath still alive. Then those who covered the pit were shot. A monument with

Hebrew writing marks that spot today. People working in the forest saw this painful moment.

She added, "After the Jewish people were murdered, our beloved priest, Father Bajko, was next. He raised our standard of living with the brickyard, sawmill, and electricity. We were loyal to him, so they singled him out. German soldiers took him to the woods. They put a bullet in his head. Somewhere between our cemetery and the road to Jankowicze. Then they burned our sheaves of wheat and rye, our homes, all of Naliboki, and took us away."

Feeling Shame

Flora shivered, telling me what my mother could not bring herself to say out loud.

Bluma was right. We *were* next. A year later, Uncle Jan and my father Michał were harvesting wheat and rye in the field as Operation Hermann was marching toward us. A few weeks later, August 1943, the two brothers and their families were headed for forced labor in Germany, their town in ashes. The cattle cars stopped in the occupied Polish city of Białystok for an evil purpose.

Flora shivered, telling me what my mother could not bring herself to say out loud. "We sat for a week crammed into those cattle cars. No place to wash. Leaving the cattle cars, we reeked with human sweat. We were made to undress. I stood naked in line. We tried not to look at each other for modesty. A male guard smeared liquid disinfectant on the private parts of my body that are covered with hair. People with lice had their heads shaved. Ceiling nozzles in the public shower sprayed us with DDT. Feeling shame, I dressed, and got back into the cattle car."

Crossing into Germany, the train stopped near towns where farmers stood ready to choose the young and strong for labor. Flora was 18. Her six siblings ranged from fifteen to two. The children in my family ranged from brother Henry at 12 and me at ten weeks old. She said, "No farmer would feed all those children who couldn't work. Families like our cousins, Janusz and Staś, with five children, a sick father, a grandmother, were seen as useless for work. They were sent back to Naliboki."

Our two families with a total of thirteen children were not sent back to Naliboki. We were discarded in a starvation camp. Flora's father and mine were trucked daily to a labor camp near the town of Kirchhellen to build rows of barracks as more people were being deported to Germany. My mother and Antonina stayed in the starvation camp as we children wasted away on a daily bowl of soup and one piece of bread. The commandant, the *Lagerfuehrer*, of the labor camp walked among his prisoners making sure he got enough work from them. He noticed two men who had exceptional building skills and produced a steady pace of work – my father and uncle. He decided they and their families should live. He

Flora Chmara and Maria Byczkiewicz pose in a studio. Germany 1946

had two guards find us in the starvation camp and bring us to the labor camp where our chances of survival were still slim, but better.

We were on the front lines of the war, but with houses and stores in the nearby town of Gladback, the older brothers and sisters helped feed the little ones like me. Flora said, "Our baby Tom had a swollen stomach, crooked legs. But with my sister Stasia's help, he lived and became a medical doctor. I'm grateful to her for going from farmer to farmer. Your brothers Henry and Chester and sister Janka begged for food to keep Marysia, Wacek, and you alive. Just a little piece of dry bread was precious."

I said, "I can't ever thank them enough for their sacrifices, but I pray for them each night."

Teen-agers worked in factories, but beautiful 18-year-old Flora was singled out. As an assistant to the *Lagerfuehrer*, she ran errands, cleaned his office, made coffee, brought him meals, and delivered messages. She said, "He taught me some German. Let me write letters to my family in other camps. He would say, '*Shmara schreibt immer* – Chmara is always writing.'"

Flora stressed, "We met all types of Germans. Some were decent. Others opened the door, saw the "P" label, and told the *Auslaenders* – the foreigners – to get out. Workers in the labor camp were East European – Polish, Ukrainian, Russian, Czech, and Slovak. Prisoners of war were West European – French, Italian, and Dutch. With all of us together, I saw good and bad in every group."

Ordinary Germans lived separate lives from those of us in the labor camps. Stores, farms, schools, and churches continued to function. Behind the scenes, foreign workers held up the German economy. Flora said, "They occupied countries, deported people. Germany got on its feet from forced labor. Hitler intended to conquer the world with our sweat and tears."

Homeless and Without a Country

Based on tradition, the older brother's family, not mine, was to go to America first.

As a child, Flora walked five miles to school, round trip, to finish grade seven, the highest level available in Naliboki. Michał Miszuk's school in Jankowicze went up to grade five. He walked six miles, round trip, to finish grades six and seven in Naliboki. Running around in the school yard at recess, she would have giggled at the idea that someday this playful boy would be her husband.

Flora and Michał were thrown together as teenagers when they were deported in the same cattle car. Their courtship took place in a forced labor camp with a barrack wall between them. Their families knew each other, and after the war, their parents chose a matchmaker. In keeping with tradition, a *swat* was the go-between who made sure the marriage arrangements were acceptable to both sets of parents. Being stripped of all they owned, the usual discussion about the dowry did not take place.

In 1946, at age 21, Flora married Michał Miszuk in the Muelheim Ruhr displaced persons camp in a small building used as a church. She wore a simple hand-sewn white dress. The wedding dinner for their families were canned goods from relief packages from the United Nations Relief and Rehabilitation Administration (UNRRA). Their honeymoon was a walk in the forest.

Now, what? Displaced persons, DPs, as we were called, had few good choices. We could stay in Germany where we had been brought by force as an inferior race.

The other choices were no better. We could return to what had been our home, but to a different life. The change of borders merged Eastern Poland into the countries of Belarus and Ukraine within the Soviet Union. With the return of Soviet rule to Naliboki, Flora's father gave up his beloved land rather than live under communism. Many refugees like us dreaded returning to their homes because they had already lived communist repression between 1939 and 1941.

In addition, Poland with its new borders had become a Soviet satellite with a communist government loyal to Moscow. Flora said, "My father refused to live under communism, but Michał parents got impatient being moved from camp to camp. It could take years to get resettled. I was now a wife and part of the Miszuk family. I left for Poland with my husband's family in 1947. After years of war, who thought about politics? We wanted stability."

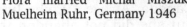

Flora married Michał Miszuk. Muelheim Ruhr, Germany 1946

The newlyweds moved to southwestern Poland, near the city of Wrocław [German: Breslau.] At first, they worked on farms for food. Then, Michał and his father got paid for cutting down trees in the forest. It was dangerous work. They found out how dangerous when a tree fell on Michał's father. He was crushed and died from internal bleeding and broken bones.

As a youth, Michał loved the abundant wildlife and trees of the forest, the *Nalibocka Puszcza*. Shaken by his father's death, he got a job as a forest ranger with a house and monthly salary. While he earned money doing work he loved, Flora gave birth to three sons, raised them, grew food, harvested and cooked it, tended the chickens, milked the cow, and ran the house. She said, "We worked hard for a simple living, but you don't miss what you don't know."

As Flora and Michał settled in Western Poland, more choices opened for our families still in Germany. Uncle Henry Mara had become an established farmer in New Jersey and offered to rescue both of our large families. Flora said, "My father was the older brother, so Uncle Henry said my family would go to America first. Your father would be next. But it didn't turn out that way."

I said, "Based on tradition, the older brother's family, not mine, was to go to America first. That custom stays with us. In the funeral procession for my brother Chester, Henry walked first, then Janka, Mary, Van. I was last, the youngest. At those times, it helps to know what is expected of you."

Flora said, "That's how we did things. Refugees were screened for contagious diseases before they could enter the United States. Your family was declared healthy while we were waiting for our clearances. Uncle Henry Mara broke with tradition, and sponsored your father, his younger brother Michał first. When he got you resettled, he would rescue my family.

I said, "Such generosity must have been repaid in heaven. But your sister, Stasia, had her own plans."

Uncle Henry Mara had set out alone into the unknown at age 21. That "pioneer gene" surfaced in the next generation. Flora's sister, Stasia, was the first to get medical clearance. Recruiters from agencies and charitable organizations visited the camps, and she took a job as a housekeeper in Canada. At age 19, she boarded a ship alone for Canada, but she did not abandon the family. Through some Polish neighbors, Stasia met Walter Ciesielczyk, a refugee who had become a Canadian citizen. As Flora put it, "He did not want Stasia to get away. She agreed to marry him, but he had to sponsor the whole family. He got a wife and eight in-laws in the bargain."

By the time they arrived in Toronto in March 1951, Stasia introduced her parents to their son-in-law and their first grandchild. The pioneer gene must have been passed down to that baby. She is now Helen Moreland, the owner of a thriving real estate business which she built from the ground up.

Uncle Jan and my father Michał were from a clan that stayed together for generations, but none of them live in Naliboki today. Three died in infancy. Only two left by choice. The oldest, Urszula, married a Russian soldier after World War I and left with him for Russia. And Henry Mara's pioneer streak took him to the United States. The other five were scattered around the globe. By the 1950's, Józef was in Nottingham, England. Jan was in Toronto, Canada. Michał lived next door to his brother Henry Mara in America. Two sisters, Maria and Józefa, had relocated to Western Poland.

For centuries, my ancestors tilled the same soil, helped with harvests, sat in church together, and were godparents to each other's babies. After exile, we have stayed connected for decades from different parts of the globe. But future generations of the Chmara clan will not know each other.

You Can't Go Home Again
I couldn't go back to the life I knew.

Grandfather Stefan stared out the window to avoid his wife's pain. Grandmother Emilia shuffled around the kitchen stone-faced packing fatback, bread, and cheese into a cloth sack. Their son Henryk Chmara, as he was then called, had broken their hearts by deciding to leave Naliboki for a new life in America. Wearing his only dress clothes, he pulled on his boots, and knelt down before them. For his peace of mind, he needed their permission and begged them to forgive him. Stefan and Emilia touched his shoulders and prayed over him for a safe journey, releasing him from his burden.

My uncle kissed his brothers and sisters one by one. He would not see his brother, my father, for another thirty-seven years. He tossed the food sack over his shoulder, picked up a small valise of clothing, and set out for the main road. Knowing his farewell kiss would have to last a lifetime, Emilia ran after him, crying she would never see her son again. She was right.

He was a tall thin man, with straight brown hair, and a square jaw. Arriving in New York harbor in 1913 at age twenty-one, he had no family or friends, only some warm clothing and a strong will. When the immigration clerk asked his name, my uncle said, "Chmara." The clerk heard "Mara" and wrote "Mara" on the form. This new identity stuck with him. Henry Mara did odd jobs until the United States entered World War I in April 1917. The army welcomed him gladly. He became an American soldier as part of the American Expeditionary Forces that fought in France.

Returning to civilian life, Henry Mara worked in the Singer Sewing Machine Company in Elizabeth, New Jersey where he met Minnie Pasternak. Her parents were from Ukraine, and he was comfortable marrying into an East European family. She was a small woman who saw the world in practical terms. That was what he needed. They lived simply and saved enough to buy a farm. Years later, she took in and fed her husband's family of eight. She must have earned her place in heaven too.

My uncle was barely an adult when he kissed his mother Emilia good-by and set out to find his manhood. By 1950, he had time and money to visit Poland in style. His wife Minnie packed a suitcase with her husband's best suit and gifts for the family he had left 37 years earlier. By then, his sisters Mania and Józefa and niece Flora were living in Western Poland with its new borders. Flora said, "I finally met this man of legend who had brought your family to America."

Uncle Henry Mara had left to escape poverty, but that had not changed. Poland had fought on the winning Allied side, spilling much blood for its freedom. After the war, Great Britain and the United States allowed Eastern Poland to become part of the Soviet Union. What was left of Poland and other East European countries became Soviet satellites, an economic disaster.

In 1948, President Harry Truman signed the Marshall Plan which provided billions of dollars for economic recovery to European countries – ally or foe alike. But Stalin refused this aid to countries under Soviet control. Excluded from the Marshall Plan, Poland remained poor long after Western Europe was rebuilt with American money. Poland recovered economically five decades later, after the fall of the Soviet Union. Uncle Henry passed away long before he could see prosperity in Poland.

Flora's father did not want her living in Soviet-dominated Poland and the poverty that went with it. When the Soviet Union loosened Poland's emigration policies, Jan insisted she come to Canada. Flora said, "My husband's parents had passed away, and the untamed forests of Canada appealed to him. We arrived in Toronto in 1959 with three sons – John, Steven, and Wally.

At first, Flora missed the European way of life. She said, "Some people don't like the fast pace here. They make money and leave. They say a simple potato with friends tastes better than eating your oranges alone. They miss the hospitality and connection. I cried for a year when I took the children to the park."

I asked, "You love being a Canadian now. What made the difference?

She said, "When our fourth son, Roman, was born we bought a house. I began feeling like I belonged in Canada. Longing for Naliboki was turning into curiosity. I went in

Flora's family waiting to leave for Canada. Front row: Vera, Tom, John, Teresa. Back row: Stasia, Mother Antonina, Father John, Lodzia. Germany 1950

1990 to see how different it was from my youthful memories of home."

I said, "It was again a quiet little corner of the world."

She said, "The little houses were close enough for the straw roofs to almost touch. They crumpled in the 1943 fires. Today two houses sit where three had been. But people living in those houses were strangers to me. The chestnut tree still stands next to the church, and cousins Janusz and Jadwiga Chmara live now on the spot where the church rectory had stood."

I said, "The massive rectangular Soviet-style building in the town center had no sign or advertising to say it was the general store. Its gray concrete felt grim against the brightly painted wooden houses and vibrant flowers that are more like the Naliboki of your youth."

Flora said, "That building had a restaurant, open from 9:00 am to 3:00 pm."

I said, "With no signs, I didn't know it had a restaurant, and most people are working at those hours."

News travels quickly in a village. As Flora savored her daily strolls, people heard she was born there. Some invited her into their homes. She said, "Their lives are easier than in my youth. We planted and harvested barefoot in the fields as soon as the snow melted. Now everyone has shoes, everyone has bread. They sit on stuffed couches, and the television seems to be turned on all the time."

She was grateful for their hospitality but felt a change in her heart. Her way of thinking was gone, along with the vanished houses. Flora said, "Maybe it's different in the cities, but in Naliboki they still think like our grandmothers. I asked a woman why she cooks a certain way. She said her grandmother did it, her mother did it, and she does it."

Flora concluded, "We had our rhythms, people born and growing old in our quiet little corner of the world. We thought it was like that everywhere, but the rest of the world is different. I couldn't go back to the life I knew, grow my own food anymore. And I don't think like that anymore."

Flora walked for miles and talked with everyone she met. This could not be during the Soviet days when staying with family was forbidden. The best part of visiting Naliboki for both of us was sitting at the kitchen table, talking and laughing with cousins Janusz and Staś, their families, and neighbors. A hotel in Minsk where I would be under watchful eyes would not feel so cheerful.

Reflections

During those air raids, I gave up. I wanted to die.

Flora began by asking, "Did you hear about Father Bajko?"

DC: All my life. I pray for him and all who perished in Naliboki – Christian, Jewish, Polish, Russian, Belarussian, Ukrainian, German, Latvian. It was a cruel way to leave our roots.

It was murder on a mass scale. We had no rights. People looked at us with disdain at the church in Kirchhellen. Friendship or romance between Polish and German was forbidden. Eating together was forbidden. Even begging for food was forbidden, but we did. In the end, the Allies were bombing Essen to destroy factories. During those air raids, I gave up. I wanted to die. The *Lagerfeuhrer* made me run to the bunker. I then left it in God's hands and accepted whatever God would give.

DC: You were a young woman, I was an infant, but our families were together.

Yes, it began with the downpour in the Jankowicze meadow, and ended by standing in the bunker the last three days of the war. Over two hundred people squeezed into a space 200 or 300 meters long. You were suffocating. Close to dying. Your mother pushed through the crowd. Got you outside and you began to breathe. When the Americans liberated us, they covered their noses. Some vomited from the human smell. Led us to an old church. We settled at the entrance to get some air. We heard scattered gunfire all night. The next morning we walked to the abandoned German houses and stores in Essen. We found food, washed, and put on clean clothes.

DC: How do you feel toward the Russians and Germans?

Danusia, people forget the horror of the war and are happy not to be living in Naliboki. Polish and Ukrainian women I know said they would still be in domestic service or herding cows for a piece of bread. Our life in the eastern *kresy* was harsh. I got to like our life in Canada. Michał set up a taxidermy business. I earned money for the first time in my life, cleaning houses until I was 75. My children lacked nothing. I paid for any education they wanted. John and Wally finished high school and Steven and Roman finished university. My children have a better life than I did. That's more important to me than anything else.

Flora always did for others before thinking of herself. My husband Henry and I attended Flora's funeral. The service was in English and Polish, but most of the people who could have prayed for her in Polish were no longer with us. I knew she wanted to be sent from this world with prayers from her childhood. Five voices joined the priest for the Polish prayers. I was glad to have made the trip to Canada so I could be one of those voices. Flora had passed down to me much family lore, and I finally got to do something for her, my Mona Lisa who remains an enigma.

Flora Chmara Miszuk was born in Naliboki on May 4, 1925 and passed away in Toronto in 2015. Her husband Michał was born in Jankowicze in February, 1922 and passed away on February 22, 1987. Their sons John (deceased) worked in sales, Steven (Zbyszek) in academia, and Wally (deceased) and Roman continued in taxidermy. They have three grandchildren.

Henry Mara was born in Naliboki in 1892 and passed away in Cranbury, New Jersey in 1966. His wife, Minnie Pasternak Chmara was born in New Jersey in 1904 and passed away in Jamesburg, New Jersey in 1986. Their son, Walter Mara, was born in New Jersey on September 30, 1923 and passed away in Jamesburg on May 31, 1995. Their daughter Eleanor Chmara Hansen was born in New Jersey in 1932 and lives in Florida. Henry and Minnie had one granddaughter.

Chapter 10 Józef
Promises and Betrayals

Families like mine with more children than workers were sent to starvation or forced labor camps in Germany. Families with mostly adult workers were a better investment. Mother's brother Józef Byczkiewicz and wife Józia had one baby. Mother's sister Eleanor Dubicki and husband Chester had one baby. In addition, five other adults were part of the family group. Their value as labor was greater than the expense of feeding them, so they were sent to work on a German farm. It was owned by Klaus and Erna Offe.

The Nazi attempt to sow hatred of Polish people did not meet fertile ground on that farm. Master and prisoner had the courage to weave a love story based on respect and compassion that outlasted the war.

After the war, Uncle Józef and Aunt Eleanor settled in Connecticut. My parents went to New Jersey. The best part of summer was going to Connecticut to visit them. We heard my uncle's take on far ranging topics: communism, morality, the next generation, rock and roll, and the moon landing. Unlike the gently rolling fields of home, Józef tamed his rocky yard by carving terraces for European specialties like gooseberries, currants, and sorrel (*szczaw*). He planted and harvested in this brave new world on his own terms as, over time, his small frame shrank almost into nothingness.

To Please the Czar

My grandparents were the first people in our family not owned by a master.

World War I was about to ignite Europe in summer of 1914 as baby Józef first opened his eyes in the East European town of Naliboki. It had no cars, electricity, running water, or newspapers. Closing his eyes for the last time 90 years later, Józef Byczkiewicz was a United States taxpayer. He drove a car, lived in a modern house, wrote poetry, spoke several languages, and followed world events.

To grasp the breadth of his journey, let us revisit Poland's erasure from the map of Europe for 123 years (1795-1918.) It was carved up by Prussia, Austria-Hungary, and Russia at a time when today's ideas of human rights would seem absurd to lords who owned the people that worked their lands. Seen as tools of work and war, men's lives within the Russian partition were sacrificed to please the czar. Józef said, "A man could be conscripted for twenty-five years. If he lived, he was used up and couldn't even work his own land."

Scholar Henry H. Hirschbiel explains that "Recruitment...was viewed by the population as a death sentence. In the pre-Reform period, the term of service was twenty-five years... Any man 20 to 35 years old was liable for the draft. If a man in his thirties was taken, his wife and family faced economic ruin, and he was very likely not to return. Younger men often returned physically broken and unable to contribute to the village economy. Instead, they became a burden on the community." [35]

As the United States fought a civil war over human bondage, my great grandparents in Eastern Europe farmed the fields of masters who owned them. This changed for their children. The Reform Period in the 1860's and early 1870's under Czar Alexander II included a degree of self-government, partial land reform, and the emancipation of serfs. Józef's parents, my grandparents, were the first people in our family no longer owned by a master, and able to own their own land.

Józef added, "The draft was cut from twenty-five to four years. Even so, the czar's army took my father Justyn in his prime at age 28 during World War I. I was a baby in 1914, your mother five. Our mother Anna, your grandmother, took care of us, the house, farm, an orchard, chickens, a cow. When the Russians pushed into our region and paid people to dig trenches to fight the Germans, she even dug trenches to earn bread money for us children. Then in World War II, they both invaded us again."

A Badge of Courage

Józef's generation was the first in 123 years to learn Polish without fear.

Józef's parents were Polish, prayed in church in Polish, but they spoke a mix of Polish, Belarussian, and Russian called *po prostu*, meaning "plain language. Teaching Polish was banned for 123 years of Russian rule, so knowing Polish was a badge of courage. Józef said, "Maryśka Farbotko, father's stepmother, taught Polish secretly in our home. An older boy stood guard. If he saw a Russian policeman, the children ran and hid. Parents could be punished, and teachers deported to Siberia."

When Poland was reborn in 1918, Józef's generation was the first in 123 years to learn Polish without fear. For a brief twenty-one years, until Poland was invaded again in 1939, the language flourished. Józef said, "I still spoke *po prostu* at home, but parents were learning Polish from their children, like I'm learning English from my children."

I said, "Your mother spoke *po prostu* to me. I spoke Polish to her. I got grandmother's jokes."

During these twenty-one years, education was free and mandatory, but not all parents could afford books and school clothes. Some children were needed on the farm. Józef rose before dawn to feed the animals and didn't always have time to eat. If Anna had a small coin, she gave it to him to buy a bun, but he saved it to buy a book. Then he walked two and a half miles to school. My uncle said, "A bus taking you to school? We didn't even have cars. Nearby villages went to grade five. Those children had to walk even further than I did to attend grades six and seven in Naliboki. We were like the Walton family on television, all ages in one room until your father built two beautiful large schools."

Józef finished grade seven with twenty classmates. He said, "With no regular transportation to towns with a high school, like Nowogródek, only one family had a daughter board out. One of the Korzenkos had rental money from their wool combing machines to send a son to high school. Beyond our reach. Our small house on 240 Nowogródzka Street, like many others, had a clay floor. Families of five, six, or ten lived in small houses. Life was hard but we felt a connection to the land and to each other."

Continuing to educate himself, Józef learned from the tax collector how to help people fill out official forms. Parents still spoke the old language, *po prostu*, so he wrote letters to their sons in the Polish army for whom Polish had become their primary language. Aunt Eleanor told me that people came to him like a lawyer to write up papers for court cases in Stołpce. He did not expect payment from people who relied on each other's good will for survival.

Józef joined the Rifle Squads (*Strzelcy*), a paramilitary group that trained boys in military skills to protect the eastern Polish border. Then as a soldier in 1932, he patrolled the border where proximity to his Russian counterparts was familiar and dangerous. They knew each other by name and joked across the telephone-equipped towers, yet, Józef said, "When I got lost in a blizzard, before I got my bearings, the men I joked with could have shot me for crossing their border."

When Józef's duty ended, his captain made two offers: stay as a military policeman or become a game warden on the estate of the Potocki nobility. Both positions carried good pay and social status, yet he turned down the chance to rise above his humble roots. His father Justyn had returned from World War I a sick man, so Józef left the army to care for his family. But with the 1939 Soviet invasion of Eastern Poland, Józef was back in the army. He was captured twice and escaped twice. When he reached home in November, the border he had protected was breached. The Naliboki of his youth where he could learn Polish without fear was under Soviet rule.

Pluralism in Old Naliboki

We lived side by side for generations.

Based on records in today's local library, Naliboki was founded as a village in 1447.[36] By the end of the 15th century, a Catholic chapel existed near the site of today's church. The fate of the chapel is unknown, but in 1636 the Radziwill family financed construction of the Church of the Assumption in that location. The church was rebuilt between 1699 and 1704.[37] After some 300 years as a place of solace, local people speak of the fires that destroyed the church and all of Naliboki in 1943.[38]

Józef had worshipped in that church as Naliboki became a municipal center governed by an executive, a *wójt*. Villages within the municipality were led by a *sołtys* and sent their property taxes to the Naliboki town hall. If owners lacked cash in this barter economy, they paid with a cow, pig, or grain.

Language and religion defined identity. Catholics prayed in Polish in a *kościół* with western style architecture that was led by a Polish priest. The Russian, Belarussian, and Ukrainian Orthodox prayed in their languages in a *cerkiew* with onion-shaped domes. Józef said, "When asked who we were, we didn't say Polish or Russian. We said Catholic or Orthodox."

According to Polish ethnographer Dagnoslaw Demski, no *cerkiew* existed within some 35 kilometers of Naliboki, a considerable distance to walk.[39] A Catholic *kościół* from the

15th to the 19th centuries as the only house of worship tells us that Naliboki was a Polish settlement for centuries within a multicultural region. Tombstones in the cemetery dated from 1833 to 1999 are inscribed in Polish and Belarussian. By the 19th century, a Jewish minority was present, growing to 95 individuals out of a total population of 2,465 in 1885, and 185 individuals in 1921. By the 1930's, half of these families farmed about 500 acres of land.[40]

Polish author, Eva Hoffman, tells us that unlike Western European countries where Jews were usually a small minority, the Jewish community in Poland "comprised a genuine ethnic minority, with its own rights, problems, and powers...in the premodern period, Polish attitudes toward religious minorities were surprisingly liberal, even by our own postmodern standards. While the young Jewish communities in Poland suffered their share of religious and folk prejudice, they were also to a large extent protected by laws and special privileges. There were times, particularly during the Renaissance, when Jews saw Poland as a refuge from other, more hostile places...This happy state wasn't always sustained. As Poland's economic and political fortunes declined, from the middle of the seventeenth century onward, relations between Poles and Jews deteriorated into suspiciousness and economic competition."[41]

In Józef's time, some 20 Jewish families lived in the *miasteczko*, the town center, near the synagogue. Children attended school together. When the priest taught religion, Jewish children were excused. The rabbi was part of the welcoming committee when dignitaries arrived, as when the bishop came to preside over the rite of Confirmation to the Catholic children. Both groups observed holidays openly. Józef said, "Jewish families were shoemakers, tailors, and store owners with land near their houses, and sometimes had jobs for the Christians. We lived side by side in peace for generations."

But as Hoffman said, the peace did not last. Józef said, "When the Russians invaded in 1939, their propaganda promised a better life. Young people, and some older ones, turned communist and sided with the partisans for protection from the Germans. A Jewish boy pummeled the statue of Saint John the Baptist with a gun. His father told me, 'I would rather see him dead than see such sacrilege.' But some of the Jewish youth started to say, 'We will wash our feet and the Poles will drink the water.'"

For generations, Christians and Jews were connected economically, and at times, by mutual aid and friendship. Yet, marriage was taboo. Józef said, "In 1939 a Jewish girl had a baby by a Catholic boy. They didn't marry. I don't know what became of the baby. When the Jews were friendly with the Russians, that boy was scared. He dressed poor walking down the street praising Stalin and mocking Poles. When the Germans came, he dressed nicely and walked around praising Hitler."

Are There Any Questions?
They stole our food and used us as beasts of burden.

Józef expected Naliboki to become a city with its school, town hall, police and first aid stations, sawmill, brick factory, electricity, and plans for a rail station. People were learning about government. The 1922 Polish constitution allowed voting for members of the legislature, the *Sejm*, at age 21 to male and female citizens in good standing, except for the military.[42] Józef said, "Mostly men voted, not like here with women's liberation. No one stopped them but they were busy at home."

Naliboki did not become a city. The Soviet and German invasions turned it to ashes. The Soviet attack on Poland on September 17, 1939, was feared by some, welcomed by others. The Polish people saw the Russians as a longtime enemy. The Jews saw the Red Army as salvation from German oppression. Hoffman describes the Soviet arrival as seen by Polish and Jewish residents in the town of Brańsk, a Polish settlement within a multicultural region, as was Naliboki. She states that, "A sizable portion of the Jewish community therefore welcomed the Soviet soldiers with flowers, banners, and expressions of joy. To the Poles, this was a distressing and an alienating spectacle...this historical episode continues to be one of the more discomfiting and delicate subjects in the Polish-Jewish dialogue."[43]

The Russians who invaded Naliboki registered each house, recorded what everyone owned, set quotas for goods to surrender. People had to dig building foundations, harness their horse and wagon to cart soil and stone for construction, and cut down trees that went to Russia. The mayor was replaced by a man named Szabunia. Having tasted self-rule, this was a betrayal by one of their own. Józef said, "Szabunia was Polish only on paper. They stole our food and used us as beasts of burden. Yet we heard at compulsory meetings that they brought us abundance. Then, 'Are there any questions?'"

Sitting mutely, Józef thought about his end of town still lacking electricity. When gasoline was delivered, he stood in line all night to buy his share before the supply ran out. This is abundance? Then one man stood up and asked, "If we have everything, why don't we have meat to eat?"

No answer. At the next meeting, they were told again that the new regime had improved their lives and brought them abundance. Then, "Are there any questions?"

Author's grandparents, Anna and Justyn Byczkiewicz. Their children are Helena, Jozef, Eleanor, and Mania. Naliboki 1930's

Another man stood up. The party leader mocked, "So you want to know why you don't have meat."

"No, I want to know what happened to the man who last time asked about the meat."

Gone was the man who dared ask about the meat. Gone were local leaders, teachers, property owners, forest rangers, and police. Gone were Józef's neighbors, Bernard Mucha and Edward Wojtkiewicz, his in-law Arciszewski, and Pius Farbotko with whom Józef had built beehives in the woods. Anyone who prospered or dared to ask questions was disposed of quickly.

The Katyń Forest Massacre

He is the first we shoot if people do not bring their cattle and food in two hours.

Józef sat on the grass in a circle of men by the chapel near his house. An armed partisan hovered over each man who was assigned ten households to monitor. They were told how much milk, eggs, meat, animals, wool, produce, and gasoline their ten households were to surrender. Józef said, "I was humiliated to look at my neighbor and tell him what he had to give away. A man with two cows met his and his neighbor's quota by giving up one cow. The neighbor repaid him in eggs, milk, or grain."

During one such meeting on June 22, 1941, the partisan leader saw the contempt on Józef's face. He said, "This one stays, he's the first we shoot if people don't bring us their cattle and food in two hours."

Sitting on the grass, my uncle wondered if the neighbor realizes Józef's life depends on him giving up a cow. The only man at home, he did the heavy work. How will his mother and sister manage if the partisans kill him? As Józef faced his mortality, high above the peaceful fields of grain and pasture came a jarring noise unwelcome in these parts. He said, "Something from the sky was coming closer. Louder and louder. Guard looked up. I looked up. We looked at each other in shock. German planes on the horizon! Germany invading its Soviet ally! The guard ran in one direction. I ran home."

The Russian partisans retreated for days. Women put boiled potatoes and fresh baked bread on open windowsills to keep hungry men from invading their homes. The local boys thought they could sneak in behind buildings and ambush the Russians. Józef was in town that day. The street was filled with people bringing cows from pasture to avoid the summer heat. A car stopped. A Russian officer got out, stood tall in a white uniform, and looked around. Józef said, "With some military training, those foolish boys would know it was hopeless to fight the Russians retreating in huge numbers. But one of them aimed at the officer. The shot ricocheted onto the cobblestone street."

In a booming voice, the Russian officer threatened to come back to destroy this village and all the rabble in it. Józef said, "They did come back. They killed Polish people for years in places like Katyń. We saw no fault with Russians in our area. They were decent. Your father's oldest sister married a Russian soldier after World War I and left with him. Some married local girls and stayed. So why did some soldiers rather die than go back to Russia? Because they would be punished for being captured. American news showed German atrocities, but not what Stalin's government did."

The Katyń massacre was the execution of 22,000 Polish military officers and intelligentsia by the Soviet Union in Russia between April and May 1940. As a multi-ethnic country, the murder of Polish citizens included ethnic Poles, Polish Ukrainians, Belarussians, and Jews. When Poland asked the Red Cross to investigate, Stalin broke off diplomatic relations with the Polish government-in-exile in London. He insisted the missing men must have escaped to Manchuria.

American historian Allen Paul states that, "Churchill and Roosevelt ...knew that massive deportations had been carried out in eastern Poland in an effort to Sovietize the region. Both knew Stalin was grooming a puppet regime to replace the legitimate government...They knew also that... crushing of the German Reich – would be a much more difficult task without Soviet manpower and economic resources. That Big Three unity should be compromised for any reason thus became unthinkable to both leaders. If preserving unity meant turning a blind eye to Katyń's mountain of evidence against the Soviets, then so be it."[44]

According to British historian, Simon Sebag Montefiore, Stalin saw these murders as "black work" and noble party service. He states, "The master of "black work" under Stalin presided over this somber but brisk ritual: Blokhin, a pugnacious Chekist [Cheka: commission to prevent counter revolutionary activities] of forty-one with a stalwart face and black hair pushed back...killing thousands personally, sometimes wearing his own leather butcher's apron to protect his uniform."[45]

"Blokhin...and two other Chekists outfitted a hut with padded, soundproofed walls and decided on a ...quota of 250 shootings a night... he began one of the most prolific acts of mass murder by one individual, killing 7,000 in precisely twenty-eight nights, using a German Walther pistol. The bodies were buried in various places – but the 4,500 in the Kozelsk camp were interred in Katyń Forest."[46]

German soldiers discovered the mass graves, and Stalin accused Germany of the murders. The initial investigation of the German discovery was used by Russia as an excuse for breaking relations with the Polish government. Although the Russian guilt was evident, the other allies could do nothing for the Poles. In 1990, the Russian government admitted the murders and blamed Stalin and other Soviet officials.

Allies in Name Only

Stalin never released them, and thousands were stranded forever.

With the 1941 German attack, the Russian soldiers became guerrilla units on orders from Moscow. Józef said, "Our forest was full of Russian, Jewish, Polish, Belarussian partisans. Jewish and Russian partisans came one dawn to steal food. My mother and cousin snuck out to alert the Polish partisans. They stopped the robbery, but they couldn't help everyone. With no flour left for bread, my mother and neighbor took wheat and rye to be ground at the mill. Russian partisans saw them, threw them on the ground, stole their grain, horse, and wagon. The women walked back empty-handed. Lucky they weren't raped or killed."

The surprise German attack on its former ally drove the Soviet Union to join the Allies – countries like the United States, England, France, and Poland. How could Poland be a Soviet ally? The Polish government knew that Stalin lied about 22,000 Polish officers escaping to Manchuria. They were imprisoned or dead, discovered later to be victims of the Katyń Forest massacre.

Although official allies, Polish men fought the Russian partisans and the German army with dire consequences. According to the Polish Institute of National Remembrance, on August 26, 1943, a Soviet partisan brigade massacred eighty members of the Polish Home Army[47] in the Lake Narach area [in northwestern Belarus]. Then in November 30, 1943, Soviet leader Panteleimon Ponomarenko issued an order to obliterate the Polish partisans in the Stołpce-Naliboki units of the Home Army. The next day, these men were invited to talks as "allies" with the Soviet partisans. As they arrived, some fifty of them were murdered. Others were flown to Moscow and imprisoned.[48]

Józef affirmed that, "After we were deported, Belarus communist party leader, Ponomarenko, set up a meeting with Polish officers to make strategic plans as allies. They left their forest dugout on December 1, 1943, and Ponamarenko had the Stalin Brigade mow them down. Many of my friends died in that ambush."[49]

From that day, the pretense of being allies ended. Polish and Soviet units fought each other openly. Józef added, "During the 1944 Warsaw Uprising, the Russians stopped their tanks outside the city and watched the

Germans destroy Warsaw and its people. Why didn't our "ally" go in and help?"

British historian, Norman Davies, adds that, "The USSR made no effort to assist the Rising for at least five whole weeks, and thereafter in only the most half-hearted and grudging fashion."[50]

Four deportations between February 1940 and June 1941 brought thousands of Polish citizens into the Soviet Union. After Germany attacked the Soviet Union, some were freed to fight Germany. Many died trying to reach the Polish army forming in Uzbekistan. The lucky ones, like Józef Chmara, reached that army and left the Soviet Union to fight Germany. Stalin never released the rest, and thousands were stranded forever. Their offspring remain in the former Soviet republics of their ancestors' exile. They may not even know about their Polish roots.

An Offer They Can't Refuse

How do I explain to a child about broken glass, the fire, a neighbor dead in front of our house?

Latvian soldiers who were German allies, walked the streets ordering local men to gather on the church steps. A German officer announced that his men were leaving for the front. The local men must accept firearms against the partisans or retribution will follow. Józef said, "A Polish Underground officer, Zenia Klimowicz, organized the self-defense units. Some criticized him for taking the firearms. Some said we'll be helpless if he doesn't."

My brother, Henry, told me, "They had no choice but to take the rifles and ammunition, but it ran out quickly. Exact number not known, maybe thirty. Not enough for the self-defense units to protect us against hundreds of partisans. Our men trying to fight back just fed the partisan fury."

As Hoffman said, Christians and Jews saw the Soviet invasion differently, but loyalties also clashed among the Christians. Józef said, "My wife was from a hamlet of twenty houses with young parents. The children had attended the Polish school. They wanted to be part of Poland. The older generation in Szemioty, also about twenty houses, wanted the familiar Russian rule. But taking sides was dangerous. I was working in my wood shop. Two Latvians, went past toward Szemioty. I heard shots. I saw them leaving. We never saw the man living there again. He was helping the Russians. When men from Szemioty left the squad that I led before the massacre, they knew it was coming. One man told me later in Germany he gave the Russians lots of ammunition."

How do neighbors absorb brutally conflicting loyalties? My brother Henry told me that one leader of the massacre had been our mother's childhood friend. Rafał Wasilewicz was among the children she used to play with. Who knew he would become a major in the Soviet army? Józef said, "Poland was swallowed up by Russia, Prussia, and Austria-Hungary in 1795. Russia had generations to turn some of our people to their way of thinking. When Wasilewicz returned from Russia, he began going to church to spy on us. He led the May 1943 massacre that killed 128 people."

Grandfather Justyn passed away before the massacre. My mother and her sister Eleanor had married and left home. Grandmother Anna lived in the south end of town with her youngest daughter Mania, son Józef, his wife Józia, and their baby Sophie. My mother was about to give birth to me, so two-year-old brother Van was with them. They were asleep as gunshots woke them at dawn.

They put the two babies on the floor against the wall, covered them with pillows to muffle the gunfire, and knelt to pray. Józef saw a Soviet partisan kick open their gate and walk toward the house. My Aunt Mania had been hiding under a bench under a window. As she crawled out, the falling glass cut her forehead and she bled. Two partisans approached, laughing about the broken window. About to enter the house, a noise on the street got their attention and they joined the frenzy.

In the town center, partisans set fire to the little wooden houses with hay roofs that almost touched. The fire spread south like a dynamite fuse but stopped at grandmother's doorstep. Józef said, "Miraculously, a strong force protected us. Russian and Jewish partisans did this. Some were Naliboki Jews, some from other villages. I saw a Jewish woman with the partisans shout, 'Here's for being in the *samoobrona*,' [self-defense group] and she shot our neighbor in front of our house."

Józef's wife Józia watched over brother Van and baby Sophie as they slept. She said, "I asked myself, 'How do I explain to a child about broken glass, the fire, a neighbor dead in front of our house?'"

The next day, Rafał Wasilewicz and Józef's former classmate, Krasowski, were surveying the burned-out town. They stopped to talk to Józef's neighbor Bernard Korzenko. Krasowski saw Józef in his yard and avoided my uncle's searing stare. But when the two men approached him, Wasilewski extended his hand, and said, "Aren't you talking to us? What's happening here?"

Disgusted by the whiff of death in the ashen air, Józef mouthed, "You – unleashed – this – destruction – and – ask – what's – happening – here!"

Wasilewicz shot back, "Why did they kill our commander?"

"Why did your commander attack us? The Germans come and do whatever they want with us. You come and do whatever you want with us. We are in between."

My mother's childhood friend spit on the ground near Józef and the two men left. That afternoon, two Russian partisans walked into Józef's house. One grabbed the watch hanging on the wall, held it to his ear, and put it back. Not knowing it had to be wound, he said it was broken. They demanded firearms. Józef insisted he had none. The tall lanky partisan loomed over him yelling, "Then how were our commander and fighters killed?"

Józef shot back, "We didn't have enough rifles or ammunition for six squads. Some men stood guard while others slept. We just wanted to live."

They walked to the barn. The short full-bodied partisan stood on a barrel with his nose inches from Józef's precious bicycle on the rafter, his main form of transportation. The he did not see the bicycle, but he took the cow – their only source of milk, cheese, and butter. Sneering at Józef, one of them said, "We're leaving. But the Red Army is coming back to finish with you."

Families hammered out 128 coffins to bury the fallen and raced to prepare food and shelter before the September frost. Some people devised secret radios, but news traveled mostly by word of mouth. They never expected to leave home, but the stomp of German boots changed their destiny.

To Please the *Arbeitsamt*

The *Bauer* pretended he didn't know we were sending you his food.

German soldiers returned three months later, August 7, 1943, and roused people from their homes. Józef dug a hole in the dirt floor of the cold storage hut and gazed at his army uniform. He folded it lovingly, put it into a cloth sack, and buried it. Surely, he would come home someday. His sister Mania had been abducted two months earlier for forced labor in Germany. Before he could find out what was happening to his sister Helena, his neighbor Bernard Korzenko was putting his own family, Grandmother Anna, and baby Sophie on his wagon. Partisans had stolen Józef's horse and wagon, so Józef and Józia walked behind to the meadow in Jankowicze.

In the morning, Aunt Eleanor's husband Chester Dubicki found them in the rain-soaked meadow. The armed guards that restrained them all night began prodding them to start walking. As they merged into the mass of hundreds who became homeless overnight, they came upon Grandfather Justyn's sister Zofia, her two grown sons and two grown daughters, making them a group of twelve. With only Chester's horse and wagon, most of the adults walked for three days to the train station 25 miles away. Józef said, "German allies, led by German officers, shot anyone trying to escape. If I was alone, I would run. But abandon my wife, baby, and mother? No!"

I said, "Before you reached Germany, you had the humiliating disinfection in Białystok."

My uncle changed the subject, saying, "The employment bureau, the *Arbeitsamt,* sent our train to the town of Pirmasens in southwestern Germany. We dug potatoes on our knees all day. In the evenings we gathered to say the rosary and sing hymns. The commandant made everyone be respectful during prayers. A week later, he told us we were leaving tomorrow, so pray for God's protection."

The cattle cars went north to the town of Parchim, then to Neumünster, near the Danish border. They dug potatoes for weeks and were not allowed to gather for prayer. Józef said, "Did Hitler give those two commandants two sets of rules about praying? No, it depended on the person's character."

Their final stop was a tiny train station where ninety people from Naliboki stood cold and hungry in a damp autumn drizzle, mothers holding crying children. Two prisoners of war from Western Poland appeared. Feliks Matelski drove a tractor pulling two open wagons with big rubber wheels. Johan Olechowski rode a bicycle. Hearing them speak Polish, a sense of relief rippled through the group.

Climbing onto the wagons, they rode three miles past the town of Gribbohm, county of Schleswig-Holstein. Arriving at a large farm, Johan showed them into a barn where they put on dry clothes and sat at rows of tables with pots of soup, bread, potatoes, pickles, and jars of milk. Not a drop of soup was left when the German farmer Klaus Offe, whom they called the *Bauer*, came to see if they had enough to eat. They were then led to a brick apartment building and assigned two large rooms. Twelve people slept in one room on wooden bunk beds, straw mattresses, and blankets. The other room was a sitting and storage area.

On the first day, the *Bauer* gave them breakfast, lunch, supper, and let them rest. Then for three days, the adults picked potatoes with one hundred Russian female prisoners while the children and elderly did chores and helped with food preparation. After the Russian women were sent to work on other farms, the *Bauer* chose Józef's family of twelve, with its nine adult workers, to stay on his farm. The man treated his workers well, so having studied French and German in the Polish school of his youth, Józef asked in German, "Could more of our group stay here? They are good workers, and they don't make trouble."

The *Bauer* said he can only keep what the *Arbeitsamt*, the employment bureau, allows. But with his male workers at war, he needed many hands to maintain the farm, two brick apartment buildings for worker housing, barns and sheds, machinery, five pair of workhorses, his wife's horse, and a horse for getting around to milk the cows. Johan was the general manager. Feliks kept the machinery and tractor in working order. The Polish people tended the fields. Józef also did general repairs. Five Russian prisoners were trucked in for fieldwork and locked up away from the farm at night. Besides the *Bauer*, wife, and two daughters, the other Germans were a woman with two children whose husband was at war, three women domestics, an old man who supervised the milking, and a German worker with his Polish wife.

They worked six days a week. After milking the cows, Sunday was a day of rest. Some Sundays, they visited Naliboki people on nearby farms. Other Sundays, Eleanor and Józia dried bread in the *Bauer*'s kitchen. The mailman took the packages of bread with him. Józef said, "Your parents were on the front with six children. The *Bauer* pretended he didn't know we were sending you his food. But his wife told Józia he knew everything that went on."

Peace at Last

His anti-Nazi reputation put him in good standing with the English.

Johan and Feliks spoke German, had responsible jobs, and shared a comfortable room. A German woman lived next door. Józef sat with them when they listened to the radio in her room. Józef said, "If authorities knew we listened to the radio with the German woman and that I had free run of the house, they would have killed us all, including the *Bauer*."

They heard about the Allied landing on French soil in Normandy, and Germany's surrender on May 8, 1945. (War in the Pacific ended on September 2, 1945.) The Nazi elite saw themselves as a superior race. As the people at the Gribbohm farm heard the news on the radio, they did not know that this elite had faced defeat with debauchery. These were the people who had expected to rule the world.

Hitler married Eva Braun on April 29, 1945, and according to Montefiore, "Hitler's secretary found in the higher levels of the bunker that "an erotic fever seemed to take possession of everybody. Everywhere even on the dentist's chair, I saw bodies interlocked in lascivious embraces. The women had discarded all modesty and were freely exposing their private parts...Two days later...Hitler tested cyanide ampoules on his Alsatian, Biondi. Around 3:15 p.m., to the distant buzz of partying upstairs, Hitler committed suicide, shooting himself in the head. Eva took poison. Goebbels and Bormann made a final Hitler salute before the pyre of Hitler's body in the Chancellery guard"[51]

The war was officially over, but as trucks of victorious English soldiers drove past, scattered gunfire continued. A German girl working in the field warned Józef that her father belonged to *Volksschutz*, men past military age who had firearms and orders to shoot the foreigners. When a policeman came insisting that my family report to a nearby village, the *Bauer* forbid them to go. Another *Bauer* rode twelve miles by bicycle to the English headquarters to let them know about the policeman's orders. They investigated and found the bodies of the unfortunate souls from other farms who had obeyed him.

After the English squelched the German resistance, the *Bauer* had Józef clean and oil his shotguns. His anti-

Nazi reputation put him in good standing with the English. They were soon hunting together. Returning from the woods with two English officers, he told Józef to bring some drinks. Józef said, "Our *Bauer* liked to drink. He liked the women too, although his wife was pretty. Whenever they brought him home drunk, he would call me to pull off his boots and join him in a drink."

Józef filled the best glasses with *spirytus*, 100% potency moonshine brewed by Feliks and Chester. The *Bauer* took a big swig. Nothing happened. Keeping up with the *Bauer*, the first English officer took a thirsty gulp as if he were drinking German beer. He let out a high-pitched moan. His throat closed. His eyes rolled. Józef got scared. The man seemed to be in trouble. But he braced himself. Put down the glass. Got his bearings. Let out a deep sigh and grinned with effort.

The second officer was content to wet his lips. Having recovered from his introduction to 100% moonshine, the first officer pulled out his camera. He snapped Józef and Chester smiling. That picture must have become part of his war stories about an unusual form of local refreshment.

Bonds of Affection

Wherever you go, my friend, if you can't find a place, you can always return to me.

Although free to leave, Józef and Chester kept working in the field. The *Bauer* 's kindness had earned their loyalty. Józef resisted his mother's pressure to look for Helena and Mania. If his sisters were alive, they would come to the farm. Otherwise, they might never find each other. Józef was right. After seeing friends in Hamburg, Józef squeezed into a train thick with people between cars and on roofs. At the end of the car, he saw a mirage of haggard faces that looked like my father Michał, Aunt Mania, and Grandmother Anna's brother Ferdinand. As they got off at Gribbohm, their sweaty embraces left no doubt they were his family still on this earth with him.

After an hour's walk, the *Bauer* and his family welcomed them and gave them supper. They barely slept that night making plans. Józef went to the main house in the morning to say what they had decided. He was feeling excited, yet sad. He told the *Bauer* he must speak with him and his family. The wife and daughters came into the room.

Józef Byczkiewicz and wife Józefa (Jozia), daughter Sophie, his mother Anna, Józef, son Stanley. Connecticut 1950's

A tense hush filled the room. They had a sense of what was coming. Józef cleared his throat and said in a shaky voice, "The time has come for us to leave you. You are such kind, good people."

Józef paused, unable to speak. He composed himself and continued, "But our family has come for us. We must start a new life with our family, wherever that may be."

The room fell silent. They looked away from each other, realizing the depth of love and trust that had grown between them. The *Bauer* stared at the floor for some time. Then looking up, he said with a tenderness Józef had never heard before from this imperfect saint, "Wherever you go, my friend, if you can't find a place, you know you can always return to me."

The wife said, "What will become of the children? Everything is torn up. At least you are safe here with us. And there is food. You must stay."

Józef replied, "God blessed us by putting us with your good family. We have all learned that Polish or German doesn't matter. We are just people. But now we must leave."

Between farm chores, the Poles and Germans ate and drank together for three days to celebrate the end of war. Józef said, "When we left, we were all crying – our family, the *Bauer*, his family, the other Germans. The *Bauer* had Felix and Johan drive us to the train station in Essen. He watched silently as they loaded the wagon. We began to move. He went into the house and didn't look back."

The industrial center of Essen was a bombed-out heap of rubble. Throngs of refugees waited on crumbling platforms. Passengers usually entered onto ledges on the side of the train. But with so few remaining trains, riders clung desperately to these ledges. As a train approached, Józef pushed Grandmother Anna inside. The others clutched the outside ledges as tall poles became a blur along a narrow track. A wrong move would mean oblivion.

Aunt Eleanor's hands became numb holding toddler Irene. About to lose her grip, she reached the car door, dropped her on the floor. A German woman put the child under her legs to keep it from being trampled. My father held baby Sophie and a suitcase. She was slipping from his numb hands. He dropped the suitcase and pushed her into the train until they all squeezed in. This harrowing journey ended in embraces with family waiting for them in the Mülheim Ruhr displaced persons camp.

After five years in five such camps, Eleanor and Chester were the first to leave. Like Henry Mara, Chester's uncle left Naliboki as a young man, and worked his way to owning a farm in Connecticut. When the same uncle sponsored Józef and Józia, they came to Connecticut with something extra: their son Stanley was born after the war in Germany. Sophie was native to Naliboki, and the youngest child, Teresa, was born in America.

Józef never saw the *Bauer* nor his family again, but their friendship continued. One of the *Bauer*'s daughters married an English officer and they lived in Africa. Józef had someone write letters in English to the daughter in Africa. She, in turn, wrote to her parents about Józef's life in America, and to Józef about the people in Gribbohm. He wrote to Johan and Feliks, who had stayed to help the *Bauer*. They read Józef's letters to his German friends on the farm.

Hitler and his retinue could not have imagined that, in place of ethnic hatred, some people would form life-long bonds of affection. Theirs was the ultimate victory.

Reflections

DC: As you speak of these events, do you feel any anger or hatred?

Danusia, as Catholics we should not hold onto anger. Every group has good and bad. But I am sad about the injustice. The Soviet Union betrayed us, but so did the United States and Great Britain.

Stalin released some of the men that were deported to form two Polish armies. One formed in the then Soviet republic of Uzbekistan. General Władysław Anders led this army out of the Soviet Union. It was made up of men like your Uncle Józef Chmara who fought for a free Europe and a free Poland.

The second Polish army stayed in the Soviet Union, led by General Zygmunt Berling, and was later used against the will of the Polish people. The Kosciuszko Division of that army was forced to march into Poland as the Soviet Union imposed a communist government that lasted for five decades.

General Anders' army was largely men from our eastern borderlands, our *kresy*. They shed their blood alongside the British and Americans against Germany as they marched through Iraq, Iran, and Italy. The Polish army succeeded in Monte Cassino where others failed. They took part in D-Day on Normandy's beaches. What did Poland get for such loss of life? Roosevelt and Churchill, United States, Great Britain gave away Eastern Europe to Stalin in Yalta and Potsdam. And in the end, we were scattered like a handful of rye. You have people from Poland and Naliboki all over the world.

Józef Byczkiewicz was born in Naliboki on July 3, 1914 and passed away on August 2, 2004 in Yantic, Connecticut. Józefa (Józia) Dubicka Byczkiewicz was born in Cielechowszczyna on June 8, 1923 and passed away in Yantic, Connecticut on September 15, 2005. In America, they worked for the Thermos Company, and Józef was a leader in the Polish American community. Daughter Sophie worked in government, son Stanley owned a business, and daughter Teresa was a school librarian. They have five grandchildren. This narrative is based on many talks with my uncle.

Uncle Józef wrote this poem for his wife Józia which I translated and read at his funeral.

When I Am No Longer Here

When I am no longer here,
As will surely be the case,
Oh, but you are still beautiful,
With silver circling your face.

Remember all my deeds,
What I held to be true,
When I was still alive,
And so in love with you.

Stroll upon these pathways
Where we walked together,
Listen to the bird song,
Under clouds of feather.

Listen to those melodies
That we held so dear,
When as a young man,
I sang them loud and clear.

Maybe then my soul
Will linger by your side,
And as one in reverie,
We will harmonize.

Our joys, our sorrows
Will come back to you,
But when my body is gone
My soul remains with you.

And when you also leave
This sphere of loss and gain,
We will be together
Untouched by time and pain.

Gdy Mnie Już Nie Będzie

Gdy mnie już nie będzie
Bo zwykle tak bywa
A ty jesteś piękna
Chociaż starsza i masz włosy siwe.

Spójrz na moją pracę
Którą wykonywałem,
Kiedy jeszcze żyłem
I ciebie kochałem.

Przejdż się po tych scieżkach
Ktoremi chodziliśmy
Słuchając śpiewu ptasząt
I chmurki liczyliśmy.

Przegraj tę melodię
Którą nagrywałem,
Kiedy byłem młody
I tobie śpiewałem

Może moja dusza
Przy tobie usiądzie,
I razem w zadumie
Wspomnień słuchać
będziem.

Nasze szczęścia, troski
Przypomnimy sobie.
Jak już ciałem nie obecny
Lecz duchem przy tobie.

A gdy już opuścisz
I ty ten swiat,
Będziemy znowu razem
Jak za młodych lat.

Endnotes

35 Henry H. Hirschbiel, "Conscription in Russia," Joseph L. Wieczynski, ed., *The Modern Encyclopedia of Russian and Soviet History* (Gulf Breeze, FL: Academic Int. Press, 1978) p. 5-6.

36 Based on author's meeting in 2017 with Valentina Buniak, Naliboki Head Librarian, this information was compiled from articles written after 1991 in Promień, the Stołpce newspaper.

37 Dagnoslaw Demski, *Naliboki I Puszcza Nalibocka – Zarys Dziejów I Problematyki* (Etnografia Polska, t.XXXVIII: 1994, z. 1-2, PL ISSN 0071-1861) pp. 71-72.

38 Ibid

39 Ibid

40 Shmuel Spector, ed., *The Encyclopedia of Jewish Life Before and During the Holocaust* (NY: NYUP, 2001) p. 872.

41 Eva Hoffman, *Shtetl: The Life and Death of a Small Town and the World of Polish Jews* (NY: Public Affairs, Perseus Books Group, 2007) pp. 8-10.

42 Antoni Peretitkowicz, ed., *Konstytucja Rzeczypospolitej Polskiej* (Poznań, 4th edition, 1928) p. 70. August Paszkudzki, ed., *Konstytucja Rzeczypospolitej Polskiej* (Warsaw: Książnica-Atlas, 1935) p. 54.

43 Hoffman, p. 210.

44 Allen Paul, *Katyn: Stalin's Massacre and the Seeds of the Polish Resurrection* (Annapolis: Naval Institute, 1996) preface pp. ix-x.

45 Simon Sebag Montefiore, *Stalin: The Court of the Red Tsar* (NY: Knopf, 2004) p. 197, p. 334.

46 *Ibid*

47 The Polish Home Army (Armia Krajowa) was an underground force organized as military units and coordinated by the Polish Government-in-exile based in London. After the German invasion they attempted work with Soviet Partisans against the Nazis which led to the Soviet betrayal of Polish soldiers.

48 Bogdan Musiał, "Memorandum Pantelejmona Ponomarienki z 20 stycznia 1943 r. in O Zachowaniu się Polaków i niektórych naszych zadaniach." *Pamiec i Sprawiedliwosc.* Instytut Pamieci Narodowej (2006-09-01): 379/ ISSN 1427-7476.

49 This event and relations between Polish and Soviet partisans are described in Adam Walczak, "Oddział "DĄB" – załążek 13 Brygady A.K. Okręgu Wileńskiego w Puszczy Nalibockiej," *Wileński Przekaz*, Olgierd Christa, ed., (Gdańsk: Swiatowy Związek Żolnierzy Armii Krajowej) pp. 3-22 and in Adolf Pilch, *partyzanci trzech puszcz* (Warsaw: Editions Sotkania, 1992) pp. 89-108.

50 Norman Davies, *God's Playground: A History of Poland,* vol 2 (NY: Columbia UP, 1982) p.477.

51Montefiore, p.487

Chapter 11 Eleanor
The *Bauer* Was a Good Man

Eleanor stood shivering in the autumn drizzle at the Gribbohm train station in Germany. Holding two-year-old Irene, she worried with a mother's anguish how she would feed her hungry child. She and her brother Józef Byczkiewicz were brought here with ninety people from Naliboki to work on a farm owned by strangers. The owners, Klaus and Erna Offe, were to be masters of their supposedly inferior, but useful, Polish labor force. They became lifelong friends instead. Her tearful memory of their parting touched me so deeply, I cried with her. Let us meet Klaus and Erne through Eleanor's eyes and heart.

My aunt's bitter exile led to a new language, a new name. When she was called Lonia, she had only been thirty miles from home. As a grandmother, she had seen Europe and much of the United States. A self-taught tailor, her suits rivaled the fashions on New York's Fifth Avenue. She kept a home, raised a family, became fluent in English, drove a car, and earned a living. Like the creamy red, yellow, and peach begonias that greeted me when I visited, Eleanor blossomed in America.

When She Was Called Lonia

Anna and Justyn toiled no less, but the land belonged to them, and they belonged only to God.

Eleanor's grandparents lived under a legal system going back to the year 1400. Polish historian, Adam Zamoyski, states that the annual rent for a farmer living on the lord's property was "fifteen *grosze* (the price of a pig or a calf) and a few bushels of grain...he had to perform up to twelve days' work a year on the landlord's fields, using his own implements and horses, usually at the busiest times."[52]

It got worse in 1496 as the Seym [legislature], "passed measures restricting the freedom of movement of peasants. Tenants...were obliged to put their tenancies in order, pay off all dues, and sow the land before they left. The economic effort involved in moving was therefore prohibitive..."[53]

"In 1520, the Seym increased the labour-rent from twelve days to fifty-two days per annum for all tenants....

they lost their right of appeal to other courts and could only seek justice in the manorial courts, in which their landlord sat as magistrate."[54]

When a general in the czar's army, Prince Piotr Wittgenstein, married Princess Stefania Radziwiłł in 1849, he received Naliboki as his dowry. This included the land and the serfs working the land, such as Eleanor's grandparents, my great grandparents.[55]

This bondage crumbled after 500 years with the emancipation of serfs during the Reform Period of the 1860's. Eleanor's parents, my grandparents, were born in the 1880's, and when they got married, they stepped out of a feudal system going back to the Middle Ages. Anna and Justyn toiled no less, but the land belonged to them, and they belonged only to God. And the work was endless.

As private farmers, they raised geese and grew linen seed which they sold to two Jewish merchants from the Machlis family. Eleanor said, "We four children had to tend geese after school. We began playing in the field, crows swooped in grabbing the baby geese. We got our behinds smacked coming home with fewer geese to sell. We cooked with butter and lard. Jewish people used butter and goose fat. So, if we lost a goose, it meant less money for necessities like gasoline, matches, sugar, and salt."

She added, "Summers weren't humid like here in Connecticut, or we couldn't bend over a sickle all day in the fields. And we carried buckets of water to the field until baby cabbages and linen seed took root. I loved walking along that waving sea of blue, blue linen two meters high. Stunning!"

Women harvested the linen as men sheared the sheep for wool. All winter, women spun the wool and linen and wove it into cloth. As a girl, Lonia learned to sew the cloth into shirts, sheets, towels, coats, and jackets. She was learning a skill she would perfect one day in a place called America.

The Pride of Naliboki

He had helpers, but you could say your father was the architect of the project.

As the region changed hands, education depended on who ruled Naliboki. As the oldest, my mother was taught in people's houses in Russian, and attended secret Polish lessons. When Naliboki became part of Poland, Józef was taught in Polish in a small building in town. Then his

Men and women digging the foundation for the new church, the only structure left standing after the town was burned to the ground during the war.
Naliboki 1930's.

younger sisters, Eleanor and Mania, joined him in a two-
building school with grades one to seven. Years later, one of
the men who built the school, Michał Chmara, married their
sister Helena. Eleanor said, "There's no trace of those two
beautiful wooden buildings, and the large gate announcing
this is a special place."

I said, "On one visit, I walked to town with mother's
childhood neighbor, Karol Sazanowicz. He remembered two
beautiful wooden buildings with big windows and pointed to
a patch of stones, near the big concrete store, that had been
part of the school foundation. I ran my hands over the stones
my father may have put in place, untouched for decades.
Eleanor said, "He had helpers, but you could say your father
was the architect of the project. Those two schools were the
pride of Naliboki."

During the school year, children walked into church
on Sunday with their teachers, sat up front, and sang at
the Mass. Every three months, teachers and parents met
after the adults' Mass that followed. Affirming their Polish
roots, they sang, *"Nie rzucim ziemi skąd nasz ród,"* (We Won't
Abandon our Ancestral Land.) Eleanor said, "Two joyful
voices stood out, my mother's alto and the forester Szerbik's
deep bass. At the end, they sang the Polish national anthem.
Our neighbor Filomena loved the meetings and couldn't wait

until her three little boys were old enough for school."

Like Józef, Eleanor could not go beyond grade seven. The local men chopped down trees in our boundless forest and floated them down the Niemen River to the sawmill for export to Germany. Justyn had no stamina for such work. She said, "I didn't dare think of high school. Father returned from World War I with severe asthma that got worse. Mother ran the farm, and we all went to work."

Józef set up a shop where he made and sold furniture. My mother Helena cleared brush on a private estate. Starting at ages fourteen and twelve, Eleanor and Mania worked in the government-owned forest tilling the soil with a hoe, planting seed, and weeding. They transplanted saplings to replace harvested trees. In the fall, they cleared and burned dead branches.

How long would my dear reader work today to buy a winter coat? A few hours, days? Naliboki had fabric stores but not ready-made suits or coats. My father took his teen-age sister-in-law to the town of Iwieniec, some twelve miles away. The round trip by horse and wagon took up the day. Eleanor entered the shop wide-eyed and gazed at the fine ladies' coats. She had worked for two months to afford the one she wanted. Then her fingers caressed the smooth fabric of suits young men bought with their first-earned money. She said, "How handsome our boys looked in church. White shirt, linen tie, deep black suits with the wide pant leg, and black shoes polished to a shine."

The Coldest Night of the Year
Lonia, I have chosen a husband for you.

Monsignor Bajko alerted his congregation that Germany had invaded Western Poland on September 1, 1939. Seeing airplanes two weeks later, they assumed that Germany was invading Eastern Poland. But as Russian planes filled the sky and their tanks crushed the cobblestone streets, Eleanor's father Justyn was barely holding on to life. He had done a father's duty to secure his daughter's future. He called his wife and daughter to his bedside. He whispered with satisfaction, "Lonia, I have chosen a husband for you. The man owns a house, a horse, works hard, and comes from a good family."

Justyn waited for Eleanor's grateful acceptance. How could she tell her father on his deathbed that she pushed away this eager suitor each time he tried to kiss her? Anna glared for her to accept. She was horrified as Eleanor's belted out, "No!" Anna pulled the defiant girl out of the room and returned to console her husband. Eleanor overheard her mother say, "She didn't expect this. Give her time. I will see that she gets married properly."

Grandfather Justyn passed away in 1940 at age fifty-four. Eleanor said, "Father was looking out for me, but I didn't want this man. The thought of kissing him made me cringe. I couldn't lie to father. He died so young.

Young men dressed for church in white shirts, linen ties, deep black suits with wide pant legs and black shoes polished to a shine bought with their first-earned money. Naliboki, 1930's

He used to smoke, most men did. No one talked about it being bad. Not even doctors. He had pneumonia and they had nothing like we do today to help my him breathe."

Losing her father soon after the Soviet invasion, she said in disgust, "Huh! They kicked out our mayor and put in charge a man called Szabunia from a nearby village. People said he couldn't even read or write. They recorded where we lived, how many cows and chickens, how much milk and eggs to take from us each week. They set up a small dairy on our property in the south end of town. Your Aunt Mania recorded the deliveries. If you refused, they took the goods and increased the quota."

Forced labor. Stolen goods. And old scores to settle as Stalin targeted men who had fought for Polish independence in World War I. After helping put Poland back on the map of Europe, my Uncle Józef Chmara had gone on with his life. He and his two brothers had built a family complex – a house for Jan, and across the road, a spacious two-family house for Józef and my father and their families. As single girls, Eleanor and Mania visited that house often to help their sister Helena with the four children, before Van and I were born.

Eleanor stayed on the coldest night of the year, February 10, 1940. She said, "Loud banging on the door woke us up. Someone was yelling in Russian, '*Atkrivaj*, open up, we know Józef Chmara lives here.' Your father rushed to Józef's side of the house. One of the men stood guard while the other one looked for weapons. They let your father say good-bye before shoving Józef, Józefa, and Stefania into the sled. It was revenge for fighting for Poland's independence."

That night of terror did not stop our plucky girl of nineteen from returning to a half-empty house to help my mother with the children. Eleanor noticed a boy as she walked two and a half miles from Koniec, in the south end of town, to Kamionka in the north end. When Chester Dubicki saw her from a distance, he found jobs to do in the front yard, and they chatted. One day, he showed up at her house. He had a feeling she would not mind.

Having eluded the man she could not bear to kiss, she liked Chester's self-confidence. He was a shoemaker, a respectable trade. His father bought cattle in villages and sold it to the military. Herding cattle for days to train stations took stamina but paid well. Chester also had ambition. Despite Soviet partisans and German soldiers swarming about, he went 90 miles north on horseback to the city of Wilno (Lithuanian: Vilnus). Pilgrims went on foot to visit the Shrine of the Blessed Mother, known as *Ostro Brama*. Grandmother Anna had gone to pray. But Chester went on horseback to show his serious intentions. His girl should have something none of the other girls had.

Our intrepid knight returned with dress material, a beret which was the rage, a purse, and a pair of summer shoes. Eleanor wore the gifts to Sunday mass where they would be seen. As she walked past Chester's house, his mother opened the window and called out asking Lonia if the shoes fit. The poor girl could feel her face turn red. She gave a tentative wave and kept walking. Proper girls did not talk to a boy's parents until all had agreed on the terms of marriage. After Mass, the gifts were admired and served notice he would soon pop the question.

Chester wore his Sunday best to visit the Byczkiewicz homestead. Eleanor's father Justyn had died, so he asked her mother Anna and her brother Józef for Eleanor's hand in marriage as was the proper phrase. The loving glances between her daughter and this young man had not escaped

Anna. He could have the priest announce the wedding bans for all to hear.

With two invaders fighting over their homeland, two young people in love walked down the aisle of the Church of the Assumption. Brides were expected to have a serious demeanor, so wearing a borrowed dress, Eleanor hid her excitement. They said "I do" with borrowed rings as family and friends looked on with approval. The bride and groom's families returned to the Byczkiewicz home for their first meal together as a new family unit.

Unlike wedding dinners of canned goods in Germany after the war, this meal was exceptional. The wife of Grandmother Anna's brother, Ferdinand, had learned fine cuisine while working for a doctor who entertained in style. Later in the day, friends joined the festivities. Eleanor said, "Both my brother and I got married during the German occupation. Some soldiers even came to Józef's wedding. Mother fermented a drink called *kwas* with hops, yeast, and rye flour. They kept saying, 'Mother, more wine!' We fed them. What else could we do?"

Brutality or Bravery

Father and son slept holding their rifles and a sack of food Eleanor had prepared for them.

The newlyweds were setting up their newly built house in Kamionka, away from the town center. A rough tapping on the window startled them. German soldiers were rounding up the Jewish residents. The fabric store owner, Haim Rubieżowski, and his son, Matus, were running for their lives. The two families knew each other well. Haim had taught Chester to be a shoemaker. They ate supper together, then with the house still unfurnished, Chester put blankets and straw on the floor. Father and son slept holding their rifles and a large cloth sack of food Eleanor had prepared for them.

Eleanor sat at the window, keeping vigil. She said, "If the German soldiers knew we hid two Jewish men, they would have killed us all."

Polish historian Eva Hoffman, states that, "The Poles, in the Nazi hierarchy, were next only to Jews and Gypsies in the order of inferior races – slated for complete subjugation and...eventual extermination. The Poles, then, were fighting against just about hopeless odds, while the Jews in their midst were being exterminated with no odds on their side at all."[56]

Referring to attempts in occupied Poland to help Jews survive, Hoffman states, "This was help offered at enormous risk, since sheltering Jews carried with it the penalty of death."[57]

Eleanor was still on guard at the window when Haim and Matus vanished before dawn. A day later, Eleanor and Chester found the houses in the Jewish section empty. They never learned if Haim and Matus had reached the forest, a haven for allies and enemies alike: Jews escaping Germans, Russians escaping Germans, Poles escaping Germans and Russians.

People in town were also in danger. Eleanor said, "Russian partisans hiding in haystacks killed some German officers. The Germans surrounded Naliboki to burn us alive in a barn for revenge. They did that to people in the village of Kleciszcze. I was at your parents' house, the other side empty now. Your father was digging an underground shelter to save us. A German woman married to a Polish man convinced the Germans it was the Russian partisans who killed their officers."

The reprieve was short-lived. Unable to subdue the Russian partisans in the forest, the German soldiers left the area. For now, with one enemy gone, the partisan fury turned upon the local population on May 8, 1943. Uncle Józef Byczkiewicz saw the slaughter in Koniec, the south end of town. Aunt Eleanor and Uncle Chester faced it in Kamionka, the north end.

Startled at dawn by gunfire, Chester stepped onto the porch, saw nothing, and went back in. Then the Russian partisans poured in from the woods, ran past the porch, and shot at the house next door. Their bullets penetrated the wooden walls and killed a neighbor's daughter who was asleep. Eleanor and Chester lay pinned to the floor for hours until the killing frenzy was spent. Chester then ran to town. He found his parents' home in ashes. The bodies of his father and brother charred beyond recognition. The sight was so repugnant, he asked Eleanor not to go to the funeral.

Naliboki resident Józef Lojko describes what led to the massacre. "German authorities had given an ultimatum to the people...to organise themselves in self-defence and not let the Russian partisans come to Naliboki for food, otherwise...they would burn down the whole town and deport the people to Germany....One of the young Polish officers,

Zenon Klimowicz, organised a defence policy... arranging a secret meeting with Russian commanders, one of these was named Wasilewicz, begging them not to come to Naliboki as the Germans threatened to burn the town if they did." [58]

Russian commander, Wasilewicz, agreed not to attack as the Poles and Russians tried to unite against the German forces. Lojko added, "Wasilewicz agreed and promised they would leave Naliboki alone...Russian and Polish partisans respected each other until the Russian partisans had grown much stronger... They wanted to diminish the Polish underground and join them or come under their command... The Polish commanders did not agree to surrender the Polish units to the Russians...The Russians executed one of the Polish officers...From that time the Polish partisans... operated at a distance from the Russians...I had already experienced what both Russians and Germans were doing... people were suffering on both sides." [59]

Surrounded by death, the euphoria of love and marriage gave Eleanor hope for a normal life someday. She got the man she wanted. They were building a house. They were not murdered that day. But they were about to lose everything except each other.

The Boys' New School Clothes

Eleanor held a secret in her heart known only to her husband.

After the May massacre and June deportations of single people, German soldiers returned in August 1943. They claimed to be evacuating villages for safety from Soviet partisans. Farmers would need their livestock in the new locations. Filomena Dubicka did not believe their promises. She saw no need to leave her home, the church where she was married, and the graveyard where her ancestors slept. After parent teacher meetings with my Grandmother Anna, she was sewing outfits for the day her three boys would start school. They would grow up and do something good for Naliboki.

She was a woman of strong will and wit, but this was different. She walked to town with a neighbor who had studied German in school. A friend told Eleanor she saw Filomena disheveled and acting disoriented as the girl told the German soldiers that this family could not be deported.

They had typhoid, an infectious and fatal disease. They told the girl to take Filomena home.

Filomena came home while hundreds were merging onto the meadow in the village of Jankowicze, three miles south of Naliboki. As she was making breakfast, a neighbor stopped by to see if her plan had worked. Yes, she convinced the soldiers to leave them alone. The neighbor left. Filomena called her husband and their three sons to the table. After breakfast, she would sit down to her favorite pastime – sewing school clothes for her boys.

As the family savored fresh baked bread and homemade jam, German soldiers approached the house. They walked in. One. Two. Three. Four. Five. Did the three boys see their parents' bodies go limp and fall. Or was it the parents who had to see their three boys sprawled out onto the clay floor? The soldiers lit a clump of straw, threw it into the house, and left. Twenty seconds to end five lives.

As five bullets ended Filomena's hopes, Eleanor and Chester's horse and wagon neared the meadow. The Lojko's wagon ahead of them was full of hay, food, pots and pans, and five children. The sick colt pulling the load lay down. Eleanor offered to watch their four-year-old girl. This would free the mother to calm the older children while the father lightened the load. As they reached the meadow, the gray sky spewed forth a nasty downpour. People scrambled for shelter under wagons. Eleanor tried to feed the child, but she refused. She put the girl under the wagon with baby Irene for the night.

Chester searched the soggy meadow in the morning. He found Józef, wife Józia, baby Sophie, and Grandmother Anna. They left with Eleanor and baby Irene in his horse and wagon. They met up with Grandfather Justyn's sister Sophia and her four adult children. One horse and wagon for twelve people, so most of them walked, but the Lojko family was nowhere in sight. While they slept in fields at night, Eleanor held a secret in her heart known only to her husband. She said, "My Lord, our house is burning, they are taking us to Germany by force, we have someone else's child, and I am pregnant."

This normally happy news did not feel happy. She cared for the little girl for three days, knowing there was another child who would need her. Then as they were packed into cattle cars, Eleanor saw the Lojkos, and the colt pulling a lighter load. What relief. As the group of twelve faced their darkest hour, fate was kindly taking them to the farm of Klaus and Erne Offe.

When quiet fell upon Naliboki, people who had been hiding in the forest found the burned bodies of two adults and three children in the ruins of Filomena's house. The boys' new school clothes, which the doting mother had sewn with care, were somewhere in that heap of ash. The boys would never grow up to do something good for Naliboki.

Prisoners of Klaus and Erna Offe

On Christmas Eve, the Offe's kindness began to blossom into friendship.

Two Polish prisoners of war, Johan Olechowski and Felix Matelski, came to the tiny train station in the town of Gribbohm and drove ninety people from Naliboki to a large farm. They were fed, given a place to sleep, and allowed to rest the next day. They then helped one hundred Russian women harvest potatoes, beets, and cabbage that would feed the German army. Eleanor said, "We got potatoes out of the ground on our hands and knees. After we harvested the crops, nearby farmers came to pick workers for their harvests. The *Bauer* put us aside so they wouldn't take us."

The farm owners were Klaus Offe, about sixty years old, his wife Erna Offe, about fifty, and two daughters, Helga and Elizabeth, in their early twenty's. Their son Eckert, in his mid-twenties, was in the army on the Russian front. Helping Klaus and Erna on their farm were Johan and Felix, five Russian prisoners of war trucked in daily, three German women domestics, a German man and his Polish wife, the twelve new Polish arrivals. Eleanor said, "A German woman with two children also lived there. The *Bauer* could not evict her while her husband was in the army, and she took what food she needed."

Chester added, "All Germans, even students who finished high school were sent to work on a farm for two years. Helga and Elizabeth went into the fields with us, but mostly fooled around and told jokes."

Foreigners replaced German men in farms, fields, and factories. American historian, Edward Homze, states that, "Well over eight million foreign workers were employed in the German war economy and most of them were forced. The term *forced labor (Zwangarbeit)*, or *slave labor*...included prisoners of war, voluntary workers from Germany's allies and the neutral states, workers recruited from northern and western occupied areas, and the brutally recruited workers from eastern Europe."[60]

Having lost their house and land, they were also denied their identity. According to British journalist, Neal Ascherson, the Soviet Union informed the Polish government-in-exile in London in January 1943 that all Poles that were living in the territories seized in 1939 were now Soviet citizens.[61]

This brought a town hall clerk to the farm who ordered my family to get their Russian *Ost* labels because they are now Russian. Klaus put a finger to his lips to say, "Don't argue now." After the man left, Klaus said to refuse the *Ost* label. The legal number of calories per day depends on a person's ethnic group. Russians got less food than Polish workers.

Felix drove my family to the town hall on his horse and wagon. Their steps echoed throughout the stone building as a tall young man led them swiftly past corridors and closed doors. They entered a room and, sitting at his desk, the clerk said in a clipped tone that they are now Russian. Józef said, "Occupied by Russia does not make us Russian. We are Polish. We will not wear the *Ost* label."

The clerk jumped up, grabbed Józef's lapel, and sputtered curses at Józef's nose. Józef felt a mist of spit on his face. Chester lunged across the desk and punched the clerk in the face! Years later, Eleanor still became agitated as she said, "Hitting a German! Oh, my God! Feliks went pale and shuffled us out. At the farm, Feliks ran to tell the *Bauer*. Klaus ran out, shaking his finger, hollering, 'Chester, what have you done? A concentration camp waits for you!'"

The dreaded punishment loomed large until Eleanor realized, "It wasn't ignored. The *Bauer* handled it quietly by giving the offended clerk a well-fed pig or calf, and we somehow got a "P" label for Polish. No one wore labels on the farm. Just in town."

Klaus and Erna understood that having lost their homes, how could their Polish workers also forfeit their identity? On Christmas Eve, they knocked on the door of the two-room apartment where the family of twelve lived. They brought smoked eel for the women, candy for the children, and beer for the men. Eleanor cried as she told me, "Their holiday wish was that we celebrate next *Wigilia* [Christmas Eve] in our own home and our own land. Such intelligent people. They knew our pain."

Chester added, "The government paid us twenty-two useless marks a month. German workers got around 80 marks and could shop for food. We weren't allowed in stores. Frau Erna bought food for us with ration cards. Toward the end, we could buy beer."

After they retired in America, my aunts and uncles applied for German pensions. Chester and Józef each got $52 a month. Eleanor tried through a lawyer, but he didn't find her work record. She said, "Probably the *Bauer* didn't enroll the women. And $52 a month is nothing for how hard we worked."

Baby John Comes into the World

We arrived in a cattle car, but they treated us like humans.

While hanging up laundry, Eleanor felt Erna Offe's gaze. Erna walked up to Eleanor. Pointing to her round stomach, she asked in German, "Are you pregnant?"

Having grasped some basic German, Eleanor said, "Yes, I was pregnant when they deported us."

Eleanor and Chester had heard that Polish children born in Germany were taken from their parents for possible Germanization. A pregnant woman on a nearby farm was sent back to Poland when she could no longer do heavy work. Her husband was kept working on that farm. Eleanor and Chester then learned that the woman sent back to Poland was struggling to feed her new baby and herself. With Naliboki in ashes, what would become of Eleanor? Or could their baby be taken from them?

Klaus put them at ease. They would all wait together for the new baby. He offered Eleanor an easier job. She could run the kitchen and be near her children. Or milk the cows. She said, "I was twenty-two. With Russians, Germans, and Polish to feed, it seemed too much responsibility. My cousin took the kitchen job. I milked the cows. Big mistake!"

Eleanor milked twenty cows each morning and afternoon alongside a Russian prisoner and a German worker. The two strong men would finish, sit on their stools, smoke cigarettes, and watch Eleanor milk her five or six remaining cows. When Erna sent daughter Helga to help, they would finish first and sit on their stools watching the men. But even with Helga's help, Eleanor would wake Chester at night to turn her over. Her hands were numb from milking twenty cows twice a day.

After milking the cows, Eleanor washed bulky milk cans, removed stable manure, and brought in hay. She shredded sugar beets, loaded them into a wheelbarrow, and pushed it to the trough for the cows. She came back to the apartment, fed and washed Irene, and milked twenty cows again. Eleanor said, "What was the big deal running the kitchen? My mother and aunt peeled the potatoes. Meat was rationed. Anyone could cook soup in a big pot. I regretted that decision."

The last month of her pregnancy, Eleanor was in the barn shredding beets. Seeing her struggle to walk, Klaus told her to stop working. He could send her to Itzehoe, a town twelve miles away with a hospital but it was being bombed. The convalescent center for the elderly had no doctor, but it was quiet. They could call a doctor if needed.

Resting in the convalescent center, the swelling in her legs went down. The patients tried to talk with her, but she was shy about speaking German. Chester visited her on Sundays. Despite legal calorie restrictions for Polish people, he brought her pork chops and pastry. Foreigners were forbidden to use bicycles. Klaus insisted if a policeman stops him, say you are with Klaus Offe and nothing else.

News of baby John's birth rippled through the convalescent home. A pink little face with eyes closed held by a beaming mother offered a respite from the wastefulness of war. Erna sent a fur coat for Eleanor to wear in the February cold and a wrap for the baby. When Feliks and Chester brought them back, everyone ran out to welcome them to their sane little enclave.

The Offe family had already embraced two Polish babies, Eleanor's daughter Irene and her brother Józef's daughter Sophie. The girls ate with them, and Helga and Elizabeth took them wherever they went. Eleanor said, "When Irene spoke German, the *Bauer*'s father shook with laughter. The cook said that when *Opa*, the grandfather, was in charge, he wouldn't even let the German children run around. Now, these babies softened the 90-year-old man's temper."

Eleanor and Chester wanted John baptized, and Klaus did not need to be asked. His family was Protestant, but he visited the Catholic priest in Itzehoe. The priest had to come discreetly to baptize a Polish baby. On his way, the sky opened. It was hard to be discreet trudging along on his bicycle in thunder and lightning. Klaus and Erna welcomed the priest, hung up his dripping coat, and put on the kettle.

Klaus kept him company. Erna and Eleanor bathed John
and put on the white clothes that Erna had prepared. With
muted pride, Eleanor and Chester brought their child to
meet the priest.

The priest led the procession from the main house
to the two-room apartment with a sense of occasion like a
bridal party entering a church. First, the beaming parents.
Then came Klaus, Erna, Helga and Elizabeth, Uncle Józef
and Aunt Józia, Grandfather Justyn's sister Zofia and her
four grown children, Feliks, Johan, and all the German
workers. Feliks and Aunt Józia were chosen as godparents.

The rain subsided to a soothing gurgle as they huddled
in this sacred moment, strangers bound by necessity and
friendship. They stood shoulder to shoulder as the wet priest
intoned the words of baptism bringing baby John into the
faith community. Eleanor said, "We were crying hard, all of
us, the Polish people, the German people. That priest came
just to baptize John. Not every *Bauer* would have arranged
this. We arrived in a cattle car, but they treated us like
humans."

I said, "I cry each time I read about this holy moment
in your little community. No labels. No thought of status.
Just people bound by their humanity celebrating a new life."

Conscience versus Demands of the Nazi Party

**Klaus was sent to a hard labor concentration camp for
Germans who disobeyed orders.**

Klaus and Erna rejected Hitler's empty promises of
glory. Packages of dried bread, barley, flour, and sugar from
their kitchen fed my family. My non-smoking aunts and
uncles planted tobacco. No questions asked. Eleanor said,
"We sent your parents food and dried tobacco. Your father
sold the leaves to people who made their own cigarettes.
With the money, he bought bread for you children."

Klaus and Erna let prisoners on nearby farms come
and sit by the coal burning stove. They were nourished by
warm soup, a piece of meat set aside for them, and human
kindness. She said, "They were Ukrainian, Polish, Russian.
Some had little to eat, some had a spot in a pigsty, or a
cold room near the cows in the barn. Their lights went off at
seven. Klaus left the lights on all evening."

Chester and Eleanor Dubicki holding daughter Irene and son John at the Klaus and Erna Offe farm. Gribbohm, Germany 1945

Klaus and Erna refused to join the Nazi party, but had to supply produce, grain, milk, and livestock to feed the German army. Klaus, Eleanor, and a Russian prisoner set out to herd twenty castrated bulls three miles to the train station. Klaus rode in a carriage harnessed to his wife's horse. The two foreigners herded the bulls. When out of sight, Klaus got off, took the whip from Eleanor, and put her in the carriage. The two strong men herded the bulls. Nearing the station, they exchanged places.

They took turns each week boiling laundry in a washroom while the children played outside. When it was the German week for laundry, they included John's diapers. When the little boy of a German woman was outside hitting Irene, Erna ran into the yard and scolded him. Eleanor said, "Frau Offe scolded the mother too, told her we have no reason to mistreat these people."

Polish people were not allowed in stores. Klaus and Erna shopped for all food not produced on the farm. Eleanor said, "Klaus brought us horse meat. The redness repulsed us. He said if we slaughter a pig, he doesn't know about it. We shared the pork with five Russian prisoners who ate with us. When that was gone, he "didn't know" we slaughtered a calf. If the authorities knew, they would hang him. Where would you find such kindness?"

As a tool of totalitarian government, Germans were to spy on foreigners and on each other. Someone noticed the kindness – the priest baptizing a Polish baby, workers from other farms seeking refuge, Eleanor riding in the carriage, Klaus ignoring the legal calorie allowances. I said, "My cousin Stefania told me how the Russian grannies were afraid their children would report them for praying."

Eleanor responded, "In Germany, parents were also afraid of their own children reporting them."

One Hitler admirer reported Klaus for holding back on government quotas and feeding his workers well. Klaus was arrested. An accusation from an ardent supporter of Hitler carried more weight than the word of a man who refused to join the Nazi party. Klaus was sent to a hard labor concentration camp for Germans who disobeyed orders. He cut down bamboo shoots thick enough to be roofing material. Klaus was released a few months later with the intervention of Erna's brother, an army general. Eleanor said, "When he came back so thin, he and Frau Offe were even better to us."

The man who put Klaus in the hard labor camp was not in the military. The uniform he wore with pomp and swagger was one reward for spying on civilians. When he died, he got a lavish funeral with full military regalia. Eleanor and others were in the barn feeding the cows. They looked out to see dignitaries in uniforms covered with medals marching with solemnity to the sound of a dirge. The Bauer came up to them and said, "Why are you watching this obscenity?"

Eckert Will Live

Soviet soldiers captured by the Germans dreaded being sent back to their own country.

People on farms were safer than my family in a forced labor camp on the front. But when bombs began showering Hamburg 50 miles away, lamps and dishes rattled and collided on the floor. Eleanor said, "We were working in the field. Erna would rush my mother and children into the bunker. If your stubborn grandmother refused, Erna grabbed the children and ran for the bunker."

As bombings intensified, Klaus and Erna worried that their son Eckert could be taken prisoner on the Russian front. Captured Soviet soldiers dreaded being sent back to their own country. They faced punishment or death for being caught by the enemy. Eleanor said, "Klaus and Erna said if that's how they punish their own boys, what will they do if they catch a German soldier?"

Klaus and Erna shared their anguish with their Polish prisoners, now friends. Feliks and Johan told Klaus to write his son to wear his shoes without socks. He could get frostbite and be removed from the front. Eleanor said, "They told us about the letter to Eckert. One day they came running to tell us. Eckert would live! Americans, not Russians, had captured him. He was in an army hospital behind the front lines with frostbite. We never met Eckert, but we felt like our own son had been saved."

As Eckert recovered in the American hospital, the German army was retreating. What to do with their "surplus prisoners?" Eleanor saw two ghoul-like creatures approaching the farm. They had black teeth, matted hair, and yellow skin. Coming closer, they vaguely resembled two teen-age boys. The guards had run away, and they were transported aimlessly in a packed cattle car for weeks. They lived by cutting off flesh from someone who had died and swallowed it for sheer survival. The cattle car was abandoned with the boys locked inside. Someone heard moans and got help. Survivors were roaming the countryside looking for shelter. After a month of food and rest, Wacek and Wiesiek looked like teen-age boys able to do farm work. Klaus let them stay.

When peace came on May 8, 1945, the people on the farm celebrated for three days with food and drink, knowing they must part. Describing the farewell, Eleanor cried. I cried too. They were thrown together by notions of racial superiority, but instead, their humanity had grown. She stood afraid and hungry on that misty September day in 1943. Two years later, the Polish and German people hugged and cried as they said good-bye. She said, "Klaus and Erna worried about Irene, Sophie, and baby John. They packed food and clothes. Elizabeth and Helga kissed the children hard. Erna hugged them a long time as if she couldn't let go."

Chester saw Klaus and Erna one more time. After the war, Chester traveled from city to city buying and selling goods. When he was in the area, he knocked on the door of the Offe family. They welcomed him with smiles and embraces. He ate with them and stayed the night. His German was fluent by then, so in the evening, they all sat in the Offe living room and talked like old friends.

From Refugee to U.S. Taxpayer

West Europeans still had countries. We had no place to go.

Leaving the Offe farm, the group of twelve, plus baby John, survived the perilous train ride described by Uncle Józef in the previous chapter. Arriving in the Mülheim Ruhr displaced persons camp with fewer suitcases but their children intact, they were among millions of homeless. American author Mark Wyman states that, "German prisoners of war were able to...return to their old neighborhood and to sympathetic countrymen. This was true as well for many of the foreign laborers, especially the Dutch, Belgians, French, Norwegians, Danes, and Italians...A reporter watching the exuberant Western Europeans pass along the highway in throngs noticed that "a sadder sight is presented by the Poles...the Polish current "sets toward the West" instead of toward Poland."[62]

Eleanor said, "West Europeans still had countries. Russia took Poland in the east and forced communism on Poland in the west. We had no place to go. People I know returned to Naliboki and faced poverty and hardship. Danusia, you saw for yourself when you went to Naliboki."

Eleanor, brother Józef, and sisters Helena and Mania stayed together for five years in five displaced persons camps. The urgency to resume normal lives grew each time Chester wrote asking his uncle in Connecticut to sponsor them. Like my Uncle Henry Mara, his uncle came to the United States before World War I and eventually owned his own farm. Chester kept writing, with no reply. When he began writing again,

Chester and Eleanor Dubicki with son John and daughter Irene. Connecticut 1950's

Eleanor snapped, "Can't you see they don't want us? Leave it alone."

He wrote again and did not tell her. He also tucked in a picture of little Irene and John. He checked the post office every day for months. Then one day he startled his wife, running, shaking, and yelling, "Papers! Papers! We got the papers! The papers! Papers for America!"

Eleanor and Chester were the first to leave for Connecticut in August 1949. Józef followed with his family. Mania had married Wincenty Szalczyk and they left for Canada. My family came to New Jersey in November 1950. Grandmother Anna was held back waiting for papers allowing her to enter the United States. Eleanor said, "If it wasn't for that picture of the children, we might not be here today. The aunt and uncle later told us how that picture melted their hearts."

Eleanor and Chester worked on the uncle's farm until a Polish neighbor found Eleanor a factory job with year-round work. She and her husband looked after the children until Anna arrived. Eleanor then worked at the Yantic Wool Mill where the manager was a Polish Jewish man who came to the United States at age nineteen. He learned the textile business in the Polish city of Łódz and often spoke with Eleanor. He proudly told her that, at age seventeen, he had stood next to Marshal Józef Piłsudski who had recreated Poland after it had been erased from the map of Europe for 123 years.

Eleanor learned to weave patterns in knit material on a complex machine. The going rate was 60 to 80 cents an hour, but she got $1.70 for her skilled work. When the factory moved to Boston, she took a local job as a drape maker for 14 years before retiring.

Reflections

We loved our country, but it is no longer the country we knew.

My aunt asked, "Are you curious about the things I am telling you?"

DC: *I can't get enough! But tell me, do you forgive what was done to you?*

(Long pause) Yes and no. Frau Offe protected us. The *Bauer* was a good man. Wiesiek from the abandoned cattle car settled in Detroit, Michigan. He came to Irene's wedding. He wrote to Klaus and Erna and they always asked about us, especially Irene, Sophie, and John. Even from a distance, we remained lifelong friends. We grieved and prayed for them when the *Bauer* and Frau Offe died in the mid 1960's. God was merciful for putting us together.

We weren't brutalized like some. Your cousin, Casimir Wolan, was in the Naliboki Home Army. Along with our neighbor, he was imprisoned at Bergen-Belsen concentration camp. Our neighbor survived. He told us that as the guards were marching them, he saw Casimir's eye hanging from his face before they finished him off. I don't know what those people would say about forgiveness.

The Russian partisans were our worst nightmare. Poland is free now, but with Naliboki part of Belarus and under communism, I am grateful not to be there. We loved our country, but it's no longer the country we knew. We are American citizens. Our children were educated here. We like this way of life. I would be curious to see Naliboki again, but I don't miss it and we were better off than some.

Eleanor paused to get her emotional bearings. She then intoned the song I have known all my life that opened the parent-teacher meetings at the Naliboki school. My grandmother's alto and the forester Szerbik's deep bass were with us in spirit as I joined her in singing:

Nie rzucim ziemi skąd nasz ród.	We won't abandon the land of our birth.
Nie damy pogrześć mowy.	We won't let our language be buried.
Polski my naród, Polski lud.	We are a Polish nation, Polish people.
Polski szczep Piastowy	Descendents of our Piast ancestors.
Nie damy by nas zgnębił wróg	We won't be vanquished.
Tak nam dopomóż Bóg.	So help us God.
Tak nam dopomóż Bóg.	So help us God.

She concluded, "Danusia, the first morning in America Chester looked out the window and said, 'My God, as soon as Poland is free, I'm going back to her.' That was 1949 and we are still here."

Eleanor Byczkiewicz Dubicki was born on March 27, 1921 in Naliboki and passed away in January 2018 in Yantic, Connecticut. Chester Dubicki was born on November

29, 1915 and passed away on May 7, 1993 in Yantic. He worked at the Thermos Company in Norwich for thirty years. Their late daughter Irene worked in retail and their son John worked as a business manager. He earned a Purple Heart and a Bronze Medal for Valor in Viet Nam. They had five grandchildren. I learned about Eleanor's life during my visits to Connecticut.

The Church of the Assumption which the author's father helped build in the 1930's, renovated in the 1990's. The interior of the church prepared for the consecration in 1994.

Endnotes

52 Adam Zamoyski, *The Polish Way: A Thousand-year History of the Poles and their Culture* (NY: Hippocrene, 1996), pp. 56-57.

53 Ibid

54 Ibid

55 Dagnosław Demski, *Naliboki i Puszcza Nalibocka. Zarys dziejów i problematyki* (Warsaw: Instytut Archeologii i Etnologii PAN, Etnografia Polska, t.XXXVIII: 1994, z. 1-2) p. 60.

56 Eva Hoffman, *Shtetl: The Life and Death of a Small Town and the World of Polish Jews* (NY: Public Affairs, Perseus Book Groups, 2007) pp. 6-7.

57 Ibid

58 Józef Lojko, *The Wound That Never Healed* (Kidderminster, England, 1999) pp. 139-140.

59 Ibid

60 Michael Berenbaum, ed., *A Mosaic of Victims: Non-Jews Persecuted and Murdered by the Nazis.* Edward Homze, "Nazi Germany's Forced Labor Program, (NY: NYU Press, 1990) pp. 37-38

61 Neal Ascherson, *The Struggles for Poland* (NY: Random House, 1987) p. 122.

62 Mark Wyman, *DPs: Europe's Displaced Persons, 1945-1951* (Ithaca: Cornell UP, 1998) pp. 17-20.

Chapter 12 Mania
A Quota to Fill

The number of able-bodied workers determined whether a family was sent to a forced labor camp or to work on a farm in Germany. Single people, like my Aunt Mania, toiled in factories or as domestic servants. Two months before Helena, Józef, and Eleanor were deported, their nineteen-year-old sister Mania left at gun point with only the homespun clothes on her back to work in a German factory.

I knew her after the war as upbeat, except when she spoke about wartime hunger. Then, her face twisted in pain, tears hugging her cheeks. She patted them dry and continued in a soft voice. We met in the safety of her American kitchen as she made delicious soups from what seemed like a few carrots and potatoes. While we ate, I asked about the delicate matters of life I could not ask anyone else. Over a bowl of sorrel or beet soup, our girl talks ended either in tears or in laughter.

My godmother's small size and soft manner housed a core of power and wisdom. She knew that one's worst enemy is bitterness of heart and soul. When I asked about her abductors, she replied, "Forgive us our trespasses, as we forgive those who trespass against us." Amazing.

Bolsheviks Are Coming

Your life is better. We have liberated you.

My Aunt Mania said, "The Russians and Belarussians east of the Niemen River seemed like anyone else to me. People are people no matter what you call them. But I was scared when I heard the Bolsheviks were coming. Soviet tanks crushed our smooth cobblestone streets in town, and my cousin, Stefan Byczkiewicz, was among the boys forced into the Red Army."

Despite Red Cross attempts to find him, they could only guess young Stefan died fighting a war he did not believe in. Mania added, "They said our sons and fathers would return, but it was all treachery. They cut the electric pole wires, and for two years, they stole our food and fed us lies at required meetings. They said Stalin is wonderful. Your life is better.

We have liberated you. From what? They brought us poverty and put-up signs saying they are our friends. Like hell, our friends. They filled their bellies on our food and made sure Stalin had his share while we went hungry."

The first invader had a local Jewish man run the big dairy, and Mania was put in charge of a small dairy they set up on her parents' land. Farmers had to bring milk based on how many cows they had. Mania weighed, recorded, and poured the milk into large cans. Another woman loaded it onto the horse and wagon and took it to the main dairy. Meat was scarce, so whole milk provided dietary fat. But the Russians separated the cream, kept some milk, and gave back skimmed milk to the farmers.

For young girls, such robbery was secondary to rape. The German army appeared in 1941, pushing the Russians into the forest. These partisans snuck back into town as guerrilla fighters to steal food and rape. Mania said, "They went into a house, held down the husband, and raped the woman. They attacked women working in the fields. We girls covered ourselves and tried to look old."

Unable to defeat the Russian partisans, the German soldiers left temporarily. This opened the way for hundreds of angry partisans to sweep in on May 8, 1943, burn half of Naliboki, and kill 128 people. I was born twenty days later and baptized with Mania cradling me in her arms. In June 1943, the soldiers returned to kidnap young people. By August 1943, as Naliboki burned, my godmother was already working for two months in a German factory.

The Day the Music Died

During this orgy of killing, I was sleeping in my mother's womb.

The German invasion lessened the chance of rape but had its own cruelty. Benedict Klimowicz had taught himself to play the violin. A man in his twenties, he played for hours as teen-agers danced Sunday afternoons on the meadow near Mania's home. She danced to Benedict's violin until Russian partisans killed eight Latvians, German allies, during a food raid. Mania said, "The Germans laid them out near the lake and made our women wash them before burial. Poor Benedict had no shoes. He took a pair off a dead Latvian. Someone told the Germans."

Mania heard the same account I was told by one of Benedict's relatives. German soldiers took him to the forest. Some local people were working there and watched secretly for fear of their own lives. The soldiers made Benedict dig a pit. He dug the pit and asked if they were going to shoot him.

"Yes."

"Will you let me play the violin a while?"

"Play."

He played, "Kto cię w opiekę – He Who Seeks Your Protection."

Again, "Are you going to shoot?"

"Yes."

He played "W mogile ciemnej, śpisz na wieki – In a Dark Grave, You Sleep Eternally." As the notes of this well-known dirge filled the forest, a bullet found his heart. The last note fell silent. He swayed, then hit the pit caressing his beloved violin.

Benedict's music died as German soldiers were rounding up the Jewish population in 1942. Mania said, "Christians and Jews lived near each other. A Jewish man and his son came to buy our geese. When he was ready to butcher them, we went to his house to pluck the feathers. We bought biscuits, sewing needles, and soap from Jewish shop owners. They bought berries we picked in the forest. We got along but didn't marry. They didn't come to our church. We didn't go to their synagogue."

Looking back, Mania realized there were tensions not apparent to her as a young girl. She said, "The Jews had grievances that came out when the Russians invaded, so they welcomed the Russians. When the Germans came and marched the Jews through town, past our house to the woods, we were terrified for our lives. The Jews who escaped into the forest joined the Russians for protection, and together they wiped out our self-defense units. I heard that some of the Jews hiding in the forest left money with people in town for safekeeping. They returned during the May 1943 massacre and demanded the money from a certain couple. They didn't have it, so they killed them both. And their stores had been robbed. It was a time for settling grievances."

When the massacre hit the south end of town, Mania lived with her mother Anna, her brother Józef, his wife Józia, and their baby Sophie. My mother was expecting my birth, so my two-year-old brother Van was with them. Awakened by gunfire at dawn, they put Sophie and Van under a bench by the wall and covered them with pillows. Mania crawled under the bench. As the babies slept, the adults said the rosary. Feeling cramped, she crawled out just as a partisan smashed the window above her with his rifle. She said, "The glass cut my face, blood covered my clothes. I saw through the window a partisan laughing at the broken glass, then ran back to the street. A Jewish woman cursed our neighbor Hodyl for being in the self-defense unit, then shot him dead in front of our window."

When the fury subsided, Mania said, "I saw Russian and Jewish partisans going past our house toward the forest. They had wagons full of food, clothes, and livestock. I then ran north through fields to avoid dead bodies and burned houses. An hour later, I reached Kamionka and found your parents and five children alive. The next day, two Russian partisans came and took the cow from our barn."

During this orgy of killing, I was sleeping in my mother's womb. Coming into the world surrounded by killing on the ground and bombs in the air may be why loud noises from ambulances, fireworks, and sirens make me tense as I go into survival mode until the apparent danger is over.

Nineteen and Alone

She knelt before the soldier towering above her, and pleaded that he not take her daughter.

I was born twenty days after the Soviet massacre and baptized quickly. Before Mania could fuss over her godchild, German soldiers returned to kidnap young people for work in Germany. Mania and Józef hid in the field of their Uncle Antoni Byczkiewicz whose son, Stefan, had disappeared forever into the Soviet army. They sat for hours, then crept home to feed the animals and have supper.

After a supper of beet soup and boiled potatoes, Mania was knitting and Józef was reading, both sitting on wooden benches he had built. Their mother Anna was sewing a shirt from home spun linen. The roar of trucks broke the silence. With father Justyn's death, Józef was the man of the house doing the heaviest work. If abducted, how would the women manage? Hearing the thump of boots, he bolted out the back door. He heard the bullets whiz past him.

With Józef out of reach, the soldiers set up tables on the street and ordered people outside to be registered.

Pointing to Józia holding baby Sophie, the soldier asked Grandmother Anna in Polish who she was. Anna replied, "This is my daughter-in-law."

"Whose child is she holding?"

"My son and daughter-in-law's."

The soldier continued, "Where is her husband?"

Not knowing if Józef was dead, wounded, or lying safely in the potato field, Anna said, "In the army."

Pointing to Mania, the soldier asked, "Who is this?"

"My daughter."

A single girl. He grabbed her. Anna shoved her petit frame between him and Mania. She knelt before the soldier towering above her and pleaded that he not take her daughter. He pushed her and left. Anna told Mania, "Go to the stable, turn a sheepskin coat inside out, and hide with the sheep."

"No! They steal our livestock for food. If they come to steal sheep, they could shoot me by mistake."

Trucks rumbled past the house. As Mania glimpsed some friends on those trucks, two soldiers burst into the house to fill their quota. Mania heard her mother's painful moan. Her husband had recently died. Her son could be dead in the field. Her daughter was being kidnapped. Mania whispered to her mother, "Don't cry. I won't abandon our Blessed Mother. She won't abandon me."

The soldiers drove Mania to a truck. She said, "I was nineteen, wore a homemade blouse, skirt, and shoes on my bare feet. I couldn't even grab a piece of bread. We rode past the wheat and tobacco I had planted for your father. I learned later how he tried to comfort my mother. He promised when they get a letter from me, he would send me a food package. But your family was next."

Mania was put into a ghetto where Jewish prisoners had been kept before their executions. Twelve girls were squeezed into a closet-like room. They all shared food from home, although Mania had nothing to offer. A few days later, guards were yelling, "Raus polische Schwein, get moving you Polish pigs," as they were pushed into a cattle car.

During stops on the way to Germany, guards gave out salty soup to thirsty people. When no one ate it, a soldier screamed in Polish that they are obstinate Poles. Mania said, "I had no sense of time. The train stops. We run out to go in some bushes. Everything inside you is dry. Before you're done, the train starts to move. We run to jump in. We can't be left in this no man's land."

They were unloaded at a transit camp with Russian and Ukrainian prisoners. Mania stood in line for a piece of bread and soup. A man in front of her dropped dead from hunger. They slept in barracks on flea infested wooden pallets where earlier prisoners had carved their names. Mania said, "I saw carved in Russian, 'Whoever wasn't here, will be. Whoever was, will never forget.' Your family was brought there two months later and saw my name on one of the pallets."

They were led to a building at the German border. Her face twisted in pain, she said, "We had to strip naked. We had to lift our arms, you know, people didn't shave. A man sitting on a chair put disinfectant under my arms and between my legs with a foul-smelling brush. They checked my scalp for fleas. Some people had their heads shaved. We went into a room like a shower and were sprayed with DDT. We put on our clothes and got into the cattle cars. They could do anything with us."

The Iron Furnaces

East Europeans – Russian, Ukrainian, and Polish – got less food, did heavier work.

The cattle car stopped near the Dutch border at Duisburg Hamborn, county of Westphalia. Three more women from Naliboki were added, making them a group of fifteen. A truck took them to the Blechwaldswerk factory. Each got a blanket, a pair of wooden shoes, one blouse, and a pair of slacks. They slept on wooden beds and straw mattresses in a low barrack with a coke stove, a sooty by-product of burned coal. Mania said, "I had never worn slacks. At first, it felt strange."

Workers fell into three categories. German men beyond military age earned salaries, bathed at the factory after work, put on a suit, and went home to their families. The second category were prisoners of war. West Europeans – French, Italian, Dutch, and Belgians – were fed better, got packages from home, and wore civilian clothes. East Europeans – Russian, Ukrainian, and Polish – got less food, did heavier work, and wore work uniforms.

The third category were civilians like Mania. The commandant tried to label them as Russian, until the interpreter, a woman from Naliboki, convinced him to let them wear the 'P' label for Polish. But he enforced the law harshly. Mania said, "My friend and I weren't wearing the 'P.' He took us to his office and hit us in the face so hard I lost my balance."

Foreign workers sustained the German war effort on farms and in factories like this one with its huge furnaces for smelting iron. The smelt iron was poured into machines that expelled table-size sheets to build airplanes. Mania said, "I flattened each hot sheet by moving it from side to side with tongs and a leather piece wrapped around my hand. We worked in three shifts for nine hours. No breaks, a little water, and never enough food."

On Sunday, potatoes and red cabbage was considered a good dinner. During the week, Polish workers got cabbage or turnip soup and provisions for three days at a time: three bread slices, a pat of margarine, a few teaspoons of sugar, and a slice of Blutwurst – a grain and meat by-product. Tears ran down Mania's cheek as she said, "I could eat it in one gulp. But I put it away. Go back. Smell it. Nibble on it. I drink water and go to work. But if one of us got food, we shared it with each other."

The better-fed French and Italian prisoners of war sometimes brought them food in a small canister. The women had learned enough German to sit and talk with them while sharing the food. When the *Lagerfuehrer* did room inspections, their benefactors left via a window in the barrack. All this time, Mania kept writing to learn if brother Józef was alive. A woman in Naliboki came across one of the letters and wrote that Naliboki was burned and her family was in Germany. But no word about Józef.

One day, Mania got a letter post marked Schleswig-Holstein, near the Danish border. Relief! Józef was alive! He and his family, sister Eleanor and her family, and their mother Anna were working on a German farm. Mania said, "Some Polish men were forced into the Russian army or into the German army. They met people on their marches, took addresses. If they ran across their relatives, they shared the addresses. That's how we found each other."

Mania wrote to Józef and Eleanor that my parents and their six children were in a forced labor camp on the front. We soon got food packages from the kitchen of Klaus and Erna Offe, the German owners of the farm where her brother and sister were working. This food helped keep us alive.

Guardian Angels

Going from prisoner to young lady was complete by hiding the "P" on their clothes.

Contact between Polish and German workers was forbidden. Armed guards stood watch to make sure. But some of the German men shared food secretly. Voice trembling, Mania said, "A German man walked past, pointed to a ledge, and whispered, 'Butterbrot, essen.' By then I knew this meant, 'Bread with butter, eat.' I swallowed the bread and went back to work."

One man went past and whispered in Polish that his name is Staś. Some days later, he whispered that his mother wants to meet her. The women sometimes got Sunday passes to leave the barrack, and the next week, he whispered, "Look for me by the bridge on Sunday."

By then, Mania and a friend each had a skirt and blouse. Going from prisoner to young lady was complete by hiding the "P" on their clothes. Unlike the grimy factory worker, at the bridge stood a stylish man in suit and hat. Staś walked toward the tram station. They followed and entered the tram. They sat apart, pretending not to notice him. The tram stopped, he walked out. They strolled behind. He entered an apartment building. In case someone was watching, they lingered and looked at something far off, then went in. Standing in the doorway, he said, "Come, mother is waiting."

Mrs. Ceglarek was short and stocky with a round face and warm embrace. Mr. Ceglarek was thin, tall, and a man of few words. Staś had a younger brother who was in the German army, both of them born in Germany. His German wife had been sent to a farm for safety. Mrs. Ceglarek said, "Come into our humble apartment. Tell us about yourselves. You must be hungry."

The Ceglareks became Mania's guardian angels. Another Polish German family took Mania's friend under their care. On Sundays when Mania could get a pass, a real dinner waited for her along with some motherly care. Mania said, "I couldn't keep eating without helping, so I washed her windows. Then, she had me lie down and covered me with the feather quilt. Such sweet sleep. She wasn't repulsed I might have lice. We washed every chance against fleas and lice."

Mania was the daughter Mrs. Ceglareks had wanted. She invited Mania to Wigilia, Christmas Eve supper. With nothing good enough to wear on the holiest night of the year, my aunt declined. When Mrs. Ceglarek coaxed the reason out of her, she gave Mania one of the daughter-in-law's good dresses. She came properly dressed for a few sacred hours with her guardian angels.

The iron smelting factory was near Kirchhellen where we were kept. Despite the harsh slap for not wearing the "P" label, the *Lagerfuehrer* let her and her friend visit us. Mania said, "Two German men were our guards. They were decent, paid for our train tickets, bought your mother flowers. They went to a bar while we visited. I lived on soup and saved the sugar, margarine, and kielbasa from the Ceglareks for you six children. We asked the German men to leave us there. They said they would pay with their heads if they didn't bring us back."

Bombs and Phosphorus

Mania did not know she had already met her future husband.

Mania's visits to the Ceglareks stopped abruptly. By spring 1945, Allied and German forces were trying to bomb each other out of existence. Hearing the wail of an air raid siren, Mania and her friends grabbed their precious civilian clothes and raced for the bunker. They sat up all night with no supper to the pounding of explosives. The six Ukrainian women they had befriended did not leave in time. A bomb shattered their thin bodies and moved the ground with enough force to seal off one end of the bunker. Another bomb shoved enough soil to seal off a barrack door. As the women left the bunker in the morning, an airplane dropped low to the ground shooting at them from a machine gun. They ran for the bushes, heads hung low, bullets whistling by.

Mania said, "The Ukrainian women wanted to live, but three Russian men gave up. Refused to leave their barrack. A bomb fell on them. It didn't explode, but the force threw one of them up against the wall. He burst open, skin, bones, and blood. The legs of the other two flew into the air without their bodies. But I saw more death in Naliboki from Russian partisans. In Germany, they covered it up fast. An ambulance removed pieces of the men; guards cleaned

Women abducted to work in the iron smelting factory, liberated and wearing civilian clothing. Maria Byczkiewicz is on the left sitting in a chair. Germany 1945

up the rest. Russian prisoners defused the bomb that didn't explode. If they succeed, fine. If they are killed, the guards don't care."

I said, "Human bodies bursting open like pumpkins. I'm amazed you came out of it so normal."

She added, "That was just the beginning. One night the *Lagerfuehrer* woke us up shouting "Fire." An Allied plane dropped phosphorus on the barrack we lived in. We ran out just as a bomb smashed the barrack. I hit the ground. The barrack exploded. Another bomb covered us with soil and flying debris. We yelled to each other, 'Are you alive?' One by one, fifteen shaky voices answered, "Yes." The factory was gone. Only the tin bowls and spoons we ate from with the swastika survived."

Wincenty Szalczyk and his friends at another factory had heard about Polish girls working nearby, and sometimes visited on Sundays. Viewing the explosions in a distance, the young men rushed by tram to see if their potential girlfriends were alive. The women stood embarrassed in nightshirts until guards brought them factory uniforms. Mania and Wincenty glanced at each other as the women were loaded onto a truck. Mania did not know she had already met her future husband.

Mania survived the phosphorus, but she was cut off from the Ceglareks. Hard as she tried when peace came, she never found her guardian angels. She never again sat at Mrs. Ceglarek's table or felt her warm embrace. If they lived, they never knew what became of the girl they loved like a daughter.

With the barrack in pieces, the women were trucked to work as domestics for German soldiers who did factory maintenance in town. They lived in a complex of makeshift shelters in a forest for safety. The women boiled and scrubbed the men's laundry on a washboard. They mended their clothes. As they cooked, they increased their own meager rations. Mania said, "One woman puts a potato in her pocket, another does the same. One skims some fat off the soldiers' food. We cook potatoes in the metal pan we use to wash. Hearing the *Lagerfuehrer's* voice, we hide our supper under a bed."

Surplus Prisoners

Walking for days, the rain drenched Mania's clothes, the sun dried them.

When bombs reached the forest, the women hid under a railroad trestle with the kitchen manager whose family was evacuated to a farm. He welcomed them and added brick walls for protection. But when his wife returned, he was embarrassed to tell them that she did not want her children near Polish women. Mania said, "We found a big water cistern, climbed in, replaced the cover, and sat on the pipes. By then, we weren't afraid of much, except the bombs. That terrified us to the end."

As Germany was losing the war, the soldiers who did factory maintenance disappeared. Amid the chaos, other soldiers on horseback showed up with snarling dogs. They marched Mania and other prisoners away from the front. Mania said, "Rain drenched my clothes, sun dried them. We slept under fences, begged for food if guards weren't looking. Some gave bread; some said get out, you Polish swine. I ate a type of raw beets used to feed animals, then fell to the ground with pain. Too weak to carry my girl civilian clothes, I left them on the road."

On the tenth day, they collapsed under some trees. Mania said, "We didn't care if we lived. But they abandoned the infirm and kicked the rest of us in the ass to get moving. They fed us at some farm a big pot of potatoes with peels. We slept on straw in the stable. In the morning, we opened the creaky door. No soldiers. No dogs. No bombs. Was it over?

Everyone went looking for food."

Walking down a dirt road, Mania saw a small dairy. She needed food. The German couple with two children and a grandmother needed a worker. She fed sheep and pigs, dug up potatoes, cleaned house, cooked, and polished the children's shoes for school. They ate together, then she slept deeply in a clean cozy room with a bed and feather quilt. One day, she was feeding animals when the grandmother ran into the yard, bewildered by two men screaming at her. Familiar with Russian, Mania asked what they wanted. The war was over. They were killing and robbing bad Germans. She convinced them this family was good to her. They went on to plunder the next farmer.

One Sunday, she walked into town. She saw American soldiers putting people onto trucks. It made her uneasy. She had been put on a truck and kidnapped from home. She asked a woman, "Who are these men and why are they putting people on trucks?"

She said, "American soldiers. Taking us to refugee camps. You'll get food and a place to stay."

Mania knew she had to leave the German family, but not yet. A bond was forming between them and their accidental visitor. Laughing, she described the parents and children teaching her to ride a bicycle. So their inevitable parting was sad, like the sadness Eleanor and Józef felt leaving the Offe family in Gribbohm. Carrying a sack of food and clothes the German family had given her, Mania walked into town. She hopped onto a truck, not knowing that my father and her mother's brother, Ferdinand, had been going from camp to camp for months looking for her.

Two Reunions in One Day

My mother struggled to connect this woman's face with that of her lost sister.

Two woman standing next to her on the truck were talking about a displaced persons camp in some place called Muelheim Ruhr. When the barrack at the iron smelting factory exploded, Mania and Wincenty glanced at each other as she was loaded onto a truck. But who thought of romance? Not while being marched around the countryside with snarling dogs. Wincenty survived such a march and was a security guard at the Muelheim Ruhr displaced person's camp. Mania

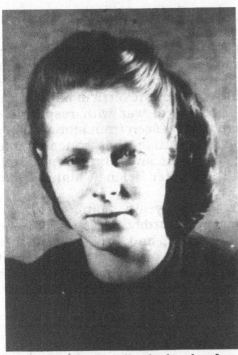

Mania Byczkiewicz after finding her family at the Muelheim Ruhr displaced persons camp. Germany 1946

said, "The truck pulled in. He saw me. He ran after the truck yelling, "My pal, my buddy. Where have you been, my pal?"

When the truck reached the registration tent, the search for Mania was over. Still amazed to be standing next to Wincenty, she was told that her sister Helena, husband Michał, and their six children had found shelter at this camp. Wincenty walked her over to the barrack where my family was living. As she entered the room, my mother struggled to connect this woman's face with that of her lost sister. Then came embraces, tears, and talking long into the night.

The next morning, Mania joined my father and her Uncle Ferdinand to look for brother Józef and sister Eleanor. Nearing the farm in Gribbohm, a man standing at the end of the train car could have been her brother's double. He was returning her stare! Józef had been visiting friends, and happened to be on that train, that day, that time! The universe was looking out for them. Walking to the farm, they learned how the war had forced itself upon each of them. My father and Uncle Ferdinand had been on the front in forced labor camps. Mania's brother and sister had been working on the farm they were now approaching. At nineteen, Mania was alone in an iron smelting factory.

An hour later, the owners Klaus and Erna Offe and their two daughters welcomed them to the farm. For three days, between farm chores and packing, the German and Polish people celebrated the end of the war. Then came time for the unwilling actors in this drama to find new homes. They would have to create the rest of their life story away from Naliboki, something they had never expected to do.

Eleanor and Józef had waited with dread in the autumn mist at the Gribbohm train station. Two years later, they cried and embraced the German friends they had come to love. Sixteen people climbed onto an open wagon hitched to the tractor. In addition to my father, Mania, and Ferdinand, the group of twelve was now thirteen with the birth of baby John. Felix and Johan, Polish prisoners of war with responsible jobs on the farm, drove them to the Essen train station. They stood for hours at the crumbling station, then squeezed into a packed train. Reaching the Mülheim Ruhr camp, Józef, Eleanor, and Mania joined their sister Helena. Mania could finally be my real godmother.

Robbed of her youth for two years, Mania never sat out a dance at the canteen on Saturday nights. Someone accidentally stomped on her hand, and broke one of her fingers. A few days later, we were assigned to a different barrack. The floor had to be washed before moving in. With Mania nursing a broken finger, Wincenty washed the floor. He began visiting her, but their courtship had no frills.

Mania Becomes a Bride

Their wedding dinner was canned goods from the United Nations relief packages.

Wincenty proposed, the family approved, and Mania accepted without any of the fuss made over the bride – no bridal shower, fancy gown, bridesmaids, reception, gifts, or little nest of her own to feather. It was not the spirited feasting for three days given to her brother Józef and her sister Eleanor at their weddings in Naliboki. Let's see what Mania was missing.

The dowry was settled before the wedding. Józef brought over Józia's wooden wardrobe full of linens, clothing, and towels woven and sewn by her and her mother. The cow from Józia's parents was already in the stable. Mania said, "People gave whatever dowry they could afford, sheep or pigs, so the bride had something of her own in her new household."

Before the big day, food was grown, gathered, marinated, dried, cooked, or baked. Animals were slaughtered. After the church ceremony, the groom's family and bridal party were driven by horse and wagon to the bride's parents for a dinner that would join them as one family. Children along the way cheered as the bridal party threw them small coins and candy. The next feast was at the home of the groom's parents where the newlyweds would live. During the ride, the maid of honor held a picture of Jesus or the Blessed Mother, draped with cloth. Reaching the groom's home, the maid of honor entered and said, "Praise be the name of Jesus." Everyone replied, "Forever and ever." His parents removed the cloth and hung up the picture. Mania said, "We put up holy pictures on walls. They hide holy pictures here and put up the Beatles."

The wooden houses were small, so friends came later for dancing and refreshments. For Józef's wedding, the musicians gathered at his uncle's larger house across the street. The wooden floor was better for dancing than the clay floor in my grandmother's house. In summer, they danced outside. A German plane had crash-landed, and all three officers survived. Hearing about the wedding, they decided to come. Mania said, "They had Józef lock up their guns in the grain bin. Then they ate their fill. Mother brewed kwas, a drink from rye bread, hops, and yeast. Did they like it! They kept saying, 'Mother, more wine.' They drank it in pitchers."

The German officers ate, took back their guns, and left. Mania said, "A man who had too much kwas started a brawl in the crowded house. Your father pointed a knife to scare him. Your mother grabbed baby Van. You weren't born yet. Eleanor and I took the older children outside. The Germans returned and dragged the troublemaker from under the table. Standing with a torn pant leg, he begged not to shoot him. They kicked his behind and shoved him out the door."

Unruffled, the guests went across the street to dance.

The girls in Naliboki became brides in the little wooden church built in 1636 by the Radziwill family and rebuilt in 1699. Mania was the first in many generations not to be married in the 17th century church. She married Wincenty in a makeshift church, and their wedding dinner was canned goods from United Nations relief packages. They lived with my family in two rooms. When Mania became pregnant, there was no baby room to decorate. No cute little outfits and blankets to choose. No magazines or books to tell her what to expect. Soon after Steve was born, we were all sitting in a truck taking us to the next displaced persons camp near the town of Raderhorst.

At that camp, Wincenty and a friend ran a beer and soda stand in a dance hall. He was saving money for passage to Australia or South America. When Irene was born, he did not want to raise his children as refugees. He left for Canada as an indentured laborer. Working for a year in a gold mine in Red Lake, Ontario, Wincenty saved enough for Mania, Steve, and Irene to join him. She said, "With only three months of mild weather, trucks crossed the frozen lake most of the year. I wanted to leave after Wincenty had some accidents. But at sixty-five cents an hour, it took five years to pay off his passage."

They left Canada with an addition, their youngest daughter Helen. To enter the United States legally, an American citizen had to sponsor them. Uncle Henry Mara opened his heart again and signed the papers. The family of five lived with my family of eight until Mania and Wincenty got factory jobs and rented an apartment in the town of South River. When they saved enough to buy a house in the city of Trenton, Mania worked in a factory all day. Then she cleaned, decorated, cooked, and grew flowers next to the cherry tree she planted – the first real nest befitting her status as wife and mother.

The First Nineteen Years

The tall, lanky keeper examined the knee, rubbed it with ointment, and whispered words Anna did not know.

Mania never returned to Naliboki, but lovingly reconstructed her nineteen years at home. She said, "Our town center was beautiful. We had a town hall, stores, a two-building school, infirmary, community center, Catholic church, synagogue, a Radziwill family estate, and a large open space to gather on market day. The policeman on bicycle had a rifle but rarely dealt with crime. If he saw animal droppings or grass sticking out between the cobblestones in front of your house, you got a fine. But we kept the streets clean out of pride. It hurt to see our beautiful roads crushed by Russian tanks."

The brightly painted little wooden houses were tucked into yards full of vegetables, flowers, and fruit trees. People swept the streets clean for the weekend. The Jewish merchants closed their stores on Saturday and strolled along the miasteczko, the town center, in their good clothes. Stores were open the next day, and the Christians walked to church in their good clothes. Friends walked arm in arm, singing. They met in Skniut's tavern and tearoom or in the home restaurant of one of the Klimowicz women. Boys got into scrapes. Girls giggled and gossiped about the boys.

One day, as Mania left school, she saw people decorating the town. The President of Poland, Ignacy Mościcki, was coming. His visit was part of the history lesson, and children got cake to celebrate. Mania took hers home in her hand. Some children bumped into her. The cake fell on the ground. Mania said, "I had never had cake. I cried looking at the crumbs on the ground."

To Mania, the school my father helped build were the two most beautiful buildings in town. Children hung coats on hooks in the hall and left their shoes under the coats to keep the shining wood floors clean. The teacher's desk faced rows of benches for some twenty-five students, boys and girls sitting apart. With no running water, toilets were in another spacious building ventilated by large windows. The caretaker and his family lived on the grounds. He set up a volleyball net for recess. In winter, he stoked the tile stoves in the classrooms, and poured water onto a platform in the yard for sliding.

Mania was not an eager student like Józef and Eleanor. She did not miss school when she stayed home with a swollen knee. Her father took her to the doctor who began pushing on her knee. Mania screamed in pain. Justyn shoved him aside and carried his daughter home. Anna took Mania to the infirmary the next day. The tall, lanky keeper examined the knee, rubbed it with ointment, and whispered words Anna did not know. She took Mania home. He returned the next day before sunrise. He had Anna mix a leaf called tryputnik with sweet cream, apply the poultice, and cover it with a cloth. He walked back that night and reapplied the poultice with more incantations. He came the next morning before sunrise and did the same. He then told Anna, "I won't need to come back."

It was Sunday and Anna and Justyn took the other children to church while Mania slept all day. Justyn's sister across the street came in the evening. She removed the cloth, stained by a yellow secretion, and touched the knee. Yellow pus releasing fluid burst onto the ceiling. Mania said, "I have an indentation in that spot, but my knee never hurt again."

When Mania returned to school, she was offered a job by a Jewish family. The families depended on each other. The father and son came to the Byczkiewicz house to buy geese. When Mania's parents came to see Dr. Klimowicz or to shop, they left her in the care of the Machlis family. Mania liked staying with them, but one time, gloom filled the house. Both daughters were crying and kissing the father's black coat hanging by the door. Mania said, "They were beautiful children, and happy. It scared me to see them like that. On the way home, my parents told me their father had died."

The son came to the house after the funeral. He said that while his sisters do their chores all day, the mother is home alone. Could their little girl come to keep his mother company? Anna asked her daughter if she wanted to go. Mania sat staring at the floor, playing with the edge of her blouse. Her mother repeated the question. Her eyes still on the floor, Mania shook her head "no." She told me, "The house was dark, the sisters were crying and kissing the coat. I couldn't say I was afraid of the father's black coat. It was a stupid childhood fear."

I said, "As a child, you did not understand, but kissing the father's coat was not so unusual. My mother and sister Janka are gone now, but I kiss the quilts and pillowcases they made for me."

Four Seasons of Work

We carried our shoes to church so they would last.

Mania did not take the job and found no rest at home. She rose before dawn, helped prepare the daily bread, then walked half an hour to school. After school, she cut grass for the cows and pigs and picked sorrel leaves for the evening soup. The south end of town still lacked electricity, so sleepy little Mania did homework by a gas lamp. Sunday was a day of rest only after they cooked, fed the animals, and milked the cows. Mania said, "I worked at home, I walked to school, homework at night – too much for me. After fifth grade, I left school to work in the forest with my sister Eleanor. We spoke Polish, most girls east of the Niemen River spoke Belarussian, but we understood each other."

Our twelve-year-old working girl was fixated on a new pair of shoes. Her uncle had sewn a fine pair of leather boots for her. She forgot them outside and a rabbit chewed the soles. Another good pair would mean working two weeks. She said, "I bought a cheap pair after working a few days. We carried shoes to church so they would last, but I wore mine on a rainy day. My feet felt damp. I turned back. I would have reached the church barefoot. The soles were made of pressed paper. So, I worked for two weeks, then I bought a good leather pair. They were truly mine. I earned the money."

Working in the forest and doing daily chores at home, she also helped with seasonal work. In early spring, the family plowed fields and planted barley, wheat, rye, vegetables, and linen. They picked mushrooms in the forest, cleaned them, marinated some, and dried the rest. They picked wild berries, ate them, then cooked and stored the rest in little wooden barrels.

In summer, women harvested the linen and prepared it through many stages. Men sheared the sheep and took the wool to the washing machines owned by the Korzenko family. They then butchered some of the animals and tanned the hides. In late summer, women, men, and children were in the field harvesting grain to be ground at the mill for flour.

Schools closed for weeks in the fall so all hands could dig potatoes, as they still do today in Naliboki. Potatoes, cabbage, beets, and onions were kept in a cold storage cellar near the house. Embers from tile stove in the house kept the cellar from freezing. While sauerkraut was fermenting in barrels, they dug pits in the woods, lined them with straw, stored more potatoes, and covered the pit with soil to prevent frost. When the potatoes in the cold cellar were eaten, the pits were unearthed.

Once, as Mania and her father were opening a pit, she noticed a big dog run by. Chuckling, Justyn said it was a wolf with eyes like searchlights. They sneak into barns to kill sheep, chickens, or little pigs. And they made their way into local legend. Mania said, "There's a story about the Blessed Mother walking through the woods with a candle. The wolves saw her and ran away, so she protected the village. I'll recite a playful poem Józef wrote about them."

A wilczek nie cnota.	Don't expect a wolf to be polite.
Wyskoczył z za plota	He jumps the fence at night.
Chyc prosie za szyje	Grabs the little piggy's neck.
I już on nie żyje.	Poor thing becomes his snack.
A kto nabrał się strachu	So if you are afraid of his hoof,
Niech nocuje na dachu.	Sleep more soundly on the roof.

After the fall harvest, heavy snows arrived and Mania was spinning wool and linen into thread, then wove it into fabric. She turned the fabric into jackets, slacks, blouses, shirts, underwear, tablecloths, bedspread, and towels. She said, "Summers, we worked in the field. In winter, the men didn't do much, but women worked all day. Boys and girls had fun walking around the outdoor market on Mondays. I didn't go. Why freeze out there looking at the boys?"

Despite constant work, the family's only money came from selling linen seed, chickens, and geese, and sometimes from bartering eggs with the Jewish storekeepers. Stores in town had baked goods, fabric, liquor, scarves, stockings, shoes, smoked meats, herring and fish. But Anna and Justyn could only afford the essentials – kerosene, salt, matches, and sugar.

Ethnic groups mingled on Mondays at the outdoor market to buy and sell milk, butter, eggs, grain, potatoes, and wool. Jewish merchants sold stock from their stores or fruit from their orchards. The Eastern Orthodox from beyond the Niemen River sold cows, pigs, and hay. One such Russian family stayed with Mania's family. They ate together, spent the evening in the house, and slept in the barn. Seeing Mania's fine knitting, they gave her wool to make sweaters and paid her with money or hay.

Mania never missed Święto Morza, Holiday of the Sea, at Lake Kroman eight miles south of Naliboki. People rode bicycles, harnessed the horse and wagon, or walked through the thick forest to reach the lush vegetation. They paid an entrance fee and gathered at the lake where an altar stood on a bridge. After the priest said Mass, the altar was removed. An orchestra took its place and dancing began. Tables were laden with food for sale. People took boat rides on the lake.

Mania repeated a legend I had heard in Naliboki. She said, "Long ago, Lake Kroman had a town. The priest was away and wasn't there to say Mass. When he returned, the whole town was drowned except for the church Missal floating on the water. Legend or real, that's what people say."

Reflections

When a hungry soldier with a rifle asks for food you give it to him.

There's a saying, "Hora placze, hora skacze, I hora piesienki piejot." In hardship we cry, we dance, we sing. We had clean water, clean air, rolling fields, forests. We knew each other. When work was done, we sat on little benches in

Residents enjoy the Holiday of the Sea, *Święto Morza* as described by Mania.

front of the house and talked to people passing by.

DC: They still do. When I visit, I sit on those little benches and talk to people as they walk by.

Teenagers met by a bench, took out a harmonica, sang. Benedict Klimowicz played his violin. When boys asked younger girls to dance, the older girls chased us out. So we practiced dancing to keep up with them. Life was fun. It seemed the whole world lived like this. Józef got a monthly pamphlet but we didn't write away for a newspaper. No time to sit and read every day. We had no radios or telephones, no factories, no buses. Why did they force themselves on us? The Germans wanted to destroy the Polish race, but we suffered more from the Russians.

DC: When I studied World War II in school, the Soviet atrocities were never discussed.

They were killing and deporting Polish people even before the war. When we broke free after 123 years of Russian rule, they took vengeance on us. Then, the Germans came and pushed them out. At night, Russian partisans would knock on the window for a piece of bread. I felt sorry for them. When a hungry soldier with a rifle asks for food, you give it to him if you have it.

Young people enjoy a boat ride on Lake Kroman accompanied by a chaperon on the right.

(DC: Aunt Mania got up and poured me a generous bowl of her beet soup.) Danusia, have some more soup. I was always hungry. We have food now, but I watch my diabetes. I wanted to dress nice. Now, I have closets full of clothes now, but don't go out much.

DC: Do you feel any anger or hatred?

I say forgive us our trespasses as we forgive those who trespass against us. Every group has good and bad. Not all Germans or Russians were bad. The governments were bad. Look at the wrong ideas some people have about Polish people. You can't judge everyone the same.

We were always attacked. World War I, World War II. I'm glad not to live there. They are still out in the field cutting hay. At least, in your video from the church consecration, they have shoes. We worked barefoot in the woods on that surface like needles. In winter, we wore a wooden sandal tied to our feet with leather straps and carried our shoes to church. That one pair had to last you a lifetime.

We learned to survive, but I worry about young people with their steaks and McDonalds. What would they do? When dry provisions weren't enough in one of the refugee camps, we found beets, a potato or two, some sorrel in a field to make soup. We thought it was terrific. Who in this country would eat like that? I'm grateful to be alive and living here. All I can say is, God bless America.

(DC: Mania took a deep breath, gazed out the window.)
I hope my children read this.

Maria (Mania) Byczkiewicz Szalczyk was born
in Naliboki on November 22, 1923 and passed away in
Philadelphia, Pennsylvania on July 11, 2001. She worked
in manufacturing for thirty years. Wincenty was born in
Poland on June 26, 1916 and died in Trenton, New Jersey
on September 18, 2005. He worked as a laborer. Their son
Steven worked for NJ Bell Telephone Company and Verizon.
Daughter Irene worked for the State Department of Justice.
Helen worked for the Mercer County Judicial system. They
had seven grandchildren. My aunt's account is based on
our numerous talks over homemade soup at her home in
Trenton, New Jersey.

Chapter 13 Antonina
Just Keep Working

As my Aunt Mania was snared at age nineteen to work in a German factory, Antonina was yanked from her family at age fifteen to be a domestic servant in a German household. After the war, she became a wife, mother, and a widow before her time. She lived in several refugee camps, then she came to the United States, remarried and, like many survivors of trauma, created a family life that kept at bay the whispers of bygone terror.

Antonina and her second husband built a cozy Connecticut home furnished in American colonial style. As she moves contentedly from house to yard, she fusses over the flowers of many hues and heights that wave gloriously at anyone who walks by. The way they do in Naliboki.

When we first spoke, this small woman with a ladylike demeanor showed no emotion in response to my questions. She needed time to unlock the memory of being young and waiting to die in a bombed-out cellar of a house. Yet in time, this gentle soul generously stepped out of her safety zone. Her willingness to relive dreaded memories was a gift that I received gratefully.

Everything Changed

They were grabbing our boys to be their soldiers. We never saw those boys again.

Antonina made her way through four languages, some forced on her, before she spoke English. She first spoke *po prostu*, meaning plain speech. This mix of Polish, Belarussian, and Russian was a remnant of 123 years of Russian rule. When Naliboki was again in Polish hands, the new generation still spoke *po prostu* with parents and grandparents who had grown up under Russian rule. But young people were learning Polish in school and speaking it on the street. I understood *po prostu* with my Grandmother Anna, spoke Polish with my parents, aunts, and uncles, and English with my brothers, sisters, and cousins. All in one family.

Antonina looked up to the big kids who spoke Polish among themselves. She was eager to talk like them. Kazimierz and Anna Dubicki wanted their four children to finish all seven grades paid by their taxes. The family rose before dawn to prepare their daily bread. While it was baking, they fed the animals. Then the two oldest, Zofia and Antonina, washed, dressed, ate breakfast, and walked five miles round trip to school in Naliboki.

Antonina learned to read and write with thirty other boys and girls, and dove into math, music, science, geography, and German and French. The parents had the priest come a few days a week to teach religion. Most teachers were local, and those who came a distance boarded with families.

Her love of school changed drastically in third grade. She said, "The Russians came in 1939. Made the priest stop teaching religion. We still used it in church, but in school they punished us if they caught the children speaking Polish to each other. We had to learn a new alphabet, new language. They were telling us what to do. Some people, some of them young, were turning to communism. They spied on us for the Russians. We were afraid to talk to anyone."

This first invader decided who would stay and who would be banished to the vast hinterlands of the Soviet Union. Like my Uncle Józef's cousin, Stefan Byczkiewicz, who was forced into the Soviet army, Antonina said, "They were grabbing our boys to be their soldiers. We never saw them again."

Stalin was also taking revenge upon thousands of men now in middle age. They had fought in World War I and revived a Poland that was erased from the map of Europe for 123 years. The revenge on the night of February 10, 1940 included my Uncle Józef Chmara, wife Józefa, daughter Stefania, and my brother Henry's future in-laws, Jan and Zofia Kaniewski and their five children.

And people living above the poverty line were punished for not being poor. Antonina said, "The Russians called them *kulak*s if they had regular jobs and were a little better off. We didn't know any rich people. They were just what we call regular people, middle class people – teachers, policemen, forest rangers. Some of my family was taken the night of February 10, 1940. They died in Siberia."

As lives ended in the Soviet Union through cold, exhaustion, and starvation, Antonina kept going to school in Naliboki. She struggled to learn Russian until the language changed again. When the German army invaded in 1941, she put aside the Russian alphabet. German became dominant.

Another Invasion, Another Language

Next Year I'll finish grade seven and hold that precious diploma in my hand.

Another invasion did not stifle our sixth grader's grit. She said, "Walking to school was horrible. If anyone said something against them, or did something they didn't like, or squealed on them, the German soldiers killed them. They hanged them on electric poles to show what happens if we make them mad. They left Russian partisans so long, flies covered their faces and bodies. They left dead horses on the ground where we walked with flies all over them. I still see it before my eyes."

She walked past rotting bodies swinging from electric poles, and kept repeating to herself, "Don't look. Keep walking straight. Next year, I'll finish grade seven and hold that precious diploma in my hand."

By summer 1944, as a proud owner of a diploma, she would be considered an educated person – and a girl, at that. But Naliboki would disappear in summer 1943. When the German army pushed the Russians into the forest, they became guerrilla fighters living in underground shelters called *ziemianki*. They stole chickens, cows, grain, eggs, and milk from villages located near the forest. And they overpowered the German soldiers and their Latvian, Lithuanian, and Ukrainian auxiliaries.

Unable to defeat the Russian partisans by August 1943, the German army tried to starve them. If they stopped them from stealing food from villages near the forest, they would leave the forest. That was the thinking. Antonina said, "The Russian partisans were powerful. To get rid of them the Germans threw bombs deep into the woods to blow up any partisans hiding there. They also burned Naliboki, then Szemioty, and my village of Cielechowszczyzna. They burned Prudy, Niescierowicze, Niwno, Kleciszcze, and Rudnia. But it didn't work. The partisans stole food from villages away from the forest that weren't burned until they had orders to leave for the front."

During this mass arson, armed German soldiers on horseback were screaming for people to leave with their livestock to be relocated for safety. Terrified villagers loaded belongings onto wagons and drove three miles to the meadow in the village of Jankowicze. Russian partisans had stolen

Antonina's family horse and wagon. Such families were loaded onto trucks and driven to the meadow where they spend the night in the pouring rain. People who resisted were shot.

Leaving the drenched meadow in the morning, they walked for three days and slept in the fields at night until they reached the train station in the town of Stołpce, twenty-five miles away. She said, "My older sister Zofia and I had to help the two youngest, our sister Teresa and brother Pawel. We carried their little sacks of clothes and picked them up when they fell. We were not relocated for our safety. We were deported to Germany for work."

Antonina reminded me, "When the Germans first invaded, Russian and Polish partisans tried to work together. But in the end, they were against each other and against the Germans who loaded us into those big trains like they do to cows."

Antonina is Given as a Reward

She wonders where she is going with this strange man.

As Antonina's world burns, hundreds of prisoners are stuffed into cattle cars going northwest toward the German cities of Bremen, Oldenburg, and Wilhelmshaven near the Dutch border. She said, "We stop. They scream at us to go over there in the bushes. We go. There's no other way."

The cattle cars stopped near the German border for assembly-line disinfection. Antonina said, "They line up groups of women and children, men and boys. We are naked. You know, some women have their monthly sickness and all that stuff and the kids were looking at them. Horrible. They spray us and put our clothes in a machine, then tell us to dress in the same clothes."

Disinfected with the chemical DDT, they were brought to a transit camp near a railroad terminal. The bread from home was gone. The meat smelled rank in the summer heat. While they stood in line for a piece of bread and bowl of turnip soup, the *Arbeitsamt*, the central employment agency, was deciding how to use them. Some people were immediately sent to work sites. Antonina's family was taken to a row of barracks in a transit camp near the city of Bremen.

Standing in line for their daily ration, Antonina heard the stomp of boots. This meant trouble. Guards rushed in, clubs in hand. Pushing aside women and children, they grabbed the first men they saw who looked strong. They shoved them into cattle cars going to locations where the *Arbeitsamt* had decided there was a need for heavy labor. Antonina said, "It was so fast, until the end of the war, women and kids didn't know what happened to their husbands and fathers or if they would ever see them again. Some families never found each other."

People who remained after their husbands' and fathers' abduction were transported to a railroad terminal near the city of Oldenburg. There, the armed guards began to take children away from their parents. As Antonina spoke of families being torn apart, I understood why my mother was so proud that her husband, my father, had helped reunite families after the war.

The two youngest of the four Dubicki children, Teresa and Pawel, stood clutching their parents as the guards decided whom to pull out of line. Kazimierz and Anna Dubicki stood with sinking hearts as guards pulled out their two daughters, Antonina and Zofia. The parents watched the guards take them away with no explanation. Antonina said, "We rode on a passenger train holding each other and lost any idea of time. The train stopped. A woman in uniform got on. She gave Zofia some papers and pointed to get off. We were crying and hugging each other. The woman in uniform pulled Zofia away from me and yelled at her to leave fast. The train started again. I was scared without my parents on this train all by myself. Fifteen and alone."

The next moments felt like a film noir in black and white and slow motion. The train stops. A man in dark uniform boards the train. He hands her a piece of paper, points to the exit. Antonina steps off into the black night. She stands alone on an unlit platform. She hears unfamiliar sounds but sees no human face. A woman in somber uniform appears. She points to a car. The car lights go on. The woman motions for Antonina to get into the car. The male driver is not in uniform. The bewildered child gets in the back seat. Sitting on the edge, she wonders where she is going with this strange man.

The driver maneuvers through unlit streets to a residential area on the outskirts of the town of Barssen. He comes to a large house with a barn in the back. He stops the car. Checks papers. Motions for Antonina to get out. She grabs her bag of clothes and walks to the front door. A heavy-set blond woman in her thirties opens the door. The woman walks slowly with large varicose veins on her legs. Four children run up to see who is at the door. Antonina realizes she was brought there to be a domestic servant. A few months earlier, she was determined that walking past those rotting bodies was not going to stop her from getting her seventh grade diploma.

The four children she would take care of ranged from toddler to pre-teen. The husband was a high-ranking officer. Antonina was given to this family as a reward for his leading the men on the front lines of the war. She said, "They treated me good because I was obedient. I was doing lots of things for the kids, the family. They kind of liked me, I guess. I was babysitting and playing with the children, washing clothes, cleaning house, taking care of the yard and vegetable gardens, cooking, milking two cows. The government paid me twelve marks a month. It was worth maybe a dollar. We ate together. That was forbidden by law."

Waiting for the End

The whole house became a death trap when a bomb hit the side of the house.

Antonina did not know that her father Kazimierz was also in Barssen, working on the railroad. His boss knew that high-ranking officers had been rewarded with Polish girls as domestics. The man was also a father. He risked telling Kazimierz the area where he might find his two daughters. Whenever he got permission, he left his post. With the same pluck that got Antonina past partisans hanging from telephone poles on her way to school, he walked for miles from house to house looking for Antonina and Zofia. His determination paid off. Antonina was peeling potatoes in the kitchen. She heard the door rattle. She turned around. There stood her father! Shock. Tears. An embrace. Many questions.

Satisfied that she was alive, her father kept walking from house to house until he found daughter Zofia milking cows on a farm two miles from Barssen. After Kazimierz found them, the German officer's wife let Antonina visit her parents once a month in the barrack where they were living. She also allowed occasional Sunday visits to her own home from sister Zofia.

For two years, June 1943 to April 1945, the family was not cruel to her, but her value was in her working like a robot. Instead of getting that precious diploma, Antonina was an unwilling servant, morning to night, for the benefit of the German family. As Germany was losing the war by spring 1945, towns were not much safer than forced labor camps on the front where my family was being held. The Allied and German air battles reached residential areas.

As bombs swooped down on Barssen, Antonina would help the mother get the four children into the dark, damp basement. It seemed safer to sit there for hours than being upstairs. But one day, the whole house became a death trap when a bomb hit the side of the house. The jolt threw them all to the floor. Antonina saw her own terror in the eyes of the little ones. With broken lamps and dishes underfoot, they made their way into the basement.

After some quiet moments, the foundation shook. Antonina's eyes burned from the smoke filling the basement. She tasted the acrid dust in her mouth and nose. The basement walls were beginning to crumble. The ceiling was sagging. The stairs had collapsed. There was no way to leave. They were trapped. Antonina and the mother held the little ones in their arms as they waited for the house to become their burial chamber. She said, "We expected to die. The children knew. The horror grabbed me. I was robbed of my education. I will never grow up to be a woman. I will never have a husband. I will never have children, a home of my own. All I knew was to work like some kind of machine."

As Antonina agonized over the injustice she knew, a rescue crew happened to look through the shattered basement window. They could see one child beneath the sinking house. But they pulled out six people through that window, cut and bruised by broken glass. The impact of the bomb had charred their hair and clothes. As the rescue crew cleaned the cuts on their bodies, the house crashed with a deafening thud into the basement from which they had been pulled moments before. The new world the woman's husband was fighting for ended with the destruction of his home, family photos and mementos of value gone, his children traumatized, and his wife having to cope without him.

With nothing to salvage, Antonina helped the officer's wife walk the children to a relative's farm three miles away. Baarsen was no longer a town. It was a pile of multi-story houses that had collapsed like stacks of pancakes. It was a heap of ruined dreams, family photographs, heirlooms, and dead bodies. So different from the glory Hitler had promised.

Thank God for America

Antonina never learned what happened to her husband.

The war ended soon after Antonina's near death, but she was cut off from her family. Her parents, Kazimierz and Anna, and their two youngest, Teresa and Pawel, had survived and were living in a displaced persons camp near the city of Oldenburg. Kazimierz again got on his feet.

He no longer needed permission to look for his daughters. He walked thirty miles from Oldenburg to Barssen. He found a pile of debris. It used to be the house where Antonina was working. Could his daughter have died there? Walking from farm to farm, he asked what had become of the two Polish girls working in the area. He happened upon a relative of the family where Antonina was working who told Kazimierz where they were. Antonina could be alive, but no one knew about his Zofia.

Kazimierz approached the farm where he might find Antonina. Without knocking, he walked through the back door of the house to reclaim his daughter. She was in the kitchen washing a big pile of pots and pans. Without a word to anyone, he took her by the hand. With no explanation, he pulled her out the door with only the dress and shoes she was wearing. They began a long hard walk toward freedom.

Antonina had put herself as if on "automatic pilot" walking to school. Again, she plodded on by sheer will. Antonina said, "They told me I did this, but I don't remember. I walked in a daze for hours with father to the barracks in Oldenburg. My hair stood up like wire from the bombs. I was black and blue all over. My mother washed me and brought a pail of water to soak my feet."

The warm soapy water felt good, but she had no strength to sit upright in the chair. She slowly sank to the floor. Her parents carried her limp bruised body to a bed where she slept for three days. When she awoke, her joy at seeing her family was mixed with sadness to learn that sister Zofia was missing.

A few months later, a letter from Zofia reached the family. Cut off from them, she had married a fellow prisoner and they got on a cattle car leaving Germany. The cattle car took them to the country of Ukraine, but they eventually returned to Naliboki. Antonina said, "All those people in Germany – Russian, Ukrainian, Polish – they didn't have to work anymore, and the farmers didn't want to feed them. So, they put people like my sister back in those cattle cars to get them out of Germany."

With Zofia out of reach, Kazimierz wrote to a Catholic agency in New York. He asked their help in finding his brother, Paul Dubicki, who had come to the United States after World War I. He began as a farm hand, and with years of determination, he worked his way to buying his own farm in Connecticut. They waited for an answer.

As refugees were trying to find permanent homes, the camps took on a vibrant life. Resettlement could take years, so aid agencies helped set up schools, churches, and medical facilities. Refugees organized theatre groups, religious celebrations, sports events, and dances in the canteen. During a Saturday night dance, Antonina met a young man she liked. The feeling was mutual. No longer a servant, she allowed herself to hope for a family and home of her own. Two years after the war, Antonina became a bride. Like other brides in the camps, she celebrated her passage into womanhood with a wedding dinner of canned goods from United Nations relief packages. As the newlyweds kept looking for a place to emigrate, she became pregnant and gave birth to their daughter Janina.

People like my father found jobs to supplement the United Nations packages, and to save money to leave the camps and start new lives. Germany was in ruins and needed to be rebuild. Antonina's husband had a steady job in construction. When daughter Janina was a year old, Antonina's husband was late for supper one evening. She waited up all night. Morning came, no husband. The family searched from barrack to barrack and found no trace of the man.

Kazimierz reported the missing son-in-law to the camp authorities. They tried to find him, but with so many war dead, wounded, and missing in action, one human life went undetected. Antonina never learned what happened to her husband. Our eager student, instead of earning her diploma, had become an unwilling domestic in Germany. And when she was free to decide her own destiny as a bride and beaming mother, she was suddenly presumed to be a widow.

Still stunned by the case of the missing husband, the family got good news. The Catholic agency in New York had found Kazimierz's brother Paul in Connecticut. He offered to sponsor them. But good news was followed by bad. The rigorous immigration process included a medical exam. Doctors found a spot on Kazimierz's lung, suspecting tuberculosis. Recovery could take years if he recovered at all. He could not come to America without a clean bill of health. As a single mother, Antonina's parents told her to accept the uncle's offer.

While the rest of the family waited for news of Kazimierz's health, Antonina and daughter Janina came to Norwich, Connecticut in 1949. She worked in a box manufacturing factory while her Uncle Paul and his wife took care of her child. And she was determined to learn English.

The spot on Kazimierz's lung was a false alarm. He did not have tuberculosis. Antonina's parents, sister Teresa, and brother Paul boarded an army transport ship in May 1950 and joined her in Connecticut. After the siblings grew up and married, Antonina, Teresa, and Pawel lived near each other for the rest of their lives, with one missing. Zofia was on the other side of the ocean.

Antonina's second marriage gave her the home she did not expect while crouching in the basement of the house in Barssen and watching the sagging ceiling about to drop. She married Marian Dubicki in 1959, a man with the same surname as hers. He managed a small dairy owned by his family. They worked, raised Janina, and built the house they enjoyed together for forty-four years until Marian's passing. She lived in that house, surrounded by the flowers she nurtures. She no longer spoke *po prostu*, the language of her childhood. She was not eager to learn the Russian forced on her, nor the German. But she grasped English enthusiastically to go with her new country, her new life, and feeling safe all day.

Reflections
I wish this never happens to anybody else.

DC: Were you ever reunited with Zofia? (Antonina's face lit up with joy in response to my question.)

Yes. Fifty years later. I could not see my sister during the Russian years. I went to visit her in Naliboki after the fall of the Soviet Union.

DC: How do you feel about what happened to you?

Now, I don't feel much. But when I went to Poland in 1974, we stayed in a hotel in Gdańsk. I saw Polish authorities meet German authorities with big bouquets of roses. They were like friends and that hurt me because they tried to destroy us. That war was the worst nightmare in my life. We never knew if we would live or what they would to do with us.

DC: Before Germany, the nightmare in Naliboki was walking to school past corpses of Russian partisans hanging from electric poles. Your determination to earn that diploma is amazing.

But then I was robbed of everything. My education. My family. Almost my life. They just expected me to work. They were dropping bombs on Barssen. I was shaken up from all that. When I came here, I always had that fear of going into basements. We had safety drills when I was working in the box shop. We had to go down the cellar. I started shaking. Someone walked me down and held me, but I was so scared, I never stopped shaking. What happened in Germany was still in my head.

DC: You felt trapped and expecting to die. This is still with you.

How can you forget? I dream about it. When I think of everything that happened, I wish this never happens to anybody else. Thank God we got through it and lived. Thank God for America.

Antonina Dubicka was born in Cielechowszczyzna, also called Zaścianek, a short walk from Naliboki, on June 26, 1930. She passed away in her daughter's home in Texas in 2017. In the United States she worked in a box shop for fifteen years, several years in the Yantic Wool Mill, and twenty years in the John Meyer clothing factory. Her daughter is a laboratory technician in a hospital. Her husband, Marian Dubicki, was born in 1918 and passed away on January 23, 2003 in Norwich, Connecticut. I knew Antonina Dubicka from various social occasions, and we spoke at length in October 1995 in Yantic, Connecticut.

Part Three Resistance: Because I am a Human Being

Faces of Resistance

Chapter 14 Stefan: A Marked Man

Chapter 15 Krystyna: I have to Be Somebody

Chapter 16 Czesław Miłosz: The Big Taboo

Chapter 17 Father Hyacinth: Auschwitz, Dachau, and the Mosquitoes

Chapter 14 Stefan
A Marked Man

Stefan and Krystyna worked in the Polish Underground Resistance in Western Poland until they were deported to Germany in 1944. By then, people from Eastern Poland like my family were existing on turnip soup and a sliver of coarse bread in Germany and in the Soviet Union.

Stefan and Krystyna were strangers during the underground years, but by the time they were my parents' dear friends in America, they were married with two daughters. They were different in temperament and appearance, a case of "opposites attract." Ruggedly handsome with a strong jaw, his lean frame stood six feet tall. He spoke slowly, precisely, and moved with the ease of a cat. He lost her to illness after 54 years of marriage and never removed his wedding ring.

From Forestry Student to Prisoner of War
We dressed quickly and they pushed us out the back door.

Our hero who moved with the ease of a cat also had nine lives. Each close call could have ended his life – in crematoria ovens in his hometown, in a German prisoner of war camp, in the mass murder of Polish soldiers by the Soviet Union in the Katyń forest, in gun battles on two fronts, from an intestinal abscess, or by the post-war communist government that wanted revenge.

A happy boy in a happy family, Stefan could not imagine such perils ahead of him. They lived in Tczew, an industrial center on the Vistula (Wisła) River with a large railroad terminal – a dangerous place to be on September 1, 1939. It was only twenty miles south of the Baltic seaport, Gdańsk, which took the first blow as Germany invaded Western Poland. To block further invasion, the Polish army blew up the two bridges of Tczew, one for rail and one for vehicles, but the German army prevailed.

Stefan said, "I was twenty-one, working in a forest near the Ukrainian border to help pay my way at Poznań University. I was a forestry student and in the reserves. I left immediately at news of the invasion, but by the time I reached my unit, it was on the front line. So, I joined an infantry division."

Military resistance was valiant, brief, and futile. By October, Germany held the west bank of the Bug River in southeastern Poland. Its ally, the Soviet Union, held the east bank. Stefan's unit was trapped in the Biłgoraj Forest between them. Poland had a non-aggression treaty with the Soviet Union, so some of the Polish soldiers expected to be safer in Soviet-controlled territory. Stefan said, "They pushed east into the part of Poland held by the Soviets. They couldn't know it was a terrible mistake."

Stefan's decision to remain west of the Bug River saved his life.

Back row: Stefan Władyka, forestry student, with his sister Maria. Front: brother Andrzej, Mother Lucja. Tczew, Poland 1930's

The Soviet Union violated the non-aggression treaty, and the Polish soldiers east of the Bug River were doomed. On Stalin's order, they perished in the Katyń Forest, shot in the back of the head. As British historian Simon Sebag Monefiore pointed out earlier, Stalin called this "black work" which he regarded as noble Party service. Their executioner wore a leather butcher's apron to protect his uniform from their splattered blood.[63]

Stefan remained with the units west of the Bug River which fell to the Germans. By late October, thousands of prisoners of war were marched past the smoldering town of Biłgoraj, then separated into smaller groups. Stefan was with some two hundred men who were locked up in a fenced-in school yard in the industrial town of Ostrowiec Świętokrzyski in central Poland. They slept on straw-covered cement in freezing temperatures, always hungry. Stefan said, "The Germans marched us in formation up and down the streets. I heard rumors of local people helping prisoners escape during those marches. A friend and I began memorizing the town layout. With guts and good timing, a man could disappear between buildings. Why not us?"

He continued, "On a Sunday march, people were idling outside during Mass. A man turned toward us. Our eyes met. He motioned for us to slip into the side door of the church. They pulled off our prison uniforms. They had a box of civilian clothes hidden among the priest's vestments, so I knew they had helped others. We dressed quickly and they pushed us out the back door. A man and woman had us walk with them on the inside. Reaching their house, the man pointed to the back door."

These strangers gave them a place to sleep and fed them while others were preparing their safe exit. Three days later, an Underground courier brought forged passes to allow them to travel. Hitchhiking and taking trains, Stefan's friend went to Pomerania (Pomorze), a region on the southern shore of the Baltic Sea. Stefan returned to Tczew, relieved to find his mother at home.

Escape from the Ovens

Stefan's mother Lucja smelled danger even before the stench of crematoria ovens.

Stefan took a job clearing debris to rebuild the two demolished bridges of Tczew. Sensing a pervasive fear, he learned the ugly truth from his fellow workers. After capturing Gdańsk, Germany controlled the nearby town of Sztutowo (German: Stutthof). Near this small town, in a secluded, wet, wooded area, festered the evil that became one of many German concentration camps in occupied Poland. Stefan's coworkers had family members who had perished in the crematoria ovens in Sztutowo.

As American historian Richard Lukas explains, "The German policy of destroying the Polish nation focused strongly, but not exclusively, upon eliminating anyone with even the least political and cultural prominence...The German definition of 'elite' was so broad, however, that it embraced a major part of Polish society, including not only teachers, physicians, priests, officers, businessmen, landowners, and writers but also anyone who even attended secondary school."[64]

Concentration camps had already been built in Germany after Hitler became Chancellor in 1933 to punish German dissidents and communists. With the 1939 German invasion, this evil took root near Stefan's home, starting with the Polish people who had to build the ovens in which they would perish. Stefan said, "Tczew had about 25,000, mostly Polish Christians, a German minority, and a few Jews. So, hundreds burned in Sztutowo were mostly Christian. At first, ashes might be returned. Cremation was rare, but families took whatever was left of their loved ones and held funerals. I attended such a funeral for a friend's father. Later, families just got a note saying, 'Died of natural causes.'"

Stefan's mother Lucja smelled danger even before the stench of crematoria ovens. A month before the German invasion of Western Poland, she sent son Andrzej, twelve, and daughter Maria, twenty-three, to stay with friends in the town of Kielce in south central Poland. Lucja and Stefan remained in Tczew until German soldiers came knocking on their door to arrest Stefan's father. Stefan explained, "For 123 years, your eastern part of Poland was under Russian rule, but Tczew was under the German partition. Polish people knew their language from what was taught secretly at home. When Poland was reborn after World War I, my father was known and respected as teacher of Polish language and literature at the high school, a patriot. He died from a burst appendix when my mother was five months pregnant with my brother Andrzej. If father was alive...

Stefan paused, cried silently, then continued...he would have died in Sztutowo for promoting Polish culture and language."

The soldiers left without her long-dead husband, but Lucja learned that she and Stefan were next. With her many connections, she secured travel passes. She packed food and clothes, and Stefan quietly left his job. Before some bureaucrat figured out that travel passes were issued to two people on their crematoria list, mother and son were on a train headed for Kielce to join brother Andrzej and sister Maria. The next time soldiers came banging on their door in Tczew, no one was home.

Lucja and Stefan's escape from the Sztutowo ovens did not guarantee safety. Hitler had annexed western and part of central and southern Poland into the German Reich. Kielce was within the General Government, the part of Poland incorporated into Germany – making everything at the disposal of the Reich – people, civil liberties, culture, and artifacts. Stefan said, "Our diocese of Pelplin had an original Guttenberg Bible. They were precious, a few in the world. In revenge for not getting that Bible, the Germans killed most of the priests in our diocese. We escaped the ovens, but we were still under German occupation."

Guerrillas and Underground Schools

Polish people were forbidden education beyond the elementary grades.

Before leaving Tczew, Stefan and Lucja had a visitor. Mieczysław was a seaman who fought during the Gdańsk invasion. His wife had taught with Stefan's father. His words echoed as mother and son rode the train toward Kielce, "It's not over. We will meet in Warsaw, get organized, and fight back."

Stefan and Mieczysław joined a unit in Warsaw in April 1940, one of many that fought for homeland independence. Stefan said, "Amazing. Initiatives came spontaneously from people like us. Small groups joined bigger organizations in all the regions. One group started with two secret radios. They got news from France until it was occupied in 1940, then from England. We faced punishment if caught with anything printed against the Nazi regime, so couriers got the word out to people secretly."

Stefan would someday marry one of those couriers who risked her life as part of the Underground Resistance. These military and civilian operations were led from London by the Polish government-in-exile of General Władysław Sikorski. The structure of this nationwide network was based on pre-war political parties. Stefan said, "Most of the parties were against communism taking over in Poland, but some were pro-communist. Others concentrated on local issues. We could have some political differences at first because our goal was independence."

With the official Polish army defeated early in the war, armed partisans, also called guerillas, became the military arm of the Underground. Stefan said, "When Gestapo were destructive, the Underground planned their elimination, and a small unit did the work. We sabotaged German communications, helped people escape arrests. Armed guerillas fought in the countryside, forests, and mountains."

This vast network also supported aspects of civilian life denied to Polish people. With the German invasion, Polish people were forbidden education beyond the elementary grades. In response, teachers organized secret schools. If teachers or students were caught with books or notes, a concentration camp was the punishment, so time and location of classes changed constantly. Female couriers who passed on such logistical information were essential to the functioning of the Underground.

Stefan said, "In cities like Warsaw or Kraków, the Underground offered university courses. As in peace, the Underground police kept order against banditry among our own population. The Underground set up courts of law and schools to educate our young people. A law professor was helping us organize a law school in Kielce. Not many educated people were left. Most were in concentration camps. We couldn't admit just anyone to classes, they might be infiltrators. They had to be scrutinized. But those female couriers were risking their lives."

Stefan worked in a sawmill, and in the evenings, he taught military skills as part of an Underground plan for an uprising. His students also had jobs, then they came to his classes to learn offensive and defensive tactics, map reading, and use of weapons. Rifles could not be carried without being noticed, so Stefan taught them how to take apart and reassemble firearms using small guns. He began with six boys, ages 17 and 18. As classes grew, he went beyond the classroom. He formed a platoon out of small groups and taught infantry movements in a remote part of the forest where he worked. He said, "My students went into battle as soon as they finished my course. By 1944, we desperately needed to defend our country, and I joined the guerrillas with twelve of those boys."

Life and Death on the Run

...the anti-communist groups in the Underground now faced two hostile forces.

The military arm of the Underground Resistance consisted of several groups of guerrilla fighters. The Home Army (Armia Krajowa – AK) was the largest of these groups. Stefan and his 12 students joined the Brigade of the Holy Cross, named after the mountain range in south central Poland. This brigade was part of the National Armed Forces, which Stefan said was second to the Home Army in strength. They had contact with the Home Army units, but they were on their own to survive.

Stefan's brigade was over 1,000 strong, divided into fourteen companies. It included twelve female nurses, a British officer, and a Polish paratrooper called *Cichociemny* – quiet and invisible. By the end of 1944, they had captured two German officers who were later critical in negotiations that saved the brigade.

Stefan said, "Besides the two officers, we seized an artillery piece that fired munitions into enemy territory. A great prize since the men mostly supplied their own small arms. The two cars we seized were useless. Even when we could find gas, we marched unseen at night with no headlights. Horses dragged the cars through forests. When they burned down in a battle, we were glad to be rid of them."

As Stefan said, Underground political parties were unified in their goal to expel the German invader. But unity was shattered when Soviet paratroopers landed secretly on Polish soil in 1944. They came to organize communist units in the Underground in preparation for communist takeover of Poland. The anti – communist groups in the Underground now faced two hostile fronts: the German army, and Polish communist units led by Soviet paratroopers. Stefan said, "Our brigade, like most Poles, was against communism taking over in Poland. But some people felt there was injustice in Poland and expected communism to correct this."

As they fought on two fronts, their losses grew. When some of the men went to find food, they were caught by a unit of Polish communists and Soviet paratroopers working together. After a vicious battle, some of the men got away, but two were badly mutilated. Stefan said, "Our nurses tried hard, but we lost these two men."

Bullets, bombs, and guns killed many a husband and son at the peak of his manhood, his final resting place anonymous and far from home. Hiding in dugouts, poor sanitation, infection, polluted water, and spoiled food were also enemies. A Russian doctor from Georgia, then a Soviet republic, travelled with the brigade. Stefan said, "He was our prisoner of war. But to that doctor human life was more important than politics. He took good care of the men."

While fighting on two fronts, the brigade protected the local population who showed their gratitude with potatoes, vegetables, milk, and eggs. Some days, the only daily meal came from local farmers. Stefan chuckled, "Our unit captured a load of sugar from the Germans. We made sure every house was enjoying a dish with eggs and sugar called *kogel-mogel*. We enjoyed it with them."

Christmas 1944 felt almost normal as farmers took the fighters into their homes and churches to share the traditional wafer, called *opłatek*, and the sacred Christmas Eve supper. But by January 1945, the Russians had crossed the Vistula River and invaded the mainland. Against the snow and howling winds, the brigade helped families load supplies onto wagons and leave their homes. As they trudged westward toward the town of Częstochowa to escape the powerful Russian units, the snowstorm became a blizzard. The doctor from Georgia disappeared. Willingly? Killed? Died? No one knew.

But fate snarls and fate smiles at us. As the caravan of civilians and guerillas on horse and wagons pushed against the angry blizzard, a white apparition stepped out of the snowy blur. It had no coat, only a blanket over its shoulders, and pieces of wood tied to its feet. It was a man! Shivering, he asked Stefan, "Can I sit on this wagon with your people?"

Stefan said, "Sit and stay with us. I will find you something warm to drink and maybe some shoes."

The half-frozen coatless and shoeless man turned out to be a doctor, also from Georgia. He stayed with the brigade. And he saved Stefan's life.

A Gentlemen's Agreement

Two men from the brigade approached the German garrison, waving a white cloth.

Stefan almost lost consciousness during battle from a stabbing stomach pain. The white apparition that turned out to be a doctor, now wearing shoes and a coat, diagnosed Stefan's pain. Unless he operated, an intestinal abscess could poison the whole body. But with little anesthetic and poor sanitary conditions, an infection could take his patient in his prime. Stefan took the chance.

Dr. Par saved Stefan's life on a makeshift table and no gloves. Stefan said, "That Russian doctor took his work seriously. We were grateful for Dr. Par's care. Not his real name. We had Underground names for security. We didn't know our closest pals' real names until we reunited in this country."

Thanks to Dr. Par, Stefan was alive in February 1945 when the brigade was stuck between German forces to the west and Russian forces to the east. They had just buried seven men lost in battle with the Germans. In the other

Quartered with General Patton's Third Army, these officers of Guard Company 4222 guarded German prisoners of war. Stefan Władyka is third from the right. Germany 1947

direction, they faced communist units from the Polish Underground and Polish soldiers led by Russian officers within the army of General Zygmund Berling.

Who is Zygmund Berling? A short review:

When Germany invaded its Soviet ally in 1941, Stalin allowed two armies to be formed using men from the four major deportations to the Soviet Union between 1940 – 1941. The first army left the Soviet Union to fight Germany alongside the British and Americans. My Uncle Józef Chmara was part of that first army. That is how he, wife Józefa, and daughter Stefania were freed to leave Russia.

Stalin kept the second army in the Soviet Union under the command of General Zygmund Berling. Later in the war, this second army was used to force a communist takeover of Poland. Stefan's brigade was 100% anti-communist. Capture by this Soviet-led army would mean certain death. The brigade's only hope was to negotiate safe passage with the German front. Two men from the brigade approached the German garrison, waving a white cloth. The commander was willing to talk when he learned that the Polish brigade was holding two German officers.

They reached an agreement. The brigade would turn over one officer. When the brigade crossed the German defense line safely, the second officer would be freed. Their agreement required trust on both sides. Would the Germans keep their promise? Would they forgo the chance to kill many Polish men in place of one German officer? Would the brigade turn over the second officer when they could kill him? Each step felt like a mine field as the brigade crossed the German defense line. But the gentlemen's agreement held. As the last pair of boots stomped across the defense line, the second German officer was alive and joined his comrades.

The brigade marched south through the Carpathian Mountains of Poland. It then crossed the Sudeten Mountains and entered what was then Czechoslovakia. Finding shelter in schools, inns, and with Czech families, they met some skepticism about having crossed the German defense line. Stefan said, "One night we stayed up talking to our Czech host. Toward dawn, he asked, 'Did you have German officers in your unit?'

Those words felt like a hornet's sting. Living on one meal a day, dodging bullets, killer infections, and burying many men – now their survival was questioned. Stefan explained, "That question really meant, 'Were you cooperating with the Germans? Were you controlled by them?' They were not our commanders. They were our prisoners of war."

By the end of April, the brigade reached the outskirts of Prague and met General George S. Patton's Third Army, which was a major force in the collapse of Germany. The brigade had trudged some 500 miles to escape the Soviet army, only to face the next blow. The Soviet government that had occupied Poland did not forget that this brigade was 100% anti-communist. They wanted revenge.

Might Makes Right – Discarded Heroes

Stefan was now a marked man.

Stefan's brigade was quartered with General Patton's army and trained as guard companies to police German prisoners of war. But when the Soviet Union, as a member of the Allies, was assigned to patrol Czechoslovakia, it was dangerous for Stefan's brigade to remain. He said, "The Russians wanted us extradited to communist Poland to take revenge on us."

The war in Europe ended in May 1945, but the political conflict did not. Anti-communist forces that risked their lives to free Poland were now outcasts. Poland was an American and British ally, but these countries allowed the legitimate London-based government to be removed. In its place, the Soviet Union installed a communist government run by Polish nationals taking orders from Moscow. Anyone against this takeover was considered an enemy. Stefan said, "With the Soviets running our country, we would be jailed or executed if we went back."

Stefan was now a marked man. British historian, Norman Davies, points out, "On the one hand, the Soviet leaders openly declared themselves to be the loyal allies of the Western powers, and subscribed in theory to the principles of the common, democratic, and anti-Nazi alliance. On the other hand, they denounced the Polish Government-in-Exile, which was the accepted authority on Polish matters in everyone else's eyes, and they confined their dealings in Poland to persons and institutions appointed by themselves... They began attacking all non-communist Resistance groups...and by appointing local administrators subservient to themselves, in every town and village throughout Poland."[65]

To protect against Soviet revenge, the Americans moved Stefan's brigade to Bavaria, Germany. Stefan said, "They shipped us out to save our skins. I contacted the Second Polish Corps of the British Eighth Army in Italy. We agreed I would prepare thirty candidates for officers' training school. My friends drove me to Italy along with some brigade nurses. With no documents to prove my military rank, they said I would be a regular soldier, not a lieutenant. Nobody carried papers going to guerrillas, too dangerous. So, I returned to the guard company in Germany."

Stefan's military career ended when the Americans replaced foreign guard companies with Germans in 1947. Stefan risked his life to free Poland, and now imprisonment or execution by the communist government in Poland waited for him. He sought shelter in a displaced persons camp in Germany. But despite the military defeat, Stefan was not a defeated man. He joined a Polish group in Germany that provided safe passage corridors for news and people. Stefan said, "We saved families and political people that were in danger of arrest in Poland for being anti-communist. When the Russians first took over East Germany, they were lax. Later, it became risky to do this."

Stefan learned that his mother Lucja, sister Maria, and brother Andrzej were alive in Poland. He tried to get them out through one of the safe passage corridors set up by his group. Stefan said, "I tried to get my brother to the west, but when a day opened up, he was to take exams for his high school diploma. He gave up this chance, and never had another. My mother and sister stayed with him."

Stefan saw his mother one last time when she visited the United States in 1960. She returned to Poland and passed away from cancer of the eye. Until it was safe for Stefan to

Stefan's grandfather, Alexander, prior to World War I dressed in the regional finery of a Polish nobleman.

return to Poland, he saw Andrzej once. His brother was working for an import-export business owned by the Polish government. Andrzej was in Cuba on business at the time when the United States and Cuba had diplomatic relations. He got a 24-hour visa to see Stefan and wife Krystyna in New Jersey. Stefan saw his sister Maria when she visited the United States in 1980.

It was not safe for Stefan to return to his homeland for forty-five years. With the fall of the Soviet Union, Stefan and Krystyna visited Poland as it was learning to become a democracy. After Krystyna passed away in 2002, Stefan made another trip with his daughter, Elizabeth.

Reflections

We were recognized by the Polish government only decades after the collapse of communist rule.

During a visit to Stefan and Krystyna's home, my husband Henry had many questions.

Henry: *Are you still a member of the guard?*

Stefan: Yes. We incorporated others who could not return to Poland, like Veterans of Foreign War and American Legion in this country. We have our New England group in Connecticut. I recently met with a unit in Chicago. I keep our archival papers, and I kept notes until January 1945 when the Russian offensive started.

Henry: *Your underground name was "Lech?"*

Stefan: Before anyone heard of Lech Wałęsa as a Solidarity leader in 1980's Poland, my girls bought me a license plate with my Underground name, "Lech."

Henry: Many like you risked their lives for a free Poland. Did you ever get recognition from the Polish government-in-exile in London?

Stefan: That was not possible for years. The legitimate Polish government was removed, and a communist government was installed, a figurehead of the Soviet Union. Non-communist organizations like the Home Army and our unit were persecuted within communist Poland.

Henry: You got no recognition even when you did the job for the American army in Bavaria?

Stefan: We were controversial units. The Allies falsely suspected us of cooperating with the Germans because we moved through German occupied territories. We were recognized by the Polish government only decades after the collapse of communist rule. Some veterans went to Poland to receive their decorations for wartime service. I got these medals in 1995 during a ceremony at the Polish consulate in New York. This one was from Lech Wałęsa for fighting in the guerrillas. And this one is for Underground work for the armed forces.

Henry: The recognition took 50 years. And what about reparations from Germany?

Stefan: Who is going to prove it? Who proves that my wife, Krystyna, was working?

Krystyna: Right, fifty years later when most of the people are dead.

Stefan: Maybe there is something in the Polish mentality, since Poland went through so many wars, that nobody ever asked for anything. It is destroyed. People start rebuilding. The Germans marched us to Biłgoraj. Only the crumbling brick skeletons of a school and church were left. Who compensated them? Who asked for reparations for Warsaw? Nobody. People rebuilt it. My brother was studying in Poznań and going to Warsaw to push wagons full of bricks to rebuild the city.

Henry: Was it hard to have faith during this ordeal?

Stefan: Spiritually I was strong, and I was fortunate. My mother got us away from the crematoria ovens in Tczew. During the guerrillas, I was not murdered in the Katyń Forest. As a German prisoner of war, I escaped. Our brigade had our chaplain and Sunday Mass. And, quite unexpectedly, a doctor from Georgia joined us and performed an operation that saved my life.

Donna: Did you ever learn Dr. Par's real name?

Stefan: No, but I'll never forget him.

Stefan Władyka was born on May 30, 1918 in Płock, Poland and passed away in Cranbury, New Jersey in June 2015. Stefan was a research technician for the Squibb pharmaceutical company in New Jersey. Stefan's account is based on conversations throughout the years as well as a visit to Stefan and Krystyna on February 19, 1999 in South River, New Jersey.

Endnotes

63 Simon Sebag Montefiore, *Stalin: The Court of the Red Tsar* (NY: Knopf, 2004) p. 197

64 Richard C. Lukas, *Forgotten Holocaust: The Poles under German Occupation 1939-1944* (NY: Hippocrene, 1990) p. 8.

65 Norman Davies, *God's Playground: A History of Poland*, Vol 2 (NY: Columbia UP, 1982) p. 471.

Chapter 15 Krystyna
I Have to Be Somebody

She was married to a man who stood six feet tall and moved with the ease of a cat. At 4 feet 11, she was quick as a rabbit, and her soft features hid an internal pillar of steel. Dark curls encircled her pretty face as she darted across time and space to describe a life of privilege shattered in one day.

Coming to the United States after the war, Krystyna and Stefan struggled to move out of poverty as they raised and educated two daughters. Then working their way into prosperity, they were either climbing an ancient Roman ruin, guidebook in hand, or planning the next excursion to faraway places.

When my husband Henry and I visited them in their home in South River, New Jersey, we learned about the macabre events of Krystyna's youth. I did not see tears which usually flow when people surface such tragic memories. Their pain touches my heart, and we cry together. Instead, a trance like Krystyna emerged. Perhaps that was the only way she could speak of people being shot dead and collapsing onto her small frame. Instead of going away, some wounds go underground, making it possible to go on with our lives.

A Privileged World Collapses

By sundown they were not sure where they would spend the night.

Kazimierz Białobrzeski was a widower with a baby when he married Małgorzata Praisner. She gave him two more daughters, Krystyna and Zofia. As an accountant and a major in the Polish army, he provided his family an upper middle-class life in the medieval city of Kraków He even indulged Krystyna's passion for horses. She was riding by the time she was eight.

Kazimierz was reassigned to Warsaw in 1936 when Krystyna was twelve. The family enjoyed spacious quarters in the northern Praga district east of the Vistula [Polish: Wisła] River. The stately building held sixty-eight large apartments, fifty of them occupied by military families. He sent his three daughters to private schools, expecting them to establish careers. After school, Krystyna played on the manicured grounds which offered a hill for sledding, an ice-skating area, volleyball nets, and a tennis court. And he found a place for her to ride horses.

    Krystyna's privileged world collapsed in one day. The German invasion of Western Poland on September 1, 1939, put her father's regiment on the front lines of resistance. The daughter from Kazimierz's first marriage was by then a nurse in a hospital in Praga and living in nurses' quarters. As the bombing reached Warsaw, his second wife and two daughters were left to fend for themselves.

    Military families were to be evacuated, but Warsaw was under siege with no safe place to go. Krystyna said, "In all that chaos, the driver left us at the house of some friends, far away on the other side of the Wisła River. I'm only fifteen but have to take charge. My mother is sick, and never makes decisions anyway. My sister is younger. We stay the night, then I decide to go back. Leaving was big mistake. We have no money, no clothes. We walk back eight hours. Soldiers surround our building. God gave me strength, I insisted they help us. I was speaking good German, so he let us get clothes from our apartment and gave us a room. It wasn't our lovely apartment, but a roof and a few pots."

    Living in one room, Krystyna learned from her father's unit that he had been wounded in Germany. She said, "The Germans wanted to be rid of him, afraid he had typhus, but he didn't. They sent him back to Warsaw in his blood- soaked uniform."

    The hospital in Warsaw treated his wounds and needed civilian clothes to discharge him. Krystyna said, "Where could we get men's clothes? We barely had anything ourselves. I'm asking neighbors for clothes for my father, two German soldiers bang on the door of our room. They tell my mother we have two hours to leave. They push us out, slam the door, and give the room to someone else."

    Standing on the street, our fifteen-year-old was in charge of her sick mother and younger sister. Lugging all the clothes and food they could pack, they trudged toward the apartment building of a married couple many blocks away. With the invasion, these friends might also be homeless. By sundown they were not sure where they would spend the night. Reaching the building, Krystyna had her mother and sister wait outside. She said, "I walked up and down the dark hallway. I found a door that matched their apartment number. I banged on the door. I waited. Nothing. The place felt creepy and hollow."

As she lifted her little fist to try again, the squeaky door opened timidly. Inching closer, Krystyna saw the husband's familiar face. Krystyna said, "They took us in and we all shared the little food we had. The man gave me clothes to get my father from the hospital. We brought him back to this apartment and stayed with these friends a month until my father got a bookkeeping job."

Kazimierz's salary was far from his military income, but the job included two rooms in a warehouse. This solved the problem of housing and her father's precarious military status. Krystyna said, "Under penalty of death, the Germans ordered all Polish officers to register with them. My father knew they would be sent to concentration camps, so he did not register. Both my parents destroyed their documents, but he worried the Germans will find out he was Polish officer. He went to work, and the rest of the time he hid in that warehouse until a month before the August 1944 Warsaw Uprising."

I Have to be Somebody

We dressed warm in the winter to attend secret classes in buildings with no heat.

While cleaning two dusty rooms to move into the warehouse, Krystyna told her father, "I'm sixteen. I must go back to school. To help support the family, I have to be somebody. I want to be a doctor."

German authorities forbid high school education for Polish people, but they allowed photography and cooking schools. Before the copy machine, photo shops reproduced documents. Krystyna said, "Father helped me find a cooking school because it included chemistry and math. He also asked around and found an Underground school so I could study for my high school diploma."

During the day, Krystyna attended the cooking school, then walked to the Underground school. Homeowners could be jailed for such a school discovered in their homes, so classes were often held in ruined buildings. Krystyna studied physics, history, literature, biology, anatomy, and Latin. She said, "They told us we can't have books. Remember everything we put in your head. We dressed warm in the winter to attend secret classes in building with no heat. I earned my diploma this way."

While going to school, Krystyna also worked for the Underground Resistance. For an assignment in the red-light district, she had only a vague idea of the nature of the place. She said, "They taught me to destroy weapons when German soldiers were in the bordellos. I'm sixteen but look like a kid, the smallest one they have, nobody bothers me. I wait in the basement. Somebody brings me a gun. I take out the firing pin and leave. That person puts back the soldier's gun, but it won't shoot."

The next job was more dangerous. Newspapers featured German propaganda, so the Underground prepared posters with news relevant to the war effort. The posters were attached to round pillars on street corners. She said, "I walk past pillar. Ready to pounce, I slap our posters on top of posters that glorify Hitler and Germany. As distraction, I faked falling because I could be arrested."

The job requiring the most ingenuity and courage was that of courier. Krystyna passed messages from officers to their units. She provided lawyers with information that helped get people out of prison and save them from concentration camps. These lawyers used bribery or other deals to free them. She said, "They were loading me up with numbers and addresses. You can't write it. You can't be caught with proof of where I'm going. You can't ask for directions on the street. I mostly succeeded, but once I couldn't find the place and my boss got angry. The building numbers didn't always run in order and electricity was shut off early in the evening. On a dark day, I couldn't see the numbers and goofed. It bothered me a long time. I never knew what happened to the person who was arrested."

Polish diplomat, Jan Karski, states that female couriers like Krystyna, "were a vital link to our operations and were in many ways more exposed than those they helped bring together... No one, not even the closest liaison woman, was entitled to know my secret name or the forged document I carried constantly in my pocket. Under conditions of these kinds, communication between members of the Underground was often nearly impossible. The liaison women took care of this problem."[66]

"They on the contrary, were completely exposed...She could not be permitted to go into hiding or get lost to us. To allow this would have meant to break down the contacts between the members and branches of the Underground... If arrested she was unable to betray us, even under torture, because within two or three hours all people in contact with her changed their names and addresses." [67]

"She constantly carried compromising documents... and treated with bestial cruelty in the Nazi jails. Most of them carried poison and were under order to use it without hesitation when the need arrived...the Underground could not take the risk of their succumbing to torture...of all the workers in the Underground their lot was the most severe, their sacrifices the greatest, and their contribution the least rewarded...They neither held high rank nor received any great honors for their heroism." [68]

Her Wounded Warsaw

They don't all die in a split second. Some were still alive and moving like a wave.

Krystyna was among hundreds of unrecognized heroes who worked for the Underground. Despite the brutal circumstances that Karski describes, her mind continued to serve her well as a courier, until it disconnected from her body during the next ordeal.

Krystyna faced dangers that would be daunting to any teenager, yet she found joy. When her father began running St. Stanislaus Hospital on Leśnia Street summer of 1944, Krystyna said, "My father's salary wasn't much but included an apartment. We left the warehouse. I finished high school. I got a job at St. Lazarus Hospital, across from where my father worked. They gave me white uniform. I cared for the sick. No pay, but good experience for becoming a doctor. I couldn't be happier."

Krystyna walked to work with a sense of purpose in her crisp white uniform. She washed and ironed it gently each day. The last time she wore it proudly, she was assisting a doctor in the men's ward and learning the procedure when the mass murder began. Sitting stone-faced, she said, "The German soldiers and their helpers walked in, took over the place. They grabbed nurses and doctors. They led us outside. Stood us in front of the hospital. Began shooting. They executed 276 people. When people die in a group like that, they don't all die in a split second. Some were still alive and moving like a wave. I was lucky to be small, because some man knew me and pulled me out of those bodies falling on top of me. He spoke good German. The guard saw this man also pulling a wounded German soldier from the street, so he let us pass."

As she spoke, Krystyna's body was still in South River, New Jersey, but her spirit was back on the street in Warsaw trying to escape the massacre. Her voice became trance like, as if coming from a tunnel. Her voice said, "That man kept pulling me away from those bodies falling on top of me. But the second guard didn't recognize him. He hit the man and split his skull. I knew the man who was trying to save me, but he didn't seem to have a face. I don't know what happened to him."

The voice continued, "Then, I'm struggling to pull a dead body through the street. To this day, I don't know who or why. It must have been someone dear to me."

This butchery was repeated throughout Warsaw, often by drunken soldiers of various ethnic groups under the command of German officers.

British historian, George Bruce, states that, "On 5 August the hospital of Marie Curie Radium Institute had been invaded by drunken Cossacks who assembled the staff and patients, about one hundred and seventy in all, robbed them, drove some of them into the hospital garden and thence to a camp near Mokotov Field, where the women were raped. Those patients still in their beds were shot dead, the building was pillaged, saturated with petrol and set on fire. Later the staff and patients who had been taken to the camps were shot through the head by a German officer. Similar barbarities were carried out at the Wola Hospital and the St. Lazarus Hospital." [69]

Sounding almost like herself, Krystyna said, "They struck St. Lazarus Hospital where I worked, but not St. Stanislaus where my father worked. That's where they put their own wounded. Being in white uniform, they grabbed me with twenty-six other people. My father's office was the first one as you walk in, so they used him as interpreter. We stayed two days, taking care of German soldiers."

Then the voice returned speaking in a whisper, "I lost that dead body someplace. The man pulling me from those dead bodies falling on me, at first I knew him. Then his face was blank. We nursed German soldiers for two days. Then I'm walking away, streetcars turned upside down as barricades, people fighting back. Some place I lost it. That dead body. I lost it."

Krystyna lost the dead body of someone who must have been dear to her in the middle of the 1944 Warsaw Uprising. In April 1943, the Jewish ghetto had rebelled, and the insurgents were butchered in reprisal. Then in August 1944, the Polish Underground rebellion lasted two months. Poland's official ally, the Soviet army, sat across the Vistula River and let these Poles, who were against the communist takeover of Poland, be slaughtered by the Germans.

British historian Joanna K. M. Hanson confirms Krystyna's account. Hanson states, "Himmler ...chose to send into Warsaw the police units from Poznań (2,740 officers and men) commanded by General Reinefarth, Dirlewangler's police and SS regiment from Lyck (881), Kaminski's SS Assault Brigade (RONA) from Częstochowa (1,700), Security Regiment 608 under Oberst Schmidt from the Wehrmacht (618), and finally an Azerbaijan Infantry Battalion (682). Thus, by 5 August, the number of forces available to fight the Uprising had doubled."[70]

"Barely half of the men of these units, although they wore German uniforms, spoke German. They were Ukrainians, Russians, Kalmuks, Cossacks, Turkomans, Azerbaijans ... Dirlewangler's brigade was 'composed exclusively of condemned criminals and political prisoners, who were promised an amnesty if they proved themselves in the fight.... They drank their way through the Uprising for as long as they were in Warsaw, committing indescribable crimes as they went. The soldiers were totally unaffected by death in any form and regarded rape as natural."[71]

Six Women and 247 Crazy Men

I was scared. I hated how they tried to grab and kiss and hug me.

Three days after the St. Lazarus massacre, Krystyna stood on a train platform with her parents and younger sister amid rumors they were going to Auschwitz. She said, "Forty people in one cattle car. They pick up more. After ten days, maybe 3,000 on the train. They kick us out twice a day for water and to do our business. No food. I have my period, covered with blood. I have only that white uniform. Some nuns help me clean up. I throw away the underwear. They give me clothes. Train stops. I see my family, then go back to nuns."

They waited in the German city of Bietigheim while the *Arbeitsamt*, the central employment agency, decided where they would be sent to work. Krystyna said, "Barracks are full. We sleep outside. At dawn, father, mother, little Zofia, and I stand in line. They check our faces and decide if they like you or not. Then, they sent us to factory in Stuttgart."

The Stuttgart factory produced parts for bombers and airplanes. Men stayed in separate barracks from the women and children. Krystyna said, "We had different jobs, so I only saw mother and sister at night. The cork soles on my shoes cracked, so they gave me large workmen shoes. I take step, shoe is on the ground. One night, I was running in air raid and lost those shoes. I stood bare foot in water in bunker for hours. Next day, my hands swelled like balloons and I couldn't move my legs."

She added, "Five weeks together, then Gestapo grab me. No good-by to father and mother, I'm gone."

Krystyna was yanked from her family in October 1944 and sent to the nearby town of Metzingen. She worked six days a week in a wax factory. The nauseating fumes of the floor polish it produced permeated the building. Breakfast was dark water and a piece of bread made with sawdust. Lunch was turnip soup. Dinner was hot water. She had no underwear. The trousers of the work uniform were so big they kept falling down. With no change of clothes, she could not wash the uniform.

They were locked up at night, surrounded by guard dogs. Krystyna said, "Six women and 247 crazy men, mostly Russian, slept in bunk beds in the basement and on two floors. I was scared. I hated how they tried to grab and kiss and hug me. I didn't know what it is all about. At night I think I'm not going to wake up, not from war, but because of those men. The worst was feeling dirty. I found cardboard to cover the bunk so person beneath can't see my behind. God blessed me that I never got period there. How would you feel with it dripping on your legs? Six women and 247 crazy men."

The French army came in April 1945. She said, "They shut down the factory, but we were on our own. We sat in the rain under the bridges in Metzingen. Some people went to town looking for food. A German woman said she would help me. She wants to prove to French she was friendly with Polish people so they don't take her house. I went to her house with only that factory uniform on my back."

The German woman fed Krystyna and provided the only clothes she could spare – her daughter's bathing suit and housecoat. Each day, Krystyna did house and yard work for the woman. Then wearing that strange get up, she would get on the bicycle to look for her parents.

Love and Marriage

Stefan was not leaving without meeting her.

Krystyna rode in and out of camps for eight days. She found her parents and sister Zofia in a barrack near the city of Stuttgart living in one room with forty people. By the vacant stare on her parents' faces, Krystyna had to rescue them, body and soul. She said, "I had to get them out of there. At least they knew who I was. I took their hands and said, "Mama, papa, I got a room, if I work, the woman gives me food, bread or something. Come with me."

Still wearing a bathing suit and housecoat, she instead put her parents and sister on an American army truck going to a displaced persons camp. She said, "The camp near Zuffenhausen was in a lovely place near woods, but we were stuck for two years. Father had destroyed his documents but as a high-ranking officer, he couldn't risk returning to Poland. The new communist regime would execute him."

Stefan was also in danger for opposing the communist takeover of his country. Unable to return to Poland, he was about to meet Krystyna. She worked as a nurse at the Zuffenhausen displaced persons camp, but her goal of being a doctor receded with each year of homelessness.

Krystyna joined a travelling theatre group that brought audiences much needed light moments. Stefan was the commanding officer of a guard company in the town of Ludwigsburg. He decided it would raise his men's morale to see a performance by a theatre company, then socialize with the group. That evening, Stefan sat mesmerized by a spunky girl with dark curls circling her face. As she sang and spoke her lines, everything on the stage faded away. He saw only her. Stefan was not leaving without meeting her. It was love at first sight.

Stefan began visiting Krystyna in Zuffenhausen. Her parents liked him, and she felt a silly flutter each time he walked through the barrack door. Krystyna and Stefan discovered that, although different in temperament, they were compatible in their approach to life. When they were married in early 1948, medical school was out of the question. Even a real home was years away. As some refugees found jobs and left, the camps were consolidated. The remaining displaced persons were frequently moved.

Such instability drove the newlyweds to look toward France. After their first child Barbara was born, Stefan left for France in March 1949. He would find an apartment, save money, and have his wife and child join him. He worked in a large steel mill, then in a cement factory near the city of Lorraine.

When his newborn became sick, he rushed back to care for mother and child. Krystyna said, "We learned that Barbara was allergic to mother's milk and had to be fed formula. After that, we decided wherever we go, we go together. No more splits."

Developments in the United States opened a new path for the couple, and for my own family. After much debate and many revisions in Congress as to who could come and under what circumstance, President Harry Truman signed legislation on June 25, 1948 and June 16, 1950 allowing an influx of war refugees into the country. Relief organizations began visiting the camps with job offers.

Krystyna and Stefan took a job as farm hands with Dr. Benson, a dentist in Maryland. They arrived in 1949 with nine-month-old Barbara. Krystyna said, "We got a rundown house, and sometimes the extra vegetables, eggs, and milk. We were paid one dollar a day."

Stefan added, "That was the going rate for farm hands in that part of the country. What can you buy on one dollar a day?"

Krystyna cooked and cleaned, took care of baby Barbara, the house, the garden, and the chickens. Stefan looked after the twelve-acre farm, the cows, and twenty pigs. Having taken classes in Germany, they listened to the radio and read newspapers to continue learning English. Krystyna said, "Stefan picked up the newspaper every day. On the long walk between the house and road, he compared the headlines to what we heard on the radio and we talked about it in the evening.

But they were not moving out of poverty. After two years in Maryland, their second daughter Elizabeth was born. A newspaper ad for farm hands in Pittstown, New Jersey, seemed promising. Stefan said, "Those two years were hard, but we parted with Dr. Benson and his family on good terms. Years later, he and his wife came to New Jersey for Barbara's wedding."

The job in Pittstown also offered meager wages to farm laborers, but now they had the confidence that came from being fluent in English. They moved to South River,

New Jersey. Stefan took odd jobs until he was hired by the Squibb Pharmaceutical Company as a technician. Krystyna was a seamstress at the Dora Dress Company and then a computer operator for Fidelity Trust. They bought their own house and began taking trips to far off places.

This all happened years after Krystyna had confessed to Stefan that it was love at first sight for her, too. Before they met backstage after the performance, she had already noticed him in the audience.

Photo Gallery

...we liberated the Polish, Hungarian, Jewish, French, and Russian women working in the munitions factory.

Over a break for tea and cookies, Stefan opened a drawer and took out the medals he received for wartime service to Poland, albeit 50 years later. He took out an album with photos taken 60 years ago. Too small and grainy to reproduce, but with some imagination, they complement Stefan and Krystyna's narrative.

DC: Stefan told us that his diocese of Pelplin had an original Guttenberg Bible. The Germans killed most of the priests in your diocese as revenge for not getting it. What happened to the Bible?

Stefan: It was hidden in Poland and returned to the Pelplin diocese. I bought this little camera from a Jewish man in the ghetto for 100 złoty. It made pictures only in the day. Here's the old bridge for trains. When Germany incorporated our area into the General Government, it rebuilt the two bridges of Tczew in another location.

Krystyna: *Photo:* This is my aunt, my father's sister. She was taken to Auschwitz early in the war. These Polish Christian friends from Tarnów were also among the first to die there. *Photo:* These are the friends who took us in when we got kicked out of that room in our building. We're on the street, it's the only place I could reach walking with my sick mother. They are the people who gave me clothes so my father could leave the hospital.

Stefan: *Photos:* This high school and university friend was killed in a concentration camp.

This is our constant, steady chaplain. He said Sunday Mass whenever possible.

Here I am on a horse. I was adjutant to the regiment commanding officer. I organized the needs of day-to-day life for the brigade.

We are marching to Prague through Sudeten Czechoslovakia in a blizzard. That's one of the Czech families we stayed with. And these German civilians are escaping from the Russians just like we were.

This man wearing a blanket and pieces of wood tied to his legs is "Dr. Par," the Russian doctor from Georgia who saved my life.

Here we are entering a village in Czechoslovakia with American soldiers. Together, we liberated the Polish, Hungarian, Jewish, French, and Russian women working in the munitions factory in that concentration camp.

During Mass, on the first Sunday of liberation, these Polish girls are thanking our commanding officer for being rescued.

This is the wife of Mikołajczyk, the prime minister of the government-in-exile after Władysław Sikorski died. She was in the concentration camp we liberated. And this government representative visited our unit in Czechoslovakia to thank us.

Here we are on trucks headed for Bavaria, August, 1945, to escape the Russians who wanted us extradited and killed for being against communism.

This is Italy with some of the guys, September 1945, when I tried to join The Second Polish Corps of the British Eighth Army.

We were guard companies of German prisoners in Dachau. First, we wore our green uniforms. Then, American uniforms which were navy. In this picture some of the men are wearing green uniforms, others are wearing navy.

DC: And the next major event was meeting Krystyna.

Krystyna: We met in Germany after the war. I was the type that had to belong to everything. I was in a theatre group, performing on stage. At 20, I wasn't thinking of marriage. I survived as a courier for the Underground, that horrible wax factory, being naked and scared with all those men, and riding that bicycle for days in bathing suit and housecoat. I just wanted to have fun.

Stefan and Krystyna Władyka with baby Barbara at the Zuffenhausen displaced persons camp. Germany 1949

Stefan: (Sits up with a big smile.) May I say the rest?

DC: (She smiles at him demurely, eager to hear the story she has heard many times.)

Stefan: We were guarding German prisoners of war. As commanding officer, I arranged some festivities for the anniversary of the formation of our guard company and invited the visiting theatre group. After the show, we had dancing and socializing. My company was strict about no alcohol at parties. But I saw some commotion near the stage and went to investigate. And there I found her...

Krystyna: You found me with a glass of water.

Stefan: There they were, my soldiers and performers breaking the rules. I got mad. But there she stood, so I had to cool it. Had to find out about her. Our first meeting, unexpectedly. And we have been together ever since.

Reflections

Was this a life for a human being?

Henry: Was it hard to have faith during this ordeal?

Krystyna takes a thoughtful pause, then says: Yes. I felt the only solution was to die. I wanted to die. You're dirty, no water, no soap. You stand in line, half naked. Food, you get in your hand. Soup, you get on a plate but no spoon. You have to lick it. Was this a life for a human being?

    I got to be extremely angry. Metzingen was the worst. Six women and 247 wild men. No clothes, no mattress, just two boards and if my bottoms fall down, someone below sees my rear end. I worked at the controls on heavy machinery. When they cursed me, I cursed back in German. They went behind people and hit them. But nobody German hit me. A girl, nothing on her and she's got guts to answer back, so they pushed me into better position.

DC: What happened to your parents?

Like us, they worked on a farm in Kansas, then outside of Chicago. When they could no longer work, they moved near us. My parents are buried in the cemetery in South River.

Seeing what happened to other people, I thank God I was so lucky. They stood us in front of St. Lazarus Hospital and began shooting, some man pulled me out. We survived the 1944 Warsaw Uprising. We were not sent to Auschwitz. I got out of Metzingen. Stefan and I came to America. We had a home, a family. We worked. We traveled. And in our souls, we were always free.

DC: You and Stefan survived physically and in spirit. I think the productive lives you have created after such brutality is the best definition of success.

Krystyna Białobrzeska Władyka was born on November 4, 1924 near Kraków, Poland and died on June 8, 2002 in South River, New Jersey. Stefan and Krystyna's daughter Barbara was a school librarian, and daughter Elizabeth was a teacher. They had four grandchildren. Krystyna's older sister Joanna remained in Poland and the younger sister Zofia immigrated to Australia. I had many conversations with Stefan and Krystyna when they visited my parents, and Henry and I spoke with them in their home on February 1999 in South River, New Jersey.

For More Information. Jan Karski

"A young Polish diplomat turned cavalry officer at the outbreak of World War II, Karski joined the Polish underground movement in 1939 after ingeniously escaping from a Soviet detention camp. Most of the Polish officers held with him were later executed. Karski became a courier for the underground, crossing enemy lines to serve as liaison between occupied Poland and the free world. Captured by the Gestapo in 1940, he was savagely tortured. Afraid that the Germans would extract secrets from him, he slashed his wrists. But after the suicide attempt failed, he escaped from a hospital with the help of an underground commando team. His work had just begun."

"Karski, a Roman Catholic, developed a keen concern for the plight of the Jews under Nazi domination. In 1942, Jewish leaders asked him to carry a desperate message to Allied leaders: the news of Hitler's effort to exterminate the Jews of Europe. To be able to carry an authentic eyewitness report, Karski agreed to tour Warsaw's Jewish Ghetto in disguise. The suffering he saw there was only a prelude to the atrocities he witnessed when he later volunteered to be smuggled into a camp that was part of the Nazi murder machine."

"Carrying searing tales of inhumanity, Karski reached London in late 1942 and set out to alert the world to the emerging Holocaust. He met secretly with top Allied officials, including British foreign secretary Anthony Eden, and with intellectuals like H.G. Wells and Arthur Koestler. Some reacted viscerally to his message. Other responded with disbelief or indifference. In July 1943, Karski traveled secretly to Washington, where he briefed President Roosevelt..." [72]

Karski's reports were a valiant effort to inform the West about the plight of the Jews in Europe, but the high-level officials in positions of authority that Jan Karski spoke with did not believe him. They dismissed his testimony as exaggerated propaganda from the Polish government-in-exile in London.

Endnotes

66 Jan Karski, *Story of a Secret State* (Boston: Houghton Mifflin, 1944) pp. 280 - 281.

67 Ibid

68 Ibid

69 George Bruce, *The Warsaw Uprising: 1 August – 2 October 1944* (London: Rupert Hart-Davis, 1972) p. 131.

70 Joanna K. M. Hanson, The Civilian Population and the Warsaw Uprising of 1944 (Cambridge: Cambridge UP, 1982) pp. 84-86.

71 Ibid

72 E. Thomas Wood, Stanisław M. Jankowski, *Karski. How One Man Tried to Stop the Holocaust*, (NY: John Wiley and Sons, Inc., 1994) front and back flaps.

Chapter 16 Czesław Miłosz
The Big Taboo

When Nobel laureate, Professor Czesław Miłosz, passed away in 2004 at age ninety-three, he was known as a writer of moral authority and compassion. But fifty years earlier, he was discredited by some of his fellow intellectuals. They did not believe him when his international best seller, *The Captive Mind*, exposed communist brainwashing methods which sacrifice human individuality for a future utopia.

Miłosz explains that, "This book was written in 1951/52 in Paris at a time when the majority of French intellectuals resented their country's dependence upon American help and placed their hopes in a new world in the East, ruled by a leader of incomparable wisdom and virtue, Stalin. Those of their compatriots who, like [the French author] Albert Camus, dared to mention a network of concentration camps as the very foundation of a presumably Socialist system, were vilified and ostracized by their colleagues. When my book appeared in 1953...the admirers of Soviet communism found it insulting... A lonely venture, it has been since vindicated by facts..." [73]

In the following years, Czesław Miłosz wrote critically acclaimed fiction, nonfiction, and poetry. He was in demand within literary circles worldwide, yet he made time to encourage my work. In a letter dated February 16, 1998, Professor Miłosz wrote, "Since you mention Naliboki, the name for me is meaningful, not only vaguely. I have heard about the "hell on earth" during the war in that neighborhood. Your project seems to be valid and I wish you success."

My husband Henry and I visited the Miłosz home in Berkeley, California in April 1998. I had just begun my research on World War II. The events Professor Miłosz described in Naliboki, and Poland's fate after the war, helped set the direction for the eyewitness narratives which you have just read.

The Day We Met

Giving us his full attention, our host radiated a peaceful energy.

We crept up winding hills overlooking the Napa Valley. I was nervous about meeting this man of insight and intellect. By the time we reached the Miłosz home, the twisting hills had set off a bout of motion sickness in me. We parked on a little street with a steep incline. My knees wobbled and my face turned pale. I held onto my husband Henry's arm with white knuckles, breathing deeply to ward off nausea as we walked slowly to the front door.

A pretty blond woman in her fifties wearing a buttercup yellow summer dress opened the door. With a warm smile, she introduced herself as the author's wife Carol and welcomed us into a spacious room filled with books and dark wooden furniture. The California sun streaming through the elegant floor-to-ceiling window revealed cottages and boats below. The other rooms were situated right and left from this central area.

We chatted with Carol about the thirty-day train trip Henry and I were taking across the United States and Canada. An elderly woman peeked in, and Carol explained that she and her husband were taking guests from Poland on a tour of the wine country. What kindness. While having guests, Professor Miłosz had made time for me. His wife's gracious manner put me at ease. My knees were no longer wobbly, and the nausea was gone.

Professor Miłosz entered the room quietly, dressed for company in a deep blue shirt, black tie, and black slacks. With his bushy eyebrows, high cheekbones, and square jaw, he reminded me of my father. He invited us to sit down near him on a wide wooden couch with thick cushions where he had, no doubt, mentored other eager writers. As we settled in, a frisky golden retriever ran into the room wanting to play. Professor Miłosz patted him gently on the head and told him to lie down. The dog sat near the couch with ears perked as if he were part of our conversation.

Giving us his full attention, our host radiated a peaceful energy. I framed the discussion in terms of two questions. At eighty-seven, he answered in a deep, strong voice, amplifying and affirming the compelling circumstances of the people you have met in earlier chapters. His hearty laughter revealed a keen sense of irony which may have been formed during those early years of communist doublespeak.

Czesław Miłosz grew up within the shifting borderlands of Eastern Europe. He is from the Vilnius area, once part of Poland and now in Lithuania. I am from the Nowogródek area, once part of Poland and now in Belarus. His novel, *The Issa Valley (Dolina Issy)*, captures the world my parents brought to life for me when I was a child. Like him, we were a Polish family living among other ethnic groups until two repressive regimes changed the boundaries of what had once been home.

Professor Miłosz has been described as a poet of witness and a preserver of memories, so my two questions focused on a peculiar kind of forgetting:

The general public is familiar with the German role in World War II through books, film, school curricula, even comedy. Yet the atrocities committed by the Soviet Union are not known to most people outside of academia. Why has this crucial piece of history been ignored?

As a high school and college student in America, the deaths and displacements of Slavic Christians were missing from my history classes and from the media. Why is so little known in the United States about the Christian victims of World War II?

Fifty Years of Silence

The place you come from, and your town of Naliboki, was an area of terrible cruelties and guerrilla movements.

DC: My uncle, Józef Chmara, and his family were deported to Russia near the Arctic Circle. Two years later, my own family was deported to Germany. The racism toward the Polish nation and the German invasion of Poland is known to many, but to the general American audience, the Soviet atrocities remain unknown.

Czesław Miłosz: Yes. The wife of my brother wrote a book based on the deportation of her mother's family. Her mother was four years old when her family was deported more or less to that same area as your uncle and his family in northern Russia.

DC: Many from Eastern Poland were deported to the Soviet Union, many perished. Yet, these deportations, and the repression in Poland after the war, were not discussed in my history classes. As a student, this felt hollow, as if my family's displacement did not matter. Why the silence?

Czesław Miłosz: I can tell you. During some fifty years in Poland, it was a subject spoken about in the families, but officially it was taboo. Because of communism, people were not allowed to talk about the realities of the war

DC: Because of the Soviet Union?

Czesław Miłosz: Because of the Soviet Union. The place you come from, and your town of Naliboki, was an area of terrible cruelties and guerrilla movements. That was the area of AK resistance activity. In English that was the Armia Krajowa – Polish Home Army. And that was a taboo subject.

DC: Even after the war?

Czesław Miłosz: After the war, Armia Krajowa was forbidden. The AK was considered to have taken politically incorrect actions by the communist authorities.

DC: It was forbidden to even talk about it?

Czesław Miłosz: Not only to talk about it. Membership in AK qualified a person for prison. And anything connected with that area was taboo.

DC: So Polish people living in Poland could not talk about how their soldiers had fought for an independent Poland and had been betrayed? This was true for other military groups, like the brigade in which a family friend, Stefan Władyka, had fought.

Czesław Miłosz: They could not talk about Poland being betrayed.

DC: After the war, Polish people could only talk about the German invasion of their country. They could not talk about the Soviet invasion of Poland because, after the war, Poland had become a Soviet satellite against the will of the Polish people.

Czesław Miłosz: They could not talk about the Soviet invasion of Poland that happened two weeks after the German invasion.

DC: *If American Indians had to pretend there was no genocide, if African Americans had to pretend there was no slavery – what level of rage would that engender? Visiting Poland in the 1960's, I saw the fear in people's eyes. I wondered if the rage was underneath.*

Czesław Miłosz: After Poland was invaded in 1939 from two directions by Germany and the Soviet Union, open defiance was crushed. In response, a Polish Government-in-Exile was established in London. It was anti-Nazi and anti-communist and its aim was to regain Poland's independence. In addition, the Polish Underground was organized to provide social and military resistance to the invasions. The Underground took its instructions from the government-in-exile, although there were some pro-communist units in the movement.

Since military resistance was crushed early in the war, Polish soldiers fought in Western Europe under Allied command. But some units of the Home Army, AK, remained in Poland and were organized as the military arm of the Polish Underground. That area you come from was in the center of fierce Home Army activity. Your town of Naliboki was an area of terrible cruelties and guerrilla movements. The situation was extremely complex. It was a peculiar triangle because the Home Army was fighting the Germans. But it was also fighting the Soviet partisans.

DC: *After the defeat of the official Polish army, the Underground Home Army became the military force inside the country. The branch of the Home Army in the Naliboki area was trying to protect the people and regain the territory.*

Czesław Miłosz: Yes. The Naliboki area, because of the Nalibocka Puszcza, was an area of terrible mutual massacres between the Home Army, the Germans, and the partyzanty – the Soviet led guerilla fighters. Those were the three forces that fought with terrible cruelties, mutual cruelties.

DC: The Nalibocka Puszcza, the beautiful primeval forest, became the staging area for all three groups trying to destroy each other within this "peculiar triangle."

Czesław Miłosz: Yes, and sometimes the Home Army was left in peace by the Germans and it controlled large areas because the Germans would prefer to have it between them and the Soviet partisans in that area.

DC: They used the Polish Home Army as a buffer against the Soviet partisans?

Czesław Miłosz: Yes, as a buffer. So the Home Army fought the Germans, occasionally Soviet partisans, and, of course, it was considered by the Soviet partisans as a criminal entity because the area, according to the view of the Soviets, belonged to the Soviet Union. And according to the view of the Home Army, it belonged to Poland.

DC: With the German invasion of Eastern Europe in 1941, Poland and the Soviet Union became officially allies, but in reality, the Home Army and Soviet partisans were killing each other.

Czesław Miłosz: Yes.

DC: Based on the rule of law, the region had belonged to Poland since 1918. The Armia Krajowa, Home Army, was defending its country. Soviets and the Germans came into the region by force.

Czesław Miłosz: Yes. The German army attacked the Soviet Union in 1941 and pushed the German-Russian front far to the East. After that, the German army occupied Naliboki for a long time. It was a question of who was going to control the area because the Home Army fought the Germans and the Soviet partisans. The Soviet partisans fought the Home Army and the Germans.

The Belarussian population was between two fires because many also belonged to the Home Army. In the Belarussian villages, if the Home Army controlled the villages, the Home Army asked for loyalty. If Soviet partisans were in control, they asked for loyalty. And so the Belarussian peasants were murdered by one and the other.

DC: That's also how it was in Naliboki. People didn't know by whose hands they would perish. This gets complicated because the circumstances and loyalties kept changing.

Czesław Miłosz: That is a puzzle. It will take some time before you figure it out (laughs).

DC: As you said, Polish people living in Poland after the war could not speak openly about the Soviet invasion of their country. But the Polish people who were living within the areas taken over by the Soviet Union, like my town of Naliboki, faced even greater repression.

Czesław Miłosz: Yes. Soviet policy toward the Polish population in that region was officially tolerant and officially there was no discrimination as to nationality. But in fact, the Soviet Union considered Polish populations living there as undesirable. They either deported them to Siberia or forced them to escape to the west. In that way, many families immigrated west to Poland.

DC: Yes. With Poland's new borders after the war, many of my family and friends in what had been Eastern Poland moved to Western Poland. This type of "ethnic cleansing" was also happening in your city of Wilno (Vilnius).

Czesław Miłosz: Yes. A majority of the population of the city of Wilno immigrated to Poland, and the composition of Wilno changed radically. Before the war, it was a city of people speaking Polish and Yiddish. The massacre of the Jewish population by the Nazis occurred in 1942 and 1943. Most of the Polish population immigrated to Western Poland in 1945. Before that, many were deported to the Soviet Union in 1940 and later. Those who wanted to avoid that fate were the ones who immigrated to Western Poland. The new population that came to Wilno was mostly Lithuanian.

DC: Thousands were displaced and millions were murdered, yet we still do not have a definitive number of how many Polish people and other ethnic groups perished.

Czesław Miłosz: No. Statistics are, I should say, misleading. It is very hard to tell. The losses of the known Jewish population just in Poland are defined roughly as three million. But it is difficult to divide into categories. It embraces all losses, namely, those who perished in German concentration camps. Those who perished in war activities. Those who perished from hunger. Those who were deported to the Soviet Union.

Even today the number of people deported to the Soviet Union is undefined. It was said to be a million and a half. But this included Polish speaking people as well as Ukrainians, Jews, and so on. But now it seems that it was lower, but still it was probably about 900,000 people. It is impossible to know. It is not established. Maybe some historian now is working on this.

DC: Then after the war, Polish people who did not move back to Poland with its new boundaries faced cultural and spiritual repression behind the iron curtain.

Czesław Miłosz: Yes, they lived through the Soviet occupation.

DC: My family that remained in Belarus had their children baptized in a far-off town in the middle of the night because they wanted to hold onto their jobs.

Czesław Miłosz: At least in the Soviet Republic of Lithuania, Polish schools were allowed. South of the Lithuanian border there were no Polish schools, only Belarussian and Russian schools. So in the Soviet Republic of Belarus, and in the Nowogródek area that you come from, there were no Polish schools, only Belarussian and Russian schools. Polish people grew up without the language and with an absolute taboo on learning the history of Poland. The history of that area under Polish rule was presented as a rule of bloody capitalists and landlords.

DC: They also faced a taboo on spiritual life.

Czesław Miłosz: Oh yes! Oh yes! The Catholic Church survived thanks to the great dedication of priests. We had reports about how people lived several identities. They went to church, the Mass was in Polish. They came home, and spoke Belarussian to each other. They watched television, and the television was in Russian.

DC: This is still the case in Naliboki. When Soviet partisans burned the town in 1943, the brick church that my father helped build was the only structure left standing. With the fall of the Soviet Union, it was restored after decades in disrepair and consecrated in 1994. The Mass was in Polish. Conversation was in Belarussian. Older people said they were Polish. Their grandchildren said they were Belarussian. And the television programming was in Russian.

Czesław Miłosz: Well, people say they are Polish because they are Catholic. Religion is a definition of nationality for them.

DC: Yes. When I ask people in Naliboki if they are Polish or Belarussian, they sometimes say, "Well, I'm Catholic." My grandmother thought that way.

Shifting Borders

A basic problem for many people in Poland was a mass exodus from the eastern lands that you come from.

DC: For my second question. In the United States, discussion of Christian victims of the war is largely ignored within school curricula, the media, and the publishing industry.

Czesław Miłosz: Yes, yes.

DC: With this lack of information, the general American population knows nothing about this.

Czesław Miłosz: No, it doesn't. It is no wonder. For instance, the Shoah, the Holocaust of the Jewish people, became popularly known through films – television and films. So it is no wonder that something that has never had any image, vivid image, is unknown, completely unknown to many people.

DC: As a poet, you know the power of the vivid image. But there is little even in print.

Czesław Miłosz: There are plenty of publications and memoirs in Polish in scholarly journals.

DC: But little has been written for the general public in this country. It is up to Polish and Polish American writers to tell this story. Is there something within our nature that makes us want to be invisible?

Czesław Miłosz: (Reflects) You see, Polish people in this country have been under a certain trauma. Poland has always been presented as a martyr and victim of oppressive powers. So people are reluctant to constantly complain, constantly show their wounds. That is one theory.

And a basic problem for many people in Poland was a mass exodus from the eastern lands that you come from. The shifting of Polish borders is a decisive fact in history. Polish borders were moved westward after the war and this created deep trauma. Many families had to move to former German areas. By now, the younger generation – actually several generations – were brought up in Gdańsk, Szczecin, in Wrocław, in Silesia, and so on. That is a main problem of healing those wounds of displacement. The transfer to the west, and adaptation of young generations to live in former German areas was a major result of the war for Polish people.

DC: Is anyone writing about this for a general audience?

Czesław Miłosz: Yes. This is a subject of literature in Poland, adaptation to the new land, finding roots. For example, Polish authors Stefan Chwin and Pawel Huelle write about finding roots in the former German city of Gdańsk. Here in the states, Professor Richard Lukas is a good source on the war and Norman Davies in England is an authority on Polish history. He presents these events objectively. Concerning your geographic area, there is much written in Polish. A periodical published in connection with the University of Warsaw, *Karta,* is dedicated particularly to the time of the war and deportations to the Soviet Union. But I am not aware of anything in English that tells your story.

DC: So I should tell that story, and you have pointed me in the right direction. I have a big job ahead of me.

Czesław Miłosz: Yes, I would think so (laughs.)

Telling our Own Story

The history of that area is so complicated that the young generation does not understand it.

DC: If we stop thinking of ourselves as victims, we might give voice to our experience. The victim mindset is a waste of energy and keeps us from moving forward.

Czesław Miłosz: Precisely.

DC: Fifty years of silence is like fifty years of an open wound. If we don't tell our story, the wound festers in silence. And we can't expect someone else to do it for us.

Czesław Miłosz: Of course. Women have been oppressed for many centuries. In order to make people aware, how much effort of feminist organizations was needed to introduce the subject of women's oppression into the general consciousness?

DC: And they didn't expect someone else to do it for them.

Czesław Miłosz: Yes, it was not so easy for women.

DC: War has a lingering impact. My nieces and nephews know their parents' stories. They even have some of the same nightmares. Has the war damaged the next generation, their spirit, and view of the world?

Czesław Miłosz: In my opinion, yes. But the history of that area is so complicated that the young generation does not understand it. I speak not only about Americans, but also Polish people. For the young generation in Poland, those are distant stories told by grandfathers and grandmothers. For the young people who were children when communism tumbled down, for them it is already history. Our history department here in Berkley has an interest in that part of Europe, in post-war Poland, but the faculty members are young. The time of Solidarity has become an object of history.

DC: Are they interested mostly in emerging democracies? My concerns are passe?

Czesław Miłosz: Yes, of course (ironic laughter).

DC: What was your experience during the war?

Czesław Miłosz: I was in Warsaw.

DC: You were active in the Polish Underground Resistance, and you published an anthology of anti-Nazi poetry when it was dangerous to criticize the Nazi regime. You were in Warsaw during the 1943 Jewish uprising, and you were an eyewitness to the almost total destruction of Warsaw during the August 1944 uprising.

Czesław Miłosz: Yes.

DC: And you stayed in Poland the whole time?

Czesław Miłosz: I was first in Lithuania, in Wilno, but then in Warsaw.

DC: (Professor Miłosz seemed reluctant to talk about himself, perhaps because so much has been written about him. Knowing that his visitors were waiting, I posed one final question.) Professor Miłosz, may I use the material from this conversation in my book?

Czesław Miłosz: Yes, it is not a secret anymore (ironic laughter).

DC: Your book, The Captive Mind, shows how a totalitarian government strips away the human capacity to think, create, and love. You are giving me courage to speak about the Polish experience through the people I am interviewing. Thank you.

From 1961 to 1998, Czesław Miłosz was a Professor of Slavic Languages and Literature at the University of California in Berkeley. He also continued to write poetry, essays, novels, literary criticism, translations, and scholarly work. He is honored as one of the "Righteous among the Nations," at Israel's Yad Vashem memorial to the Holocaust.

Professor Miłosz received the Nobel Prize in Literature in 1980, thirty years after defecting to the west. That same year, the Solidarity movement burst upon the world stage and brought down the regime that Miłosz had described in *The Captive Mind.*

Czesław Miłosz married Janina Dluska in 1944 and she predeceased him in 1986. After Poland won its freedom in 1989, he maintained residences in Berkeley and in the Polish city of Krakow. His second wife Carol Thigpen was an Associate Dean of Arts and Sciences at Emory University in Atlanta, Georgia. She passed away in 2002. Czesław Miłosz passed away on August 14, 2004 in Kraków, Poland.

For More Information: Taboo on Freedom of Speech in Post-war Poland

In Alicja's story, Professor Marek Tuszynski explains why the British and American governments did not want their citizens to know that their ally, the Soviet Union, was a repressive regime responsible for the deaths of millions even before the war. This information was withheld because they could not risk public protest and losing the Soviet military force against Germany. They found it preferable for Soviet boys to perish on the front rather than the sons of British and American mothers.

British historian, Norman Davies, explains why discussion of Soviet atrocities was taboo in post-war Poland. "Public discourse in post-war Poland was governed by two taboos...no one was permitted to speak badly of the Soviet Union....no one could speak well of the [1944] Warsaw Rising. Certainly, by the time a full-blown Stalinist regime had been established in 1948, all freedom of speech had been crushed, and all favorable mention of the wartime alliance with the Western powers was anathema. The word now was that the Soviet Union had won the war against fascism single-handed; that democracy was to be identified with something called 'dictatorship of the proletariat'; and that the ruling party could do no wrong. Anyone who dared to praise pre-war independence, or to revere those who fought during the Rising to recover it, was judged to be talking dangerous, seditious nonsense. Even in private, people talked with caution. Police informers were everywhere. Children were taught in Soviet-style schools where denouncing their friends and parents was pronounced an admirable thing to do."[74]

Since my conversation with Professor Miłosz in 1998, a number of books in English have addressed the Soviet role in the war. In his book and video, *Behind Closed Doors*, British author Laurence Rees provides a compelling account of the multitudes who perished based on Stalin's orders. In his book *Bloodlands*, American historian Timothy Snyder offers numbers killed by ethnic category and specific time periods. These two sources are listed in the annotated bibliography under Recommended Reading.

The author at the home of Professor Czesław Miłosz. Berkeley, California, 1998.

Endnotes

73 Czesław Miłosz, *The Captive Mind* (New York: Vintage, 1981) Foreword.

74 Norman Davies, *Rising '44. The Battle for Warsaw* (New York: Viking, 2003) p. 509.

Chapter 17 Father Hyacinth
Auschwitz, Dachau, and Mosquitoes

My extended family who remained in Naliboki lived under an imposed Soviet atheism known to the world. But little is known about Hitler's plan to banish God and replace religion with reverence for himself and the Nazi party. To avoid public alienation, Christianity would be allowed until the war was won. But this plan was already incubating during the war through the persecution of clergy. Removed from their communities, they faced incarceration, hard labor, physical and mental abuse, and medical experiments. Doctors doing the experiments did not see their subjects as human. They saw them as useful research tools to benefit a future race of supermen.

One such priest who survived malaria experiments was Father Hyacinth Dombrowski. He was in his eighties when we met in May 1991 at the church rectory in Manville, New Jersey. I expected someone frail, but he swung open the door, standing tall in a black suit, white clerical collar, and deep purple sweater. He described in halting English his work for the Underground Resistance, his incarceration in Auschwitz, and then in Dachau. With good health, strong will, and cunning, he lived to tell how he was used as a human guinea pig.

Trust Us

All I can offer is some straw to sleep on the floor. Or you can escape during the night.

The priest standing on the train platform did not wear his clerical collar. The two Polish army officers waiting with him were not in uniform. Given the German occupation, it was safest to travel in street clothes. The older officer said to Father Hyacinth, "I'm returning to Warsaw to my wife and two children. Trains are unpredictable these days, and my fellow officer here is restless."

The young man replied, "My wife is expecting our first child any day now. I need to be with her."

The older officer asked Father Hyacinth, "And what brings you to the mountains of southern Poland?"

"I'm a professor of theology at a seminary here. We ended the semester and I'm going home too. My family are the monks and priests at the Capuchin monastery on Kapucinska Street in Warsaw."

A German officer, with two soldiers, interrupted the conversation. He demanded to see their papers, their occupations, and purpose of travel. Father Hyacinth asked politely in perfect German, "We are not making a disturbance. Why do you wish to know these things?"

"I am doing my duty. I have to keep order and get people off the streets at night by curfew."

Having stumbled upon a Catholic priest and two Polish officers, he arrested them. If they promise not to escape and report to him in the morning, they will get travel passes to Warsaw. Father Hyacinth said, "One of the soldiers who led us away whispered to me that talking politely with his superior was very intelligent. You are in good position. Do not be afraid. You will be in Warsaw tomorrow."

The soldiers led them far out of town to a solitary farmhouse away from the train station. The main room where the farmer lived alone had a stove, cupboards, table, some chairs, and one bed. After the soldiers left, he said, "All I can offer is some straw to sleep on the floor. Or you can escape during the night. I'm a sick old man. They can't expect me to restrain three healthy men while I sleep."

The young officer said, "Out of the question. We gave our word of honor as Polish officers not to escape."

"Like I said, I can't control three healthy young men," and he laid down on his bed.

Feeling restless on the straw-covered floor, Father Hyacinth woke his companions and said, "Gentlemen, our host is right. We have to escape, or they will destroy us. We are not obliged to keep our promise because Germany occupies our country illegally."

The three men argued back and forth, the young officer insisting on being honorable. The farmer was coughing and breathing hard, unable to sleep. He rasped, "I am amazed you are so naïve. Enemies occupy our country. You are educated men in important positions. In the morning, they will put you in prison. Then, in a German concentration camp. You'll work hard until you die. Don't be stupid."

The naïve young officer realized the wisdom of the farmer's words. Thanking the farmer, they left. As they got closer to town, some passers-by told them how to find the travel permits office. Father Hyacinth said to his companions,

"Give me your documents. I will go in alone. If they arrest me, you will escape. You have wives, children. If I am arrested, no one will cry for me."

A young man and woman who spoke Polish and German ran the office. They gave Father Hyacinth three passes without difficulty. When he began joking about the Germans, the young woman's eyes darted around the room. She whispered, "We are occupied. If they hear you, they will arrest you."

Grateful for her concern, he said, "Thank you for your advice. I will follow it."

The three men caught a train for Warsaw, standing room only. Next to them stood two wives of Polish officers. They arrived after the eleven pm curfew. Some German soldiers were watching, so it could be an excuse to arrest them. Knowing the situation, a Polish woman said to the three men and two women, "I live a few blocks away. You can stay there for a small fee and leave in the morning."

The owner welcomed them to her one-bedroom apartment and put blankets on the floor in the front room for the men. She and the two ladies shared the bedroom. They were startled at night by men pounding on the door and yelling in Polish, "Open up. We are security. We have to do inspections."

Father Hyacinth shouted to the officers loud enough for the intruders to hear, "You stay on the left side with your gun, and you on the right with your bayonet. We'll show them inspections."

Hearing loud male voices, the would-be robbers left. In the morning, the owner fussed over Father Hyacinth as their hero and offered her guests breakfast. She said, "Please have some bread and cold cuts. There's even coffee with condensed milk."

Not to be rude, Father Hyacinth explained, "I'm a Catholic priest. My order does not eat from midnight until after the morning Mass."

"What a privilege for us ladies to have a Capuchin priest with us. "

"It is bigger privilege for me to find shelter with such fine ladies and not get arrested."

Father Hyacinth bid his fellow travelers farewell and left to rejoin his Capuchin monks and priests. A few days later, the two officers visited him at the monastery with good news. The younger officer beamed, "I got home in time to be with my wife. She gave birth to our beautiful son."

Father Hyacinth was a polite man. He did not remind the new father of his fate if he had ignored the words of the gruff farmer. He would not be with his wife and newborn. He would be a German concentration camp. The priest said instead, "Congratulations my dear fellow. This calls for a celebration of chamomile tea. We grow the flowers in our own gardens."

They toasted the new baby with home grown tea. As his visitors left, Father Hyacinth seemed to have no care in the world. But the work ahead of him was dangerous.

Lublin: A Lucky Streak

Father, don't go there. They are waiting to arrest you.

The Capuchins on Kapucinska Street in Warsaw were part of the Underground Resistance. Father Hyacinth helped clergy and lay people escape arrests and provided food for those in prison. A year later, by the end of 1940, he was sent southeast to the city of Lublin to help twenty-six priests and theology students in the dreaded Zamek Prison. The Massive arrests of priests were a prelude to destroying the faith of a nation and installing deification of Hitler and Nazism.

British historian, John S. Conway, explains, "... Hitler's antipathy to the churches was never announced as a public policy. Despite the unceasing persecution against individual priests, or against different aspects of church life from the beginning of 1933, many Catholics continued to believe that allegiance to Nazism and to the Church were entirely compatible. Although Hitler was violently critical of the churches in private ... he was careful not to reveal his intentions in public. Not until June 1941 were his feelings made plain, in the highly important memorandum issued by Bormann to the Gauleiters, which opened with the incisive pronouncement: "National Socialism and Christianity are irreconcilable."[75]

A few months later, a conference of Gestapo officials made it clear that, "Our final goal is the complete elimination of the whole of Christianity." [76]

American historian, Alexander Dallin, adds, "Though frequently muting its anti-Christian stand, Nazism officially fostered the revival of heathen Germanic antiquity and a devout reverence for Party, Leader, and State."[77]

Waiting out the war before they could destroy Christianity, the Gestapo allowed German military chaplains to say Mass for German Catholic soldiers and conduct services for Protestant soldiers. Father Hyacinth said, "When German chaplains visited Polish clergy at the monastery in Lublin, I complained that Polish priests in prison could not say Mass. They just maintained prison buildings and grounds. The German chaplains themselves were too scared to intervene. All they could do was warn me that I was being watched and could wind up in Zamek Prison myself."

The German chaplains' warning became more likely when German soldiers took over a floor of the monastery where Father Hyacinth was living. Avoiding the watchful eyes of their uninvited guests, he and some fellow priests moved to a nearby apartment building and said Mass secretly in the church. Once as Father Hyacinth was waiting for a fellow priest to concelebrate Mass, he heard soldiers outside yelling for people to line up. This could mean a forced labor camp.

The crowd ran frantically into the church. Father Hyacinth shouted from the pulpit to escape by the side door. A soldier pulled him from the pulpit, put a gun to his back, and took him outside. He pushed the priest into a line where documents were being checked. Father Hyacinth explained to the guard checking the documents that he was a priest. He was looking after the needs of the German officers living at the monastery. His quick wit and fluent German convinced the guard to release him.

Father Hyacinth left and joined three of his fellow clergymen in the apartment of a married couple. This six-person Underground cell organized supplies, contacts, and bribes needed to smuggle food into Zamek Prison. Their attempts to keep as many priests alive as possible continued for months until Father Hyacinth left Lublin abruptly. One evening, after planning food distribution with his Underground team, Father Hyacinth was returning to the apartment building where he lived. The owner of the building was standing on the lookout, ready to intercept him. Seeing Father Hyacinth, the man blurted out, "Father, don't go there. They are waiting to arrest you."

Father Hyacinth left immediately to stay with fellow priests in a different part of town. Leaving his clothes and books in the apartment that was now under surveillance, he returned to Warsaw in the morning, still a free man. But how long could his lucky streak last?

Warsaw: Luck Runs Out

I heard banging with foot and fist and shouting in German to open the door.

Upon his return to Warsaw, the Capuchin brothers had reached sophisticated levels of resistance. Father Hyacinth helped smuggle food to Jews who had escaped the Warsaw Ghetto. The seminaries had created a web of Underground schools where he taught theology and philosophy. To maintain morale and inform civilians, he wrote for the Underground paper. Too much exposure. Lady Luck was getting peevish.

Father Hyacinth said, "In 1941, my philosophy students took their examinations on 27 June. I was happy with results and was preparing class for one student hiding on a farm. I went there twice a week for lessons. About midnight, I paused to admire the pear tree outside my window, locked the window, and went to bed. I was healthy and slept soundly. But that night, I heard banging with foot and fist and shouting in German to open the door."

He put on the light and opened the door. A tall blond soldier in his early twenties told the priest to turn around. Keeping a gun at Father Hyacinth's back, the soldier began looking at the bookshelves. Seeing volumes by Tolstoy, he asked, "Why are you interested in Russian books?"

"In Germany, Poland, Russia, France, there are different periods of human culture, and it is necessary to know them. Look here! Books of Goethe, of Schiller in German."

The soldier saw notes for the Underground philosophy class and drafts of sermons on the priest's desk. He asked what he was writing. "I'm educated in philosophy. This is an explanation of philosophy."

"I'm taking these notes. Someone else will figure out what this is all about."

"I have nothing against you taking the notes, but I want them back."

"If you are back in your room tomorrow, you will find your notes. They suspect you write for the Underground paper. It would be more convenient for you if you dress in secular dress. They are waiting for you downstairs."

In the refectory, soldiers were looking for hidden script in clothing. They also removed the back of watches of every student, monk, and priest. Hearing bombs overhead, the boyish soldier searching Father Hyacinth asked, "Does the monastery have a bunker?

"Yes, if you wish, but we are not afraid."

"But...but...the bomb can drop right here. Right on us. Any minute and we're gone."

"To die here or in concentration camp is same, but if you are afraid, we can go to bunker."

The search ended before the lad could decide, and the student hiding on a farm realized his mentor was in trouble. Did the tall blond soldier in his twenties holding a gun at the priest's back realize he had doomed the man to a concentration camp? Would he care?

Sixty lay persons and clergy were taken to Warsaw's Pawiak Prison, including Father Hyacinth. By summer 1941, Jews were targets of open hatred, and eight Jewish men were in the group. The next year, persecution of Jews became systematic. Clergy who had smuggled food to Jewish victims were in hiding, in concentration camps, or dead.

Father Hyacinth remained imprisoned in Warsaw for two months. The in September 1941, he was taken to Auschwitz, the German concentration camp in occupied Poland. There, he saw how Jewish prisoners were singled out for hell within hell.

Auschwitz: You Will Be Free

Try to escape, you will be electrocuted.

Sixty men were hauled away from the Pawiak Prison in Warsaw. Father Hyacinth said, "Two high wagons, damp and stinking. People sat on the floor. I stood with one of my students. We spoke French to keep our conversation private. A tall young man, handsome, blond, stood looking at the sky, the streets. He asked in pure French where we were going. I replied, "To Auschwitz."

Seeing shock on the man's face, the priest asked, "Why are you so alarmed?"

"Probably you don't know, but I am a Jew."

"Why didn't you go to some Polish family, Christian, and they could have preserved you. There was not much danger to this family because you have no Semitic features."

"It was imprudent, but here we are eight Jews, and you know what will happen."

"My dear, probably we will survive, but you and your friends should not reveal you are Jews. When they kick and beat us, they will tell us to betray the Jews, and somebody under torture will tell."

They saw a high row of barbed wire flooded with lights. Father Hyacinth said, "On the gate, I saw in big letters, '*Arbeit mache frei* – work makes you free.' A nice sentence but the real meaning is, 'Work hard and from hunger and exhaustion you will die, and you will be free.'"

The two wagons went through the gate and stopped. Guards were yelling, "*Raus*, you dogs. Get out!" They threw down each man, kicked him, and beat him with clubs as dogs growled above him. Father Hyacinth said, "A guard grabbed my shoulder. I jumped and landed on my feet before he could kick me. I saw two rows with five men each and a new row forming. Before a guard could beat me, I ran to the middle of the third row. A prisoner took his place next to me. We formed twelve rows."

He continued, "A guard screamed into the face of the first man in the first row to count off in German, *eins, zwei, drei*. When they were counted, two of the men were beaten so badly they had to be carried by the first row of prisoners. The rest ran toward the camp, surrounded by guards and dogs. We thought the long building with seven chimneys was the crematorium, but it was the kitchen. On the roof was written, 'The way to freedom is hard work, loyalty, kindness, and love of country.' Oh gosh, what irony! Kindness. Love of country. What kind of country?"

Watchtower lights revealed more guards. Another gate opened. They entered. Father Hyacinth said, "They shouted our names, we had to yell '*Jawohl*, which means quite so,' and get in line. They said those Polish names the wrong way, and often people didn't hear it as their name. I was thirteenth in line so, even if they didn't yell 'Dombrowski' exactly, I said, '*Jawohl*' and ran in place."

After roll call, a guard yelled for the Jews to step forward. Six of the Jewish prisoners stepped forward. The guard shouted, "Is that all?" Silence.

Again, "Is that all?" Silence.

The third time, he screamed, "I know there are two more of you. Step out or we will kill you."

Two Jewish prisoners stepped forward, including the tall blond man who spoke perfect French.

Father Hyacinth recalled, "They kicked and beat them. Fall down. Get up. Fall down. Jumped on them. Kicked their necks. Aimed for kidney and faces. Again, fall down. Get up. Fall down."

The guards had the eight Jewish men get back in the rows. They marched the group to a building under construction and told them to sit by the outside wall. A guard asked who spoke German. They kept quiet, no one wanting to call attention to himself. A Polish prisoner was brought in to warn them. He said, "We are surrounded with electric barbed wire. Try to escape, you will be electrocuted. The guards in the watchtowers will shoot. In the morning, you will hear the alarm for roll call."

Left by themselves, the men began to look around and whisper. Father Hyacinth said, "The Jewish man who spoke French found me. He put my hand to his bloody face. I was surprised that one of our brothers had a disinfectant, our Kapucinski balsam, and cleaned the crushed faces of the prisoners."

The prisoners slept on the ground, and in the morning, they were marched to a washroom. They had to undress and get into a large vat of cold water with disinfectant. Father Hyacinth said, "The Jews had to go first. At the edge of the vat, a guard pushed the head of each Jewish prisoner down with his boot for as long as air bubbles lasted. They didn't want to drown them. It was to terrify them and show us the same could happen to us. We lost completely desire to escape, to resist."

After putting on prison uniforms, Polish Christians were taken to Block 9. Polish Jews were taken to Block 11, the punishment quarters. At one end of that yard stood a wall painted black. When a man was stood up and shot, his blood could not be easily seen against the black wall.

People They Didn't Like

He was hired by a German prisoner who wore a green triangle labeling him a thief.

On the third day, the men were allowed to drink water and given work assignments. Father Hyacinth did hard labor for almost a year until, in June 1942, he was moved to Dachau in southern Germany. He said, "They brought in political prisoners, people they didn't like, from many groups, Polish, German, Czech, Jewish, French, and so on. We lost over a thousand Polish priests in Dachau."

Dachau was first used in 1933 for opponents of the Third Reich, including German dissidents and communists. In time, more groups were incarcerated: Jehovah's Witnesses who resisted the draft, Gypsies who were seen as racially inferior, clergymen who resisted the Nazi philosophy, homosexuals, and anyone who criticized the regime. The *Encyclopedia of the Holocaust* adds that, "When systematic extermination of the Jews began in 1942, Jewish prisoners were transported from extermination camps within Germany to Dachau."[78]

Father Hyacinth worked in a warehouse lifting heavy boxes of supplies for the front. This was considered a good job, under a roof in winter and summer. Then he was hired by a German prisoner who wore a green triangle labeling him a thief. The man supervised heating systems in German soldiers' housing using several work groups called commandos. The priest knew nothing about heating, but the man offered to teach him. He wanted his fluency in Polish, Russian, French, and German to help deal with his many subordinates.

While working in basement corridors, Father Hyacinth saw a Polish civilian doing plumbing in the German soldiers' houses. When the plumber slipped him a piece of bread with margarine, it was like giving him a steak in peacetime. Then he asked, "Do you know the priest Zagrodski?"

"Yes. I am also priest. Only German priests can say Mass. They can go to Polish block to give Communion. This morning, Father Zagrodski secretly asked me for confession before receiving Communion, and we talked."

"He is my pastor. My church will gather food, and you will give it to him?"

Father Hyacinth accepted the food for Father Zagrodski but needed the foreman's help smuggling it past the guards. The man wearing the green triangle of a thief said he must see the food first. The priest said, "He took butter, cold cuts, sugar – and left some bread. The next time, I held back on the meats and gave him bread and crackers. He looked at the dry goods and said he did not want such nonsense. He wanted cold cuts, kielbasa, and good cakes. I said in war any food is good. But next time I was more prudent and gave him some good things so he would keep helping me smuggle food."

Quinine and Raisins

At night his body felt on fire and he heard a strange commotion in his head.

Prisoners used for medical experiments in Dachau were decompressed, frozen, or injected. Father Hyacinth

said, "The Nazis had different tests. They injected twenty
of our priests with gangrene and put them in three groups.
One group got no medicine. They all died in a month. To
second group, they gave one type of medicine. Half of them
died. To third group, they gave another medicine. This third
group lived."

Dr. Sigmund Rascher ran decompression experiments to see what happens with a sudden loss of pressure
experienced by pilots who made parachute jumps at great
heights. According to the *Encyclopedia of the Holocaust*,
"from mid-March to mid-May 1942, about 200 inmates were
used for these experiments; according to the eyewitness testimony of the prisoners' nurse, Walter Neff, out of this number at least 70 or 80 died."[79]

"Rascher was also responsible for the series of 'freezing experiments,' which were carried out from the middle of
August to October 1942. Their ostensible object was to deter-
mine how pilots shot down at sea who suffered from freezing
could be quickly and effectively helped...from a total of 360
to 400 prisoners used in these experiments, 80 to 90 died." [80]

Dr. Claus Schilling was a researcher in tropical medicine and ran an experimental malaria station in the Dachau
camp. Looking for immunization against malaria, he had
"about 1,100 inmates infected with the disease. The exact
number of fatalities from these experiments cannot be determined, since the survivors returned to their previous work in
the camp after the disease had subsided and many, physically weakened, then fell victim to other illnesses."[81]

Father Hyacinth was Dr. Schilling's subject. He said,
"The guards took me to the malaria station at the hospital.
Schilling's assistant took blood from a prisoner sick with malaria and injected me with that infected blood. They watched
for two weeks. No symptoms. They sent me back to the
block."

By the third week, Father Hyacinth was a changed
man. He normally listened more than he talked but he became loud like a man possessed. His body felt like a burning
log at night. After morning roll call, the block leader sent him
to the malaria station. No daytime symptoms for a week, but
at night his body felt on fire and he heard a strange commotion in his head. He was sent back to work.

Gravely sick but determined, Father Hyacinth wrote
to his Capuchin brothers who sent food to their members
when possible. He asked for quinine. But how to send the
letter? Prisoners cleaned corridors, bathrooms, gardens,

and parking lots, but not soldiers' private quarters. German women were hired to clean their rooms. Father Hyacinth said, "We were in Bavaria, mostly Catholic. The elderly housekeeper was Catholic. I whispered to her that I was a priest and could she post a letter."

The woman backed away from him and asked him not to talk to her. It could get them both in trouble. He said, "I'm asking a lot but I desperately need help. It could save my life."

"This time, father, but not all the time. They watch us. We shouldn't even be talking."

"I will pray for you. Here are some raisins from packages the French shared with us. Your grandchildren will enjoy them."

She put the raisins along with the letter in her apron pocket and ran away from him.

His Capuchin brothers got the letter. They hid the packet of quinine inside a jar of sugar. The package passed inspection at Dachau. Father Hyacinth got the medicine. He asked a Polish doctor, who was being used as a nurse, how to take the quinine. At first, the doctor refused to help him.

Father Hyacinth insisted, "This means my life. As a fellow Pole, I beg your help."

"If you are tortured you may betray me as the person who told you how to do this."

Again, the priest insisted, "This is a slow painful death, and you could help me save myself."

The Polish doctor rose above his fear. He told Father Hyacinth to take quinine in the morning, noon, and at night for three days to kill the infection. The priest's recovery emboldened him to also rise above his own fear. He decided he would not die as a laboratory specimen.

Because I Am a Human Being

You are not human being. You are hound. You are dog.

Father Hyacinth was called back to the malaria station. Having saved his own life, he would now reclaim his humanity. He would refuse the next injection regardless of the consequences.

Hearing rumors that the war was ending, Father Hyacinth wondered if he could outlast the men in white coats who claimed to be doing humanity a favor? Or were these rumors the hopeful fantasies of desperate men? He said, "I waited in the laboratory, reading Greek tragedy by Sophocles. Mosquitoes in containers were singing angry sounding melodies – whrrrrr. A prisoner, Jean, from Luxembourg was the technician. We talked in French and became friends. He said, 'Bon Jour.' Sit down. Roll up your sleeve. I will give injection and Dr. Schilling will later check your condition.'"

The insanity of prisoners forced to inject malaria-infected blood into the veins of other prisoners swept over Father Hyacinth. Gathering his will power, he said to Jean, "No, my friend, I will not sit down. I will not roll up my sleeve. I will not allow this to happen."

"How can you say this? Do you know what it means?"

"Yes, I know. But I will make the break."

"It would be inspiration for all prisoners to know you refused, but the risk is your own. I cannot advise you on this."

Jean left the room. The mosquitoes kept singing their melodies – wwwrrrrr. Father Hyacinth sat down next to their cages and kept reading the Greek tragedy. In the other room, he heard Dr. Schilling's assistant say to Jean, 'I see Dombrowski is here. Make the injection.'"

"He told me he will not accept the injection."

"Impossible!"

Jean was known to be friendly with the priest and feared being accused of influencing him. He said, "I know nothing about this. I am saying only what he told me."

"That cannot be. Send him to my office!"

In the office, Dr. Schilling's assistant, who had the rank of captain, politely asked the priest to sit, spoke kindly, and offered food. He said, "And so we will make the injection on you. As an intelligent man, you must know that our experiments are helping mankind and we want your cooperation."

"Doctor, I'm from a country where doctors and scientists experiment on mice, not on human beings."

"You cannot talk like that, but it is not my decision what to do with you. It is Dr. Schilling's decision. You will suffer serious consequences if you refuse."

"I prefer to die as human being, not as guinea pig."

"You are taking a great risk, so wait for the doctor."

As the mosquitoes hummed, Father Hyacinth kept reading the Greek tragedy. He heard Dr. Schilling's "*Guten Morgen*," and the tremor in Jean's voice, "Dombrowski is here."

"Well, get it over with. Do it now."

"He told me he will not accept the injection."

"How is it possible?" shot back Dr. Schilling.

Dr. Schilling entered the waiting room, pointed his finger at the priest. He bellowed, "You! What is this nonsense? You have to take the injection!"

"Doctor, I am needed for German government as worker and not to be killed by mosquitoes."

Red with rage, the doctor shook his fist and yelled, "You are dog. You are worthless. You will accept this injection from your fellow prisoner!"

"Doctor, I am sorry to say, but I will not accept this."

"Why?"

"Because I am human being."

"You are not human being. You are hound. You are dog. Not human being."

"It is your philosophy but, according to my philosophy, I am as much human being as you are."

"You stupid! I will instruct the commandant to execute you!"

"I prefer to be executed as human being than die as guinea pig."

Dr. Schilling sputtered in his fury, "Get out, get out you idiot! Jean, send him back, the idiot."

Father Hyacinth returned to his deadly companions, the mosquitoes. This time, his hands shook, and he could not concentrate on the Greek tragedy. Jean came in and said, "You did well, but at your own risk. I cannot say what is best for you. I will prepare the papers and ask what to do with you."

The quinine beat back the malaria, but Father Hyacinth lived with Dr. Schilling's threat to have him executed. A month later, Dr. Schilling's assistant, who had tried to bribe him with food, called the priest to his office. He said, "The commandant gave the order to execute you. Dr. Schilling went for a month's vacation. In his absence, I hid your files. He will not find them to execute you but tell no one it is safe to object."

"I am grateful to you. It is humanitarian move from your part."

Word spread that Father Hyacinth had refused and survived. Forced injections were soon stopped. Prisoners who took injections got more food and no hard labor, but almost nobody went. Yet the death toll swelled as unsanitary conditions swept a typhus epidemic into every overcrowded barrack.

As Germany was losing the war, other camps were evacuated and some of those prisoners were brought to Dachau. According to the *Encyclopedia of the Holocaust*, these transports brought "human beings who were, for the most part, reduced to skeletons and exhausted to the point of death. During this period up to 1,600 prisoners were crowded into barracks intended for two hundred. In early 1945, over one hundred inmates daily, and for a time over two hundred, fell victim to the typhus epidemic that had been raging in many of the camps since December 1944." [82]

"By early 1945, there were plans to kill the inmates by bombs and poison. But Dachau was liberated in April 1945 with 67,665 registered prisoners, among them 22,100 Jews...inmates from more than thirty countries were found... out of the total number of 206,206 prisoners registered there were 31,591 registered deaths... However, the total number of deaths in Dachau...will never be known."[83]

Thousands died in their prime, but Father Hyacinth was blessed with a long and productive life.

Reflections

It is a human tendency to judge all by one. It shouldn't be, but it is.

DC: How do you explain the madness you experienced?

The Nazis had false philosophy concerning mankind. First, they arrested Polish people. Their philosophy was that Polish people were inferior race. Then, they said Jews are degenerated race and we have to destroy it, because they will contaminate our race. It was their philosophy officially, but hidden philosophy was also this: Let us destroy Jews, take their jewels, paintings, money, factories, houses and we will be richer. This was another motivation.

If Germans found a Jew hidden by a Polish family, they saw he was a Jew because his features were different. The German law said if a Polish family is hiding a Jew, that family – children, father, mother – and this Jew will be shot. Even so, many Polish families or individuals hid them, either for money or because they were friends.

In Poland, we were forming one nation. Jews had the same rights as non-Jews and some were also committed to an Israeli state. It is hard to explain to people that this is normal. For example, I am an American citizen, and I was born in Poland. I am dedicated to America, but I am also committed to an independent Poland. In the United States, there are different groups – Jews, Spaniards, Germans, Italians. They consider the United States their own country, but they also love their mother country.

DC: I am sad about the bad feeling between some Polish and some Jewish people. Both religions teach us to have compassion for other people's suffering.

It is a human tendency to judge all by one. It shouldn't be, but it is. Compassion is difficult when it is most needed. Some Slavonic Poles judged all Jews in the wrong way, and some Jews judged Slavonic Poles in wrong way. We had good Polish citizens who were Jews – writers, architects, medical doctors, scientists, professors. Christians should know that our background is based on Old Testament. We consider Jewish Old Testament inspired by God. We accept it as the word of God – not only New Testament, letters of Apostles, Gospels – but also Old Testament. For this, we shouldn't hate Jews. We should respect them. And we should understand that many people are different. Now I will read something written by a fellow priest in Auschwitz. Probably it will interest you.

"I spent four years in German concentration camp. In a short period of time, it is impossible to tell you about the catastrophe of millions of human beings. I will limit myself to one incident. Early in 1942, a friend of mine, John Mester, a fellow prisoner of Auschwitz now living in Connecticut, asked me to visit him on the following Sunday. He told me that his friend, who had been a director of public school near Częstochowa, would like to receive the sacrament of Holy Communion.

After saying Mass in the cave under Block 24 and exposing myself to the possibility of torture and even death, I met John, but the director of the school was not there. He was a member of the camp orchestra. They were busy that Sunday entertaining the commandant of Auschwitz and his guests on his birthday. John asked me to come the next day, Monday, to bring Communion to the school principal. I didn't usually reserve Holy Communion for the next day, being concerned about possible desecration during the personal searches, but I made an exception.

On Monday after work, I met this friend of John, and ministered to him. He was happy to receive the sacrament but haunted by the idea that he would not survive Auschwitz, that he would be executed. I tried to encourage him every way I could. I told him that he had the best kind of work in the camp. He was a member of the camp orchestra. We spoke for some time, then I returned to my block.

The next day, Tuesday, we had the usual roll call. The commandant called the names of forty men who must remain in the camp that day. They were ordered to appear in the central office. For a prisoner, this was an ominous sign.

Suddenly, the principal of this school reached me and told me nervously, "Today is the feast of German heroes. We forty will be executed by being shot in the back of the head at that dark wall on Block 11. Tell my wife that I am grateful to her for everything she did for me and for our daughter. Tell her that I am proud to give my life for the honor of my country. Tell her that it is my last will and testament that she raise our daughter to be a good Christian and a good Polish citizen worthy of her father." He shook my hand and quickly left me to join the group of those condemned to die.

At noon, our group of workers returned to camp for the usual half quart of soup, actually rutabaga boiled in water. At the entrance of the dining area, the orchestra was playing waltzes. My friend, however, was no longer among the musicians. When we entered the main street leading from the death block to the crematorium, we saw streaks of blood covering the ground. Our youngest comrade, eighteen years old, explained, "Friends, we are treading on the blood of our martyrs. Let us pray for them." And this was one of the million sins of our daily lives in German concentration camps."

Father Hyacinth: (Long silence.) I guess we are finished.

DC: Yes, Thank you.

After serving parishes in the United States, Father Hyacinth passed away in his 90's at his home monastery of the Capuchin Order in Warsaw. His name does not refer to the spring flower. It comes from the Polish Jacynta which is the formal version of Jacek, or Jack in English.

I drove home in silence thinking about the forms of faith that sustained the people you have met in this book – faith in God's ultimate benevolence, in family, in country, in the land and the seasons that feed and clothe them, and in their own ability to stand upright under conditions no human being should ever have to endure.

Endnote

75 John S. Conway, "Between Cross and Swastika," Michael Berenbaum, ed., *A Mosaic of Victims: Non-Jews Persecuted and Murdered by the Nazis,* (NY: NYU Press, 1990) p. 18.

76 Ibid

77 Alexander Dallin, *German Rule in Russia 1941-45: A Study of Occupation Policies* (London: Westview, 1981) p. 472.

78 Israel Gutman, ed., *Encyclopedia of the Holocaust* (NY: Macmillan, 1990, Vol. 1) pp. 341-343.

79 *Encyclopedia of the Holocaust,* pp. 341-343.

80 Ibid

81 Ibid

82 Ibid

83 Ibid

Afterward: Our Shared Humanity

The eyewitnesses you have met were touched by the devil of brutality and the angel of compassion. In a world gone mad, sometimes decency prevailed when facing these wrenching choices:

Do I risk punishment for helping people in need?
Do I share my meager food with a neighbor or a stranger who has none?
Do I risk my family's life to protect someone else in danger?
Do I use firearms against others? If not, will the firearms be aimed at me?
Do I simply look the other way when another human being needs my help?

No matter how you answer these questions, the result can be brutal. Therefore with heartfelt gratitude, I thank those who faced such dilemmas and were able to touch the angel of compassion. At that moment, they honored our shared humanity.

Part One: From the East: Soviet Tanks Bring Communism, 1939

The train sentry who gave Józefa shelter and directed her to the correct train.

Boy soldiers, on their way to kill and be killed, who protected Józefa when she missed her train.

The commandant who released Józefa from work to care for Stefania when she had chicken pox.

The grandmother who shared a warm cup of tea and bread with Józefa as they sat away from the howling wind and secretly prayed.

The husband and wife who saved Stefania and Józefa from freezing or being eaten by wolves during their 200-mile trek to freedom across frozen Russia.

The family who saved my brother Henry's future mother-in-law, Zofia Kaniewski, from starvation in the typhoid ward in

Uzbekistan.

The family in Ukraine who took Alicja, her mother, and aunt into their home after they were allowed to leave the Soviet Union and brought them back to life.

The Naliboki man who was beaten with the butt of a rifle for offering bread to a Jewish family being led to their death.

The woman who saved the people locked inside a barn in Naliboki by convincing the commandant not to set the barn on fire. The commandant who listened to her pleas.

Villagers who shared what little food they had as Janusz and Staś and their family walked home for days after almost being deported to Germany.

The priests who secretly baptized children and prepared them for other sacraments.

The soldier who convinced his commanding officer not to kill the women and children lined up to be shot in the forest after the invasion of Pershai. The commanding officer who listened to the soldier's pleas.

The person in authority who allowed the workers in Jadwiga's unit to observe a religious holiday that honors their dead.

Weronika's father for throwing a bundle of food onto the truck as his neighbors as were being deported into the Soviet Union.

Weronika's aunt for giving potatoes to the orphaned children of Russian men and women.

The priest who honored the Russian parents' request to baptize carloads of their children.

Two women who, without permission, cut down the birch tree growing inside their church that had been turned into a warehouse. If the tree was uprooted during a storm, it could tear out a wall of the building they hoped would one day become their church again.

Part Two: From the West: The Master Race Brings Fire, 1941

The bakery owner who sent an employee to give mother two loaves of bread.

The woman who gave our family food and clothes even after my mother refused to give me away.

The second *Lagerfuehrer* who drove my mother and sick brother Chester to the hospital.

The family with seven children who took in a little boy when his parents were killed by a bomb.

The women who, while riding past on bicycles, threw down their ration cards for us to use.

The people who gave my brothers bread when they were out begging for food. The local women who let my brothers hide in their safer bunkers during the bombings.

The farmer who defied his country's law against Germans and Poles eating together by welcoming my father and brother Henry at his table.

The soldiers who risked their lives to rescue us from the bunker on the last day of the war.

The rabbi who took care of his family and the other refugee women and children on the journey to America.

My Uncle Jan for hiding a Jewish girl in his attic in Naliboki.

My parents, Aunt Eleanor, and her husband for sheltering Jewish friends escaping the roundups.

Our neighbor whose elaborate tale saved my father from being forced into a Russian partisan unit.

My grandfather's stepmother Maryśka who taught Polish secretly in her home, risking years of punishment in Siberia.

The officer who allowed the prisoners brought into Germany to gather for prayer.

The Offe family who ignored the legal calorie limits that were set at starvation levels for Polish and other Slavic people.

Klaus Offe who was jailed for his kindness to my aunt and uncle and their families.

The girl working in the field with Józef who warned him about men who were organized with firearms to use against the foreigners when the war ended.

Factory workers who secretly placed bread and butter on a ledge for my Aunt Mania.

The train yard boss whose information helped Kazimierz to find his two teen-age daughters.

Part Three: Resistance: Because I am a Human Being

Dr. Par who saw Stefan as a human being, rather than as an enemy partisan, and saved his life.

People idling near the church in Central Poland who helped Stefan and others escape imprisonment.

Underground teams who organized forbidden schools where Krystyna earned a high school diploma.

The man who pulled Krystyna out of the pile of dead bodies as they were falling on top of her.

The women couriers who risked their lives while working within the Underground struggle for independence.

The cleaning woman who agreed to mail a letter for Father Hyacinth requesting quinine.

The doctor who rose above his fear and taught Father Hyacinth how to take the quinine to fight back the malaria.

The officer who hid Father Hyacinth's file, preventing his execution.

With Heartfelt Gratitude

He may no longer be alive, and will never see my words, but I send this message into the universe for Officer Willi. You lost your arm for your country, but you gave your heart to people from a foreign land who could have meant nothing to you. You did not make women go to work as their babies lay bundled up flat all day. You ignored starvation calorie limits. And you lead us away from the bridge to oblivion.

Had we crossed that bridge, my life would have ended at age two and I would not be here to echo my brother Henry's sentiments that, indeed, you are a great human being. You remain always in the hearts of my family.

A Final Thought

Our struggle to survive involved many villains and many heroes. Some of you were powerless; some were in positions of authority. You were from many nationalities and religions. You risked your own safety, or shared a piece of bread with your fellow human beings out of compassion instead of fear or indifference. At times, such a choice required enormous courage. I will never know your names or see your faces and you will never appear in history books, but you are the unsung heroes of this war. Many of you are gone now but you live on in my heart as I extend to you my deepest gratitude and love.

Acknowledgments

Two authors who graciously provided valuable information and inspiration were British historian, Norman Davies, and Polish Nobel Laureate in Literature, Czesław Miłosz. Polish American historian, Marek Tuszynski, guided me on a path of rigorous scholarship.

I am grateful to Irene Mitta for her editorial acumen and precision, librarian Loretta Kelleher for her research expertise, my late brother Henry Chmara for vital details about our place of birth, my late husband Henry Talarsky for his moral support, Henry Ostapiej for compiling resource data, Carol Feeney for adding clarity to the early drafts, Peter Obst for guiding me forward, Richard Palazzi for his wit and kindness, David Benedetti for his technical support, Theresa Hololob for her scholarly insight, and all my family and friends who are part of these narratives directly or through their interest and encouragement.

I thank the people who were willing to relive painful memories to give voice to the devastation they survived – with their humanity intact. Their eyewitness accounts expand the knowledge of World War II for those of us who live in a democracy that is different from the totalitarian world of my childhood.

I thank all who saw the value of this work and encouraged its completion.

Ten Questions for Discussion

A Suggested Guide

These questions are suggested as a guide for classroom use, book club meetings, and other settings. They raise broad issues of war and peace, governance, humanitarian approaches to world problems, corporate responsibility beyond the profit motive, international competition and cooperation. Such discussions can be used to consider peace making strategies within our public and private lives.

One. What were some historic events in the book that you learned about for the first time?

Two. Give some examples from the book of how historic events changed private lives.

Three. Choose one eyewitness in the book who was an inspiration to you and explain why.

Four. How are today's local and world events changing your life or the life of someone you know?

Five. What is the role of eliminating poverty as a step toward creating peace?

Six. What qualities within government leaders are helpful in resolving conflict between groups?

Seven. What steps can leaders of nations take to prevent war?

Eight. Research an organization whose stated purpose is to promote worldwide peace. Give a brief summary of its goals and projects.

Nine. This book emphasizes the danger of identifying exclusively with an ideology or group, rather than with the fact of our shared humanity. What does this statement mean to you?

Ten. What can you do to promote peace on the local, national, and international level?

Appendix A Terminology

English

Genocide	Deliberate extermination of people based on group identity.
Partisans	Guerrilla fighters not officially affiliated with a formally recognized army.
Forced Labor	Hard labor under harsh or life threatening conditions involving violation of civil liberties and forced displacement.

German

Arbeitsamt	Agency that set working conditions for Germans, voluntary foreign workers, and forced laborers.
Auslaender	Foreigner.
Bauer	Farmer.
Lager	Hard labor prison.
Lagerfuehrer	Commandant in charge of the work camp

Polish

Armia Krajowa	(AK) – Home Army. Military arm of the Polish Underground.
Babunia	Grandmother.
Kresy	The rich soil and farm lands of Eastern Europe.
Miasteczko	Center of town, literally "little town".
Po prostu	Local dialect used in parts of Eastern Europe, called "*tutejszy*" in Polish literature, meaning "the plain way."
Puszcza Nalibocka	Extensive forest of the Naliboki region.
Samoobrona	Self-defense units.
Ziemianka	Underground dugout used for living space, plural Ziemianki.
Surnames.	Female last names usually end in the letter "a." Masculine names usually end in the letter "i." Example: Mrs. Jankowska, Mr. Jankowski.

Russian

Kolkhoz/ Solkhoz	Communal farm.
Kulaks	Persons considered by the Soviets to be exploiters of the working class.
NKVD	Soviet secret police, forerunner of the KGB.

Appendix B Extraordinary Exile of Józef, Józefa, and Stefania Chmara

February 10-17, 1940

Abducted from home in Naliboki, Poland

March 1940

Taken to Archangel (Arkhangelsk), northwest Russia then taken to Kolkhoz #21, between Vologda and Archangel. Used for forced labor

January 1, 1942

Freed from Kolkhoz #21, walked to Vologda train station

Mid-Jan to mid-March 1942

Headed south in cattle car across Russia and Kazakhstan

Mid-March 1942

Reached Polish army near Tashkent, Uzbekistan

End of March 1942

Sent to Uzbek donkey farm

Early April 1942

Left Uzbekistan by truck convoy with Polish army

Rode across Turkmenistan by cattle car

Mid-April 1942

Reached port city of Krasnovodsk, Turkmenistan

Mid-April 1942

Crossed Caspian Sea in a Russian ship

End of April 1942

Arrived Iran, given food, clothing, and medical care

Early May 1942

Transported to Tehran, organized community life

Summer, 1942 through Spring, 1944

Józef joined the English Army, marched through Iraq, Palestine (Israel), Egypt, Europe. Survived Monte Cassino

Fall 1942 through May 1948

Józefa and Stefania left Iran, boarded English ship for India, crawled along Arabian Sea to avoid mines, headed down Indian Ocean, reached Tanzania, Africa

May 1945 through 1948

War in Europe ends. Józef arrived in England, waited in resettlement camp

June 1, 1948

Józefa and Stefania left Tanzania from Mombasa, Kenya on British ship RMS Scythia. Sailed down Indian Ocean, around Africa, and up the Atlantic Ocean

July 1, 1948

Józefa and Stefania arrived Liverpool

July 1948

Husband, wife, and daughter reunited in military dependents' camp

Appendix C Military Resistance by Occupied Poland

One. The Polish Air Force operated alongside the British Royal Air Force.

Polish American historian Adam Zamoyski tells us that "By the beginning of 1941, there was a fully-fledged Polish Air Force operating alongside the RAF. With 14 squadrons and support services, it was larger than the air forces of the Free French, Dutch, Belgians and all the other European Allies operating from Britain combined. Some 17,000 men and women passed through the ranks of the Polish Air Force... They not only played a crucial role in the Battle of Britain in 1940, they also contributed significantly to the allied war effort in the air."[1]

Two. Like Józef Chmara, Polish soldiers fought on the ground under Allied command.

As Norman Davies explains, "After 1941 two separate Polish armies were raised in the USSR. The first...formed largely from released deportees and commanded by General Władysław Anders, left Soviet territory for the Middle East, where they were eventually incorporated into the Second Polish Corps of the British Eighth Army...Their extraordinary odyssey, from prison camps in Siberia and Central Asia to Buzuluk on the Volga, to Tobruk, Anzio, Rome, to the Sangrio and the Gothic Line, has never been satisfactorily recounted to western readers."[2] (The second Polish army remained under Soviet command. It was later used to help install a communist regime in Poland against the will of the Polish people.)

During the 1944 Battle of Monte Cassino in Italy, according to Polish historian, Jozef Garlinski, the German army held a vital stretch of mountain range, controlling access to the road to Rome and the Naples-Rome railway line – essential to Allied victory...the American Fifth Army, the 3rd division of the Algerian Army from the French Corps, Britain's Eighth Army, and the New Zealand Corps attempted to capture Monte Cassino. After severe losses, the brunt of the fighting fell on the British Eighth Army, and specifically on the Polish Second Corps.

Polish Commander General Anders chose the 3rd Carpathian Division and the 5th *Kresowa* Division to attack two neighboring hills to access the main hill. The *Kresowa* Division was made up of men from Eastern Poland. With severe losses on both sides, the German formations retreated on May 18 and the Polish flag was raised... The Carpathian Division lost 1571 soldiers, the *Kresowa* lost 2174. Seventy-two officers were killed. On June 4,

332 Surviving Genocide

the American Fifth Army walked into Rome along an open road as a result of the capture of Monte Cassino.[3]

Three. Underground resistance flourished within Poland.

The Armia Krajowa (AK), known as the Home Army, was the military arm of the Underground. It was as the largest resistance force in occupied Poland and a powerful Ally in Europe. At its height, in 1944, British historian Neal Ascherson states that, "it numbered some 200,000 men and women,...the Peasant Battalions, were nearly as numerous...Lack of arms...restricted the AK...to harrying rather than confronting the enemy, to attacking railways and roads, to sabotage, to the rescue of prisoners and the assassination of individual SS and police officers. The AK efficiently harboured Allied prisoners-of-war on the run, and set up a spectacularly successful intelligence service which provided the Western Allies with details...But the penalty for resistance of any kind was death, and the losses of the AK, in battle, by execution or in the camps, were tragic." [4]

Endnotes

1   Adam Zamoyski, *The Forgotten Few: The Polish Air Force in the Second World War*, (Hippocrene, 2001) inside cover.

2   Norman Davies, *God's Playground: A History of Poland*, Vol 2 (NY: Columbia UP, 1982) p. 272.

3   Jozef Garlinski, *Poland in the Second World War* (NY: Hippocrene, 1988) pp. 251-256.

4   Neal Ascherson, *The Struggles for Poland* (NY: Random House, 1987) 103-04.

Appendix D Four Mass Deportations to the Soviet Union during World War II

Numbers are elusive. Based on original reports of the Polish government, Polish American historian, Marek Tuszynski, offers numbers for the 21-month Soviet occupation (1939-1941).

"February 10, 1940: Under extreme winter conditions that contributed to an increase in fatalities, approximately 220,000 people were forcibly arrested and deported. In most cases they were taken to the northern areas of European Russia, particularly Archangelsk and the surrounding region. The targeted population included veteran land-grant holders and forestry service personnel together with their families." [This included Józef Chmara and family, and my brother Henry's future in-laws, the Kaniewski family.]

"April 1940: About 320,000 people were deported. They were generally taken to the southern region of Russia, Kazakhstan, and to points in the Soviet Far East." [This included the family of Alicja Pszonka.]

"June and July 1940: About 240,000 were taken to the northern parts of the Soviet Union"

"June 1941: The total ...came to about 300,000 people."[1]

Based on these numbers, over a million people were deported, higher than the 320,000 estimate in Soviet documents. Polish historian Tadeusz Piotrowski breaks down the Soviet estimates as:

"140,000 (mostly Poles) during the first [deportation], 60,000 (again, mostly Poles) during the second, 80,000 (mostly Jewish refugees) during the third, and 40,000 Polish citizens mainly from the Wilno area during the fourth deportation for a grand total of 320,000 persons."

Piotrowski cautions that, "These Soviet figures, even if accurate (and some scholars question their veracity), do not give a complete picture of that horrendous Soviet ethnic cleansing campaign aimed against Polish citizens...By including ...other... categories we arrive at approximately 750,000 to 780,000 as the total number..."[2]

Deportations to Russia/Soviet Union Before World War II

According to Piotrowski, "Similar deportations and enslavement of Polish citizens occurred under the tsars in 1832, 1864, and 1906..."[3]

Polish historian, Andrzej Paczkowski, states that, "In 1924-1929 several hundred [Poles in the USSR] were shot... several hundred Catholics were persecuted and dozens were shot or disappeared...[And]...repression against the Russian Orthodox Church...resulted in the disappearance of a church that had formed the foundation of social, cultural, and spiritual life for hundreds of thousands of Polish peasants."[4]

Piotrowski adds, "Between 1930 and 1933, during Stalin's war against the kulaks [supposedly rich farmers], 10,000 Poles were deported from Soviet Ukraine to the interior of the Soviet Union. In 1935, in the interest of securing the Soviet western borders, another 40,000 Poles were deported eastward. In 1936 there were additional massive deportations from this area for a grand total of 120,000 Poles in this seven-year period. The Poles in Soviet Belorussia fared no better: before 1936, about 20,000 ethnic Poles suffered some form of Soviet repression; in 1937-38, some 20,000 Poles were deported to the east." [5]

British historian, Simon Sebag Montefiore, picks up the thread. "...On 2 July 1937, the Politburo [ruling committee] ordered local Secretaries to arrest and shoot "the most hostile anti-Soviet elements... to "finish off once and for all" all Enemies and those impossible to educate in socialism." (My brother Henry remembers the 1937 arrest of several hundred Polish males along the Polish-Soviet border near Naliboki. Their fate is unknown.)

Montefiore continues, "...death was sometimes random: the long-forgotten comment, the flirtation with an opposition, envy of another man's job, wife, or house, vengeance or just plain coincidence brought the death and torture of entire families...the latest estimates combining the quotas and national contingents, are that 1.5 million were arrested in these operations and about 700,000 shot."[6]

Endnotes

[1] Marek Tuszynski. "Soviet War Crimes during the Second World War and its Aftermath: A Review of the Factual Record and Outstanding Questions," *The Polish Review*, 44, Number 2 (1999):196- 97.

[2] Tadeusz Piotrowski, ed. *The Polish Deportees of World War II. Recollections of Removal to the Soviet Union and Dispersal*

Throughout the World (Jefferson, NC: McFarland, 2004).

[3]Piotrowski, p. 4.

[4]Mark Kramer, ed., *The Black Book of Communism, Crimes, Terror, Repression,* Andrzej Paczkowski, "Poland, the "Enemy Nation," (Cambridge, MA: Harvard UP, 1999) pp. 364-65.

[5] Piotrowski, p. 2

[6] Simon Sebag Montefiore, *Stalin, Court of the Red Tsar* (NY: Knopf, 2004) pp. 228-29.

Appendix E Chronology of the Naliboki Region

1258
Plunder by Tatar horsemen from the east

14th century
Beginning of village life with Naliboki among the oldest; peasants provide military service and labor to Lithuanian lords until 19th century.

1387
Grand Duke Władysław Jagiełło, and later king of Poland, gives equal rights of hereditary land transfer to Lithuanian and Polish feudal lords.

1447
Naliboki established as a village (current Naliboki library records.)

End of 15th century
A Catholic chapel is built near site of present church, its fate known

Until 15th and 16th centuries
Ongoing Tatar attacks

1555
Mikołaj Czarny Radziwiłł purchases Naliboki and other villages from Szemiot and Zawiszy families.

1636
Catholic church built, funded by Albrecht Stanislaw Radziwiłł

1655
Prince Albrecht makes permanent bequest of the church to Naliboki. Radziwiłł family rebuilds the church 1699-1704. The church is burned during the fires in Naliboki in 1943 after some 300 years in use

1700's
Thriving iron ore industry

1722-1862
Glass manufacturing (Remnants found in present soil.)

1795-1820
Factory for processing potash

1795-1918
Poland partitioned by Russia, Prussia, Austria-Hungary. Russia gets Naliboki.

1800's
Presence of Jewish population (Spector, *Encyclopedia of Jewish Life Before and During the Holocaust)*

1849
Prince Piotr Wittgenstein, general in czar's army, acquires Naliboki as dowry through marriage to Princess Stefania Radziwiłł

19ᵗʰ century
Prince Hohenlohe acquires Naliboki as dowry through marriage to daughter of Prince Piotr and Princess Stefania

19ᵗʰ century
The brothers Falz-Fein purchase Naliboki from Prince Hohenlohe

November 1918
Poland becomes independent country, Naliboki becomes part of Poland

1936
Construction of new church begins to accommodate growing population

September 1, 1939
Invasion of Western Poland by Germany

September 17, 1939
Invasion of Eastern Poland by the Soviet Union

February 10, 1940 – June 1941
Four major deportations to Soviet republics

June 1941
German invasion of Eastern Europe

December 1941 – 1942
Murder of Jewish residents in Naliboki by German army

May 8, 1943
Soviet partisans burn part of Naliboki and massacre 128 residents.

August 7-8, 1943
German army burns rest of Naliboki, deports residents for forced labor

1944
Soviet Union reoccupies region

1945
New boundaries determined at Yalta Conference place Eastern Poland within Soviet Union. Some exiles return to Naliboki, some

emigrate to Western Poland

1950's
Private properties confiscated to set up communal farms

1990
Government permits Catholic priest from Poland to lead restoration of church that was begun in 1936

1991

Belarus officially leaves Soviet Union but remains under Soviet influence

1994

July 5, Consecration of restored church

July 1994, September 2000, September 2007, August 2017
Return to Naliboki by author

January 2002
First visit to USA by current Naliboki branch of Chmara family

Information for 13th to 19th centuries come from Dagnosław Demski, *Instytut Archeologii I Etnologgi* PAN, Warsaw: *Naliboki I Puszcza Nalibocka – Zarys Dziejow I Problematyki, Etnografia Polska*, t.XXXVIII:1994, z. 1-2 PL ISSN 0071-1861.

Cudzoziemcy w Nalibokach w Okresie od Pocz. XVIII do Konca XIX W., Etnografia Polska, t. XLIII: 1998, z. 1-2 PL ISSN 0071-1861.

Appendix F Family Trees

Individuals in bold were interviewed for the book.

Chmara Lineage

Stefan Chmara, d1921, wed Emilia Chilicka, d1941, mid-1800's in Naliboki. Children:

Urszula (1888) Married Russian soldier after WWI and moved to Russia

Henryk (1892 - 1966) Emigrated to United States 1913, name changed to Mara by immigration officer. American soldier, farmer in Cranbury, NJ. Married Minnie Pasternak (1904 – 1986) Children:

> Walter Mara (1923 – 1995)
> Eleanor Hansen (1932)

Józef (1898) wed Józefa Hodyl (1902). Family deported to Soviet Union. After war emigrated to Nottingham, England. Children:
> Jadwiga (1929) (died at 6 weeks)
> **Stefania Kuryło** (1931 - 2007)

Jan (1900) wed Antonina Ostapiej (1905) Her parents: Stefan and Wiktoria Ostapiej. Family deported to Germany. Emigrated to Toronto, Canada, March 1951. Children:

> **Flora Miszuk (1925)**
> Stella (Stasia) Ciesielczyk (1927)
> Lodzia Swiderska (1931)
> Pola Chmara (1933, died at 11 months)
> Vera (Weronika) Budic (1935)
> Teresa Sobieraj (1937)
> John (Jan) Chmara (1939)
> Tom (Tomek) Chmara (1941)
> Christine (Krystyna) Langston (1948)

Michał (1903) wed **Helena Byczkiewicz** (1909) Her parents: Justyn and Anna Byczkiewicz. Family deported to Germany. Emigrated to Cranbury, NJ, 1950. Children:

> **Henry (Heniek) Chmara** (1931)
> Chester (Czesław) Chmara (1932)
> Janka (Janina) Proszynska (1935)
> **Mary (Marysia) Wojciechowski** (1938)
> **Van (Wacław)Chmara** (1940 - 2018)
> Donna (Danuta) Chmara (1943)

Maria (1905) married Nikodem Adamcewicz. Relocated to Western Poland. Children:

> Józef Adamcewicz

Józefa (1910) married Wincenty Adamcewicz. Relocated to Western Poland. Child:

> Stanisława (Stasia) Lesiak (1937 - 2021)

Three children died in infancy: Stefania, Antoni and Franek

Byczkiewicz Lineage

Justyn Byczkiewicz (1886 – 1940) married Anna Adamcewicz (1879 – 1967).

Helena (1909 – 1998) married Michał Chmara (1903 – 1979). Family deported to Germany. Emigrated to Cranbury, New Jersey, USA, 1950. Children:

> **Henry (Heniek) Chmara** (1931 – 2011)
> Chester (Czesław) Chmara (1932 – 1975)
> Janka (Janina) Proszynska (1935 – 1989)
> **Mary (Marysia) Wojciechowski** (1938)
> **Van (Wacek) Chmara** (1940 - 2018)
> Donna (Danuta) Chmara (1943)

Józef (1914 – 2004) married Józefa Dubicka (1923 – 2005). Deported to Germany. Emigrated to Yantic, Connecticut, USA. Children:

> Sophie (Zosia) Marek (1942)
> Stanley (Stanisław) Byczkiewicz (1947)
> Teresa Beauregard (1951)

Eleanor (Lonia) (1922 – 2018) married Chester Dubicki (1916 – 1993). Deported to Germany. Emigrated to Yantic, Connecticut, USA. Children:

> Irene (Irena) Lynch (1942 – 2004)
> John (Jan) Dubicki (1944)

Maria (Mania) (1923 – 2001). Deported to Germany. Married Wincenty Szalczyk (1916 – 2005) Emigrated to Red Lake, Ont, Canada, then to Trenton, NJ Children:

> Irene (Irena) Blake
> Steve (Stefan) Szalczyk
> Helen (Helena) Stemmler

Two children died in infancy: Franek, Bronisława

Suggested Reading

Applebaum, Anne. *Iron Curtain. The Crushing of Eastern Europe 1944 – 1956.* NY: Doubleday, 2012. Describes how the Soviet regime bullied, threatened, and murdered its way to power over East European countries that fell under communist control after WWII and the suffering this caused in the daily lives of people within those territories.

Ascherson, Neal. *The Struggles for Poland.* New York: Random House, 1987. Attempts at independence from 17th century until the 1980's. German and Soviet invasions of 1939 and attempts to obliterate Poland through mass murders, deportations, slave labor, and punishment by death for use of the language or participation in educational, cultural, or religious activity.

Berenbaum, Michael, editor. *A Mosaic of Victims: Non-Jews Persecuted and Murdered by the Nazis.* New York: NYU Press, 1990. Chapters on Serbs, Croatians, Polish people, Ukrainians, Soviet prisoners, non-Jewish children, Jehovah's Witnesses, pacifists, homosexuals, Gypsies, the handicapped, and the elderly.

Hoffman, Eva. *Shtetl: the Life and Death of a Small Town and the World of Polish Jews.* New York: Public Affairs, A Member of Perseus Books Group, 2007. Nazi extermination of Jewish population in village of Brańsk in what was Eastern Poland, influx of Jews into Poland beginning in 11th century, historic and current complexity of stereotypes pertaining to Polish-Jewish relations.

Karski, Jan. *Story of a Secret State.* Boston: Houghton Mifflin Co., 1944. Diplomat, officer in 1939 campaign, and Red Army prisoner describes his role as courier within the Underground, its structure, and sacrifices that made it a form of resistance. He met with British and American leaders to plead for intervention in stopping the extermination of European Jews, but his information was dismissed.

Kostkiewicz, Janina, ed.. *Crime Without Punishment: The Extermination and Suffering of Polish Children During the German Occupation 1939 – 1951*. Jagiellonian University Press, 2021. Fate of children who were taken from their parents, exterminated, or Germanized if they met certain criteria.

Kramer, Mark, consulting ed. *The Black Book of Communism. Crimes, Terror, Repression*. Cambridge, MA: Harvard University Press, 1999. Details repression and murders in Soviet Union, Western and Eastern Europe, Asia, Latin America, Africa, and Afghanistan from 1917 to 1989.

Kurek, Ewa. *Your Life is Worth Mine*. NY: Hippocrene, 1996. Rescue of Jewish children by nuns in occupied Poland. Attitudes of Jews and Christians toward saving of Jews, impact on children, extent of network, and reclaiming the children. Interviews with nuns and adult survivors.

Montefiore, Simon Sebag. *Stalin. Court of the Red Tsar*. New York: Alfred A. Knopf, 2004. Daily lives, dinners and parties, intrigues, paranoia, and crimes of Stalin's inner circle and how he used them against each other to murder 20 million Soviet citizens in purges and Gulag banishments.

Parker, Matthew. *Monte Cassino. The Hardest Fought Battle of World War II*. NY: Doubleday, 2004. Hundreds of survivor, letters, and diaries describe the campaign between January and May 1944 in the mountains of Italy that left more than 350,000 dead or wounded. Polish role in capture of Monte Cassino, description of memorial ceremonies at Polish cemetery at Monte Cassino.

Paul, Allen. *Stalin's Massacre and the Triumph of Truth*. Northern Illinois University Press, 2010. Mass deportations of Polish citizens to the Soviet Union for forced labor between February 1940 and June 1941, and murder of 22,000 Polish officers in the Katyń Forest region per Stalin's order.

Piotrowski, Tadeusz, ed. *The Polish Deportees of World War II. Recollections of Removal to the Soviet Union and Dispersal Throughout the World*. Jefferson, NC: McFarland & Company, 2004. Eyewitness accounts from Polish Government Collection, Wladyslaw Anders Collection at Hoover Institution in Stanford University, General Sikorski Historical Institute Archives in London, and Karta Centre in Warsaw. Deportations to Soviet Union, formation of Polish army, refugees in Near and Middle East, India, Africa, New Zealand and Mexico. Includes relevant documents.

Poltawska, Wanda. *And I Am Afraid of My Dreams.* NY: Hippocrene, 1964. Translated from the Polish. Sent to Ravensbruck concentration camp at age 19 for activity in Underground Resistance. Imprisoned four years, used for medical experiments. Became psychiatrist helping child survivors of Auschwitz at a clinic in Kraków's Medical Academy and at Jagiellonian University in Kraków.

Pomykalski, Wanda. *The Horror Trains: A Polish Woman Veteran's Memoir of World War II.* Pasadena, MD: The Minerva Center, 1999. Happy family life and plans to study medicine devastated by war. Deported to Soviet Union in cattle cars and endured cold, hunger, and brutality in Odessa prison. Left Siberia to reach Polish Army, then crossed Mongolia, Kazakhstan, Uzbekistan, Iran, Iraq, Palestine, Egypt and Italy. Served near front lines at Battle of Monte Cassino in May 1944.

Rees, Laurence. *World War II Behind Closed Doors, Stalin, The Nazis and the West.* NY: Pantheon, 2008. Documents and eyewitness accounts newly available from archives in Eastern Europe and Russia reexamine the role of Stalin, Churchill, and Roosevelt in Soviet control of Eastern Europe.

Snyder, Timothy. *Bloodlands. Europe Between Hitler and Stalin.* NY: Perseus, 2010. Names death factories, killing fields, and starvation sites where millions of European civilians were murdered by order of Hitler and Stalin. Humanizes numbers by referring to letters and diaries found on corpses.

Szpilman, Władysław. *The Pianist.* NY: Picador, 1999. Translated from Polish. Pianist experiences Nazi brutality in Warsaw, rescued from train going to Treblinka, and survives in Warsaw ruins with heroes and villains from all ethnic groups: brave Jewish resistance fighters and corrupt Jewish ghetto police, Poles risking their lives to save him and Poles cheating him out of daily rations, cruel Germans and German officer who helps him survive. After the war, remained a concert pianist in Poland.

Bibliography

Addison-Wesley. *Addison-Wesley U.S. History*. Menlo Park: Addison-Wesley, 1986.

Ascherson, Neal. *The Struggles for Poland*. New York: Random House, 1987.

Bruce, George. *The Warsaw Uprising: 1 August-2 October 1944*. London: Rupert Hart-Davis, 1972.

Buniak, Valentina, Head Librarian, interview with author in Naliboki, 2017, and articles in *Promień*, the Stołpce newspaper, 1991-2000.

The Commission for the Investigation of Crimes Against the Polish Nation. Warsaw: The Institute of National Memory, 1993.

Conway, John S. "Between Cross and Swastika." Berenbaum, ed. *A Mosaic of Victims: Non-Jews Persecuted and Murdered by the Nazis*. New York: NYU Press, 1990.

Dallin, Alexander. *German Rule in Russia 1941-1945: A Study of Occupation Policies*. London: Westview, 1981.

Davies, Norman. *God's Playground. A History of Poland, Vol. 2*. New York: Columbia University Press, 1982.

_____. *Rising '44. The Battle for Warsaw*. New York: Viking, 2003.

Demski, Dagnosław. *Naliboki i Puszcza Nalibocka. Zarys Dziejów I Problematyki*. Warsaw: Instytut Archeologii i Etnologii PAN, Etnografia Polska, T. XXXVIII Z. 1-2, 1994.

Garliński, Jozef. *Poland in the Second World War*. New York: Hippocrene, 1988.

Gutman, Israel, ed. *Encyclopedia of the Holocaust, Vol. 1.* New York: MacMillan, 1990.

Hanson, Joanna K.M. *The Civilian Population and the Warsaw Uprising of 1944.* Cambridge: Cambridge University Press, 1982.

Hirschbiel, Henry H. "Conscription in Russia." Wieczyński, Joseph L., ed. *The Modern Encyclopedia of Russian and Soviet History.* Gulf Breeze, FL: Academic International Press, 1978.

Hoffman, Eva. *Shtetl: The Life and Death of a Small Town and the World of Polish Jews.* New York: Public Affairs, A Member of Perseus Books Group, 2007.

Karski, Jan. *Story of a Secret State.* Boston: Houghton Mifflin, 1944.

Knap, Włodzimierz. Interview with Piotr Kolakowski. "Mogło to Zrobić NKWD." New York: *Nowy Dziennik*, December 5, 2003.

Leich, Harold M., Russian Area Specialist, European Division, The Library of Congress, interview with author, Washington, D.C: January, 2005.

Lojko, Jozef. *The Wound That Never Healed.* Kidderminster: England, 1999.

Lukas, Richard C. *The Forgotten Holocaust: The Poles Under German Occupation 1939-1944.* New York: Hippocrene, 1986.

_____. *Did the Children Cry? Hitler's War Against Jewish and Polish Children.* New York: Hippocrene, 1994.

MacMillan, Margaret. *Paris 1919, Six Months that Changed the World.* New York: Random House, 2001.

Montefiore, Simon Sebag. *Stalin: The Court of the Red Tsar.* New York: Knoff, 2004.

Paczkowski, Andrzej. "Poland, the "Enemy Nation." Kramer, Mark, consulting ed., *The Black Book of Communism, Crimes, Terror, Repression.* Cambridge, MA: Harvard University Press, 1999.

Parker, Matthew. *Monte Cassino, The Hardest Fought Battle of WWII.* New York: Doubleday, 2004.

Paul, Allen. *Katyń : Stalin's Massacre and the Seeds of the Polish Resurrection.* Annapolis: Naval Institute, 1996.

Peretitkowicz, Antoni, ed. *Konstytucja Rzeczypospolitej Polskiej.* Poznań: 4th Edition, 1928. Paszkudzki, August, ed. Warsaw: Książnica-Atlas, 1935.

Pilch, Adolf. *Partyzanci trzech puszcz,* Warsaw: Editions Sotkania, 1992.

Piotrowski, Tadeusz, ed. The Polish Deportees of WWII. *Recollections of Removal to the Soviet Union and Dispersal Throughout the World.* Jefferson, NC: McFarland & Co., 2004.

_____. *Vengeance of the Swallows.* Jefferson, NC: McFarland & Co., 1995.

Rees, Laurence. *World War II. Behind Closed Doors. Stalin, The Nazis and the West.* New York: Pantheon, 2008.

Regulska-Ślusarczyk, Hanna. *Ziemia Mickiewicza.* Newcastle: 1999.

Snyder, Timothy. *Black Earth: The Holocaust as History and Warning.* New York: Penguin, Random House LLC, 2015.

Spector, Shmuel, ed. *The Encyclopedia of Jewish Life Before and During the Holocaust.* New York: NYU Press, 2001.

Spielvogel, Jackson J. *Hitler and Nazi Germany.* Englewood Cliffs, NJ: Prentice Hall, 1988.

Tuszynski, Marek. Interview on February 11, 2009. Fairfax: 2009.

_____. "Soviet War Crimes during the Second World War and its Aftermath: A Review of the Factual Record and Outstanding Questions." *The Polish Review*, 44, Number 2, 1999.

Walczak, Adam. "Oddział DĄB" – zalążek 13 Brygady A.K. Okręgu Wileńskiego w Puszczy Nalibockiej." Olgierd, Christa, ed. *Wileński Przekaz*, Gdańsk: Światowy Związek Żołnierzy Armii Krajowej.

Wood, E. Thomas and Jankowski, Stanislaw M. *Karski: How One Man Tried to Stop the Holocaust.* New York: John Wiley and Sons, Inc., 1994.

Wyman, Mark. *DPs: Displaced Persons, 1945-1951.* Ithaca, NY: Cornell UP, 1988.

Zamoyski, Adam. *The Forgotten Few. The Polish Air Force in the Second World War.* New York: Hippocrene, 2001.

_____. *The Polish Way: A Thousand Year History of the Poles and Their Culture.* New York: Hippocrene, 1996.

INDEX

About the Author

As an educator and author, Donna Chmara has turned her childhood experience of war into a lifetime quest for peace and respect for all human beings. As a refugee, she found the public education system to be pivotal in helping her make the transition from war-torn Europe to her new country of America. While attending the College of New Jersey, she was a one-year exchange student at the University of Saskatchewan in Canada. After college, she taught English for two years as a Peace Corps volunteer in Turkey where she maintains many dear friendships. In the United States, she has taught English and composition at the high school and college levels. She has also taught English for shorter periods in places as varied as Poland and the country of Myanmar (Burma).

In addition to teaching, she has worked as a public school administrator, director of communications for a professional association of school administrators, and director of the State Board of Education Office. She holds a Master of Arts degree in English with a major in medieval literature from Temple University in Philadelphia. On a personal note, she participates in inter-religious and multi-cultural projects and loves to garden, dance, swim, and learn from other people's wisdom.

Donna Chmara hugging a tree in the Naliboki Forest. 2017